BASEBALL

...THE PERFECT GAME

BASEBALL

...THE PERFECT GAME

An All-Star Anthology
Celebrating the Game's Greatest
Players, Teams, and Moments

Edited by Josh Leventhal

Voyageur Press

Edited by Josh Leventhal

Designed by Julie Vermeer

Printed in China

Jacket photo: Babe Ruth homers during the 1926 World Series at Sportsman's Park in St. Louis. Photo © Bettmann/CORBIS.

Facing page: Sibby Sisti, Boston Braves.

05   06   07   08   09   5   4   3   2   1

Library of Congress Cataloging-in-Publication Data

Baseball, the perfect game : an all-star anthology celebrating the game's greatest players, teams, and moments / Josh Leventhal, editor.
      p. cm.
   Includes index.
   ISBN 0-89658-668-5 (hardcover)
   1. Baseball--United States--Anecdotes. 2. Baseball--United States--History.   I. Leventhal, Josh, 1971-
   GV873.B294 2005
   796.357'64'0973--dc22

                              2004023541

Published by Voyageur Press, Inc.
123 North Second Street | P.O. Box 338 | Stillwater, MN | 55082 U.S.A.
phone: 651-430-2210, fax: 651-430-2211, email: books@voyageurpress.com
www.voyageurpress.com

Educators, fundraisers, premium and gift buyers, publicists, and marketing managers: Looking for creative products and new sales ideas? Voyageur Press books are available at special discounts when purchased in quantities, and special editions can be created to your specifications. For details contact the marketing department at 800-888-9653.

Part III: Legends of the Diamond

PREFACE

Baseball had earned the title of America's "national pastime" as early as the 1850s. As the game developed through its various forms—from town ball to one-ol'-cat and other interpretations—it became a uniquely American game, the benefits of which were proclaimed as superior to those of "foreign sports" such as England's cricket or Canada's lacrosse. Baseball endured a half dozen wars, several recessions, and one Great Depression. It survived and in many cases thrived in the face of new entertainment technologies such as radio, television, movies, and video games. It fended off the emergence of later American games like basketball and football. And even as those sports continue to increase their hold on the imaginations of children across urban and rural America, and as more and more cable channels offer a bewildering array of sporting events around the clock, the game of baseball stands tall as the national game.

Since the beginning, the most dominant teams, the most talented or most charismatic players, and the most dramatic moments have come to define each era of the professional game. From Ty Cobb and other masters of the "dead-ball era," through the magnificence of Babe Ruth—an era unto himself—and to the heroes of a war-torn America in mid-century (Ted Williams, Joe DiMaggio, Stan Musial, Bob Feller), one cannot explore the history of baseball without encountering these names. Baseball in the first half of the twentieth century experienced events that threatened to sully the sport's reputation—the scandal of the 1919 World Series—as well as unforgettable seasons that epitomized the grace and allure of our game—the historic hitting streak of "Joltin' Joe" and the dominance of "Teddy Ballgame's" .406 batting average with the nation on the brink of war in 1941.

On the green diamonds of postwar America, the integration of Major League baseball represented more than just a new era in a sport, but also a shift in our national consciousness. Jackie Robinson's groundbreaking entrance onto baseball's biggest stage cleared the way for such later luminaries as Willie Mays, Hank Aaron, and countless others. The experience of stars from the Negro Leagues, like Satchel Paige, who were able to get just a taste of Major League ball help to define the later experiences of such all-world pitchers as Sandy Koufax and Bob Gibson.

The second half of the twentieth century also saw the dreams of devoted baseball fans from the borough of Brooklyn finally realized with a long-awaited world championship, while the frustrations of the Red Sox Nation would take on new dimensions at the hands of the rival New York Yankees as well as a loss in one of the greatest World Series ever played, the 1975 classic against the Reds of Cincinnati.

As the twentieth century gave way to the twenty-first, Major League baseball was blessed with the amazing talents and performances of larger-than-life figures like Cal Ripken, Mark McGwire, Sammy Sosa, and Barry Bonds. Records previously thought unbreakable fell to the wayside one after another. Who knows what other towering achievements will be toppled by the next generation of superstars?

As these moments and men crossed into American lore and legend, writers, historians, poets, and even politicians and artists have shared their own impressions of the legendary heroes and games. Great ballplayers and great moments inspire great writing, and baseball's literary tradition remains unmatched by that of any other sport.

Collected here are nearly thirty such inspirations. From the earliest powerhouse clubs like the Brooklyn Atlantics and Cincinnati Red Stockings to such twenty-first-century superstars as Sosa and Bonds, writings from across generations tell the story of baseball's pivotal events. The first part of the book introduces the game of baseball and its impact as the national pastime. The seasons and teams that have left their imprint on fans throughout the decades are recounted from newspaper articles, memoirs, and historical essays. Lastly, we meet some of the greatest figures ever to grace the baseball diamond, through first-hand accounts, biographies, and literature.

The history of baseball and its place in our national identity is revealed through the words and images across two centuries. It is a history that continues to be written.

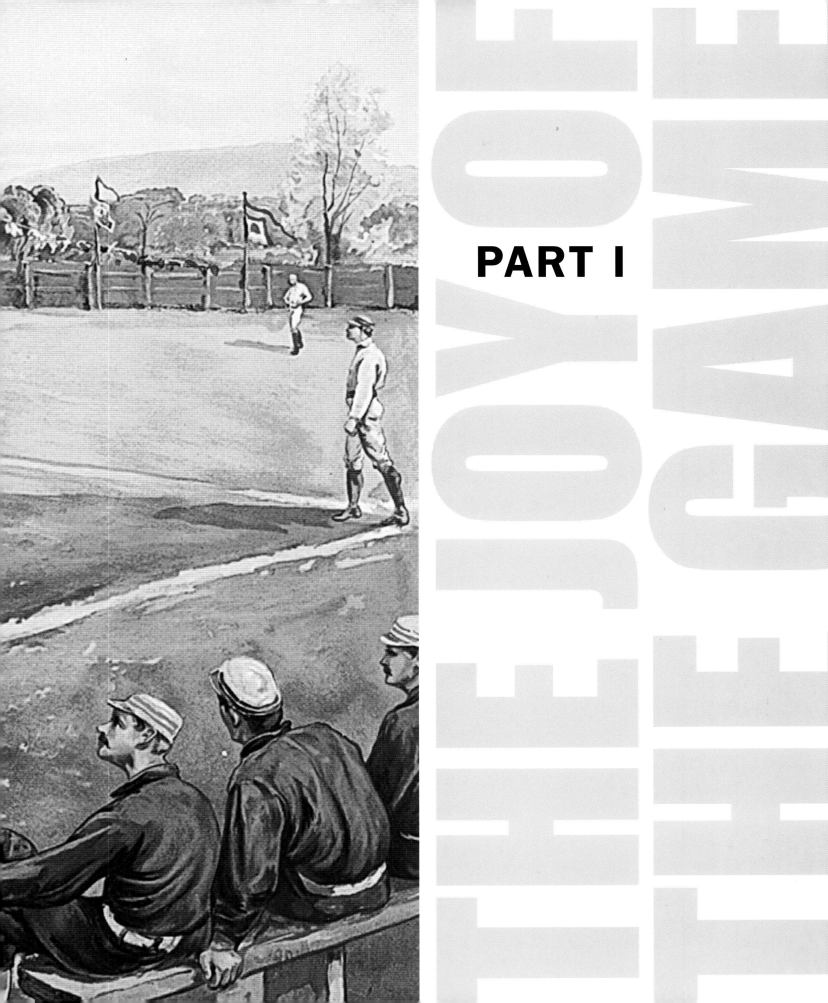

PART I

THE JOY OF THE GAME

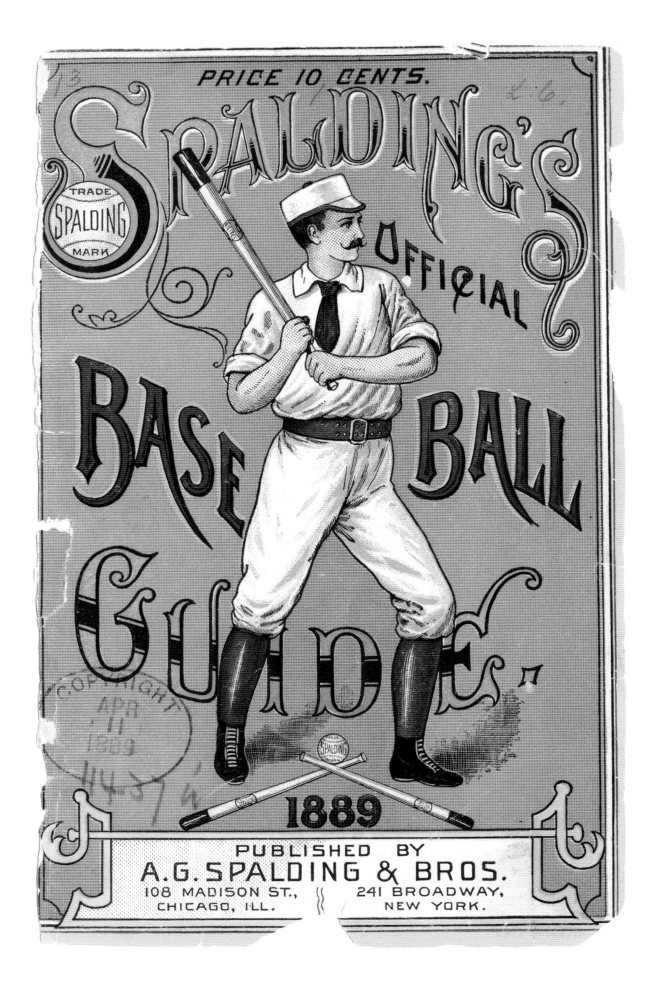

PRICE 10 CENTS.

SPALDING'S

TRADE SPALDING MARK

OFFICIAL

BASE BALL

GUIDE

1889

PUBLISHED BY
A. G. SPALDING & BROS.
108 MADISON ST.,   241 BROADWAY,
CHICAGO, ILL.   NEW YORK.

THE NATIONAL GAME

from *Spalding's Official Base Ball Guide, 1882*

AFTER SIX SEASONS **as a dominating pitcher for the Boston Red Stockings and Chicago White Stockings, Albert Goodwill Spalding left the playing field for the business office. In addition to serving as team president of the White Stockings, he founded the A. G. Spalding & Brothers sporting goods company in 1876.**

Beginning in 1878, A. G. Spalding & Bros. produced the annual *Spalding's Official Base Ball Guide*, which included the official rules, reviews of the previous season in the professional and amateur ranks, statistical analyses, and descriptions of the developing game of baseball. The following excerpt is from the introduction to the *Official Base Ball Guide* for 1882.

There is no out-door sport now in vogue in America that equals our national game of base ball, either as an exciting sport to witness, or as a game affording ample opportunities for healthy, manly and recreative exercise. In comparison with every other field game known in the existing arena of out-door sports, base ball bears off the palm in all those features which are calculated to secure the popular favor of the American public. A match at base ball scarcely averages two hours of time, from the opening innings to the close of the contest, even at the hands of amateur experts, and still less when the contesting nines are trained and experienced professionals. From the moment the ball is in play to the end of each innings of a match, the interest is kept up unceasingly. Then, too, in the accomplishment of the work in those departments of the game which the nine in the field have specially to attend to, opportunities are afforded for the most attractive displays of manly courage, pluck and nerve; while activity of mind as well as limb comes into active play through the medium of pitching, catching, fielding, throwing and holding the ball, involved in the work of an attacking party in a contest; while, on the other hand, there is the great skill needed in handling the bat, and sound judgment as well as remarkable agility required in running the bases, this being the work of the defense in the battle for the prize of victory; the whole affording scope for active exercise of mind and body, unequaled by any field sport. In the English game of cricket far too much time is wasted in playing it, and results are not arrived at in match games until the majority of the spectators have become wearied with waiting. In the Canadian game of lacrosse, on the other hand, a game is frequently finished in two or three minutes, while a series of games constituting a match may be prolonged to a wearisome length; besides which there is not that interesting variety in lacrosse that there is in base ball, though it is far more exciting for a mixed crowd of spectators than cricket is. In the popular sports of the turf, too—running and trotting races—all the interest in the racing centers in the money invested in wagers on the result, as the race itself only occupies a few minutes of time. In fact, take any sport in its season, and it will be found, by a fair comparison of its special merits, that each will "pale its ineffectual fire" in contrast with the more brilliant and electric light of our national game.

What can present a more attractive picture to the lover of out-door sports than the scene presented at a base ball match between two trained professional teams competing for championship honors, in which every point of play is so well looked after in the field that it is only by some extra display of skill at the bat, or a lucky act of base running at an opportune moment, that a single run is obtained in a full nine innings game. To watch the progress of a contest in which only one run is required to secure an important lead, and while the game is in such a position to see hit after hit made to the field, either in the form of high fly balls splendidly caught on the run by some active outfielder, or a sharp ground hit beautifully picked up in the in-field, and swiftly and accurately thrown to the right baseman in time, is to see the perfection of base ball fielding, and that surpasses the fielding of every other known game of ball. Then there is the intense excitement incident to a contest in which one side is endeavoring to escape a "whitewash," while the other side as eagerly strives to retain their lead of a single

The Currier and Ives lithograph *The American National Game of Baseball* illustrates an early match at Elysian Fields in Hoboken, New Jersey. Elysian Fields was the home grounds for the New York Knickerbockers, who were throttled by the New York Nine by a score of 23-1 in the first official game here, held on June 19, 1846.

run; and with the game in such position a three base hit sends the runner to third base before a single hand is out, only to see the hit left unrewarded by the expected run, owing to the telling effect of the strategic pitching and the splendid field support given it. Add to this the other excitement of a high hit over the outfielder's head, made while two or three of the bases are occupied with the result of a tie score or the securing of the lead at a critical point of the game, and a culmination of attractive features is reached incidental to no other field game. When it is considered, too, that the pursuit of base ball is that of a healthy, recreative exercise, alike for the mind and body, suitable to all classes of the community, and to the adult as well as the mere boy, there can be no longer room for surprise that such a game should reach the unprecedented popularity that the American game of base ball has done.

Yours Truly
A. G. Spalding

Albert G. Spalding was successful both on and off the baseball field, posting a career record of 253 wins and 65 losses as a pitcher, leading the White Stockings to three titles in ten seasons as club president, and founding the number one sporting goods company of its time. He also led a team of all-stars on baseball's first traveling world tour in 1888–89.

At a legal Meeting of the Inhabitants of the Town of Pittsfield qualified to vote in Town Meetings, ~~or their~~ ~~[strikethrough]~~ holden on Monday the fifth day of Septr 1791 — Voted, The following Bye Law, for the Preservation of the Windows in the New Meeting House in said Town —— viz,

Be it ordained by the said Inhabitants that no Person an Inhabitant of said Town, shall be permitted to play at any Game called Wicket, Cricket, Base ball, Bat ball, Foot ball, Cat, Fives, or any other Game or Games with Ball, within the Distance of Eighty Yards from said Meeting House — And every such Person who shall play at any of the said Games or other Games with Ball within the Distance aforesaid, shall for every instance thereof, forfeit the Sum of five Shillings to be recovered by Action of Debt brought before any Justice of the Peace to the Use of the Person who shall sue and prosecute therefor ——

And be it further ordained that in every instance where any Minor shall be guilty of a Breach of this Law, his Parent, Master, Mistress or Guardian shall forfeit the like Sum to be recovered in Manner, and to the Use aforesaid ——

THE ORIGINS OF BASEBALL

THE QUESTION OF **when and where baseball began has long been a subject of debate. For years, myth and folklore held that baseball was invented by Abner Doubleday in Cooperstown, New York, in 1839. That assertion was quickly disputed, and other evidence suggested that baseball could be traced back to the 1820s in New York City.**

In 2004, baseball historian and author John Thorn discovered a document that pushed baseball's origins back to the eighteenth century. A law from Pittsfield, Massachusetts, in 1791, prohibited the playing of "Baseball . . . or any other Game or Games with Balls within the Distance of Eighty Yards from [the] Meeting House."

At a legal Meeting of the Inhabitants of the Town of Pittsfield qualified to vote in Town Meetings, holden on Monday the fifth day of Sept. 1791, voted The following ByeLaw, for the Preservation of the Windows in the New Meeting House in said Town—viz,

Be it ordained by the said Inhabitants that no Person, an Inhabitant of said Town, shall be permitted to play at any Game called Wicket, Cricket, Baseball, Batball, Football, Cat, Fives or any other Game or Games with Balls within the Distance of Eighty Yards from said Meeting House—and every such Person who shall play at any of the said Games or other Games with Balls within the Distance aforesaid, shall for any Instance thereof, forfeit the Sum of five schillings to be recovered by Action of Debt brought before any Justice of the Peace to the Use of the Person who shall sue and prosecute therefore—

And be it further ordained that in every Instance where any Minor shall be guilty of a Breach of this Law, his Parent, Master, Mistress or Guardian shall forfeit the like Sum to be recovered in Manner and to the Use aforesaid.

Baseball was a popular enough activity in 1791 that the residents of Pittsfield, Massachusetts, passed a law prohibiting the playing of baseball near the town Meeting House. Today Pittsfield is home to Wahconah Park, one of the oldest minor league ballparks in the country.

The New York Baseball Rules

If the sport of baseball was pursued as a recreational activity as early as the 1790s, it took more than half a century for someone to codify the rules and organize a formal club. That accomplishment was realized by Alexander J. Cartwright of the Knickerbocker Club of New York. In 1845, Cartwright outlined the basic rules of play, as well as certain standards of decorum. His twenty rules form the foundation of the modern rules of baseball.

1st Members must strictly observe the time agreed upon for exercise, and be punctual in their attendance.

2nd When assembled for exercise, the President, or in his absence, the Vice-President, shall appoint an Umpire, who shall keep the game in a book provided for that purpose, and note all violations of the By-Laws and Rules during the time of exercise.

3rd The presiding officer shall designate two members as Captains, who shall retire and make the match to be played, observing at the same time that the player's opposite to each other should be as nearly equal as possible, the choice of sides to be then tossed for, and the first in hand to be decided in like manner.

4th The bases shall be from "home" to second base, forty-two paces; from first to third base, forty-two paces, equidistant.

5th No stump match shall be played on a regular day of exercise.

6th If there should not be a sufficient number of members of the Club present at the time agreed upon to commence exercise, gentlemen not members may be chosen in to make up the match, which shall not be broken up to take in members that may afterwards appear; but in all cases, members shall have the preference, when present, at the making of the match.

7th If members appear after the game is commenced, they may be chosen in if mutually agreed upon.

8th The game is to consist of twenty-one counts, or aces; but at the conclusion an equal number of hands must be played.

9th The ball must be pitched, not thrown, for the bat.

10th A ball knocked out of the field, or outside the range of the first and third base, is foul.

11th Three balls being struck at and missed and the last one caught, is a hand out; if not caught is considered fair, and the striker bound to run.

12th If a ball be struck or tipped and caught, either flying or on the first bound, it is a hand out.

13th A player running the bases shall be out, if the ball is in the hands of an adversary on the base, or the runner is touched with it before he makes his base; it being understood, however, that in no instance is a ball to be thrown at him.

14th A player running who shall prevent an adversary from catching or getting the ball before making his base, is a hand out.

15th Three hands out, all out.

16th Players must take their strike in regular turn.

17th All disputes and differences relative to the game, to be decided by the Umpire, from which there is no appeal.

18th No ace or base can be made on a foul strike.

19th A runner cannot be put out in making one base, when a balk is made on the pitcher.

20th But one base allowed when a ball bounds out of the field when struck.

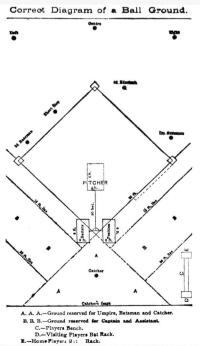

Correct Diagram of a Ball Ground.

A. A. A.—Ground reserved for Umpire, Batsman and Catcher.
B. B. B.—Ground reserved for Captain and Assistant.
C.—Players Bench.
D.—Visiting Players Bat Rack.
E.—Home Players Bat Rack.

Above: The *Brooklyn Eagle* of June 12, 1858, had the following to report about the Excelsior Club of Brooklyn, one of the city's earliest baseball teams: "There was an error in our notice of the Base Ball matter yesterday which requires correction. It was stated that the defeat of the Excelsiors was owing to the *bad feeling* existing amongst them. It should have read that they were beaten in consequence of *bad fielding*, which makes all the difference in the world."

Left: The baseball infield had assumed its familiar diamond shape by the 1850s. Although Cartwright didn't specify a measurement, the New York Baseball Rules did establish the distance between the bases at forty-two paces, which evolved into the 90-foot base paths of today. Note that the "pitcher's box" was placed just 50 feet from the plate, compared to the 60 feet, 6 inches standard today.

OPENING DAY

from *The Long Season* by Jim Brosnan

FOR EVERY BASEBALL player and fan, Opening Day is a moment of great excitement and anticipation, the beginning of a new life, in a sense, for the coming summer. Jim Brosnan saw nine Opening Days during his Major League career, and the 1959 season opener had its share of ups and downs for this journeyman pitcher.

In 1960, Brosnan published his daily diary of life as a baseball player in *The Long Season*, taking the reader from spring training through the conclusion of the 1959 season. Brosnan the author followed *The Long Season* with *Pennant Race*, his diary of the 1961 pennant-winning season with the Cincinnati Reds.

APRIL 9—ST. LOUIS

"The night before" is one of those peculiarly personal phrases that frequently repeats itself in a man's memory. It can refer to a wild time, or to a sad moment, or to the traditional misty haze of dim reckoning. For the professional ballplayer, the night before Opening Day is full of extreme nervous tension. All of winter's fond hopes and daydreams, all of the spring-training trials and successes, all of the promise-filled publicity focuses eyes, in the baseball world, on the players. There's no more time to think and dream, to plot and scheme, for this is it . . . the championship game. Only the first of 154, perhaps, but to eight teams it's the only chance to be as good as any other team in the league for one whole day. You may have won every game in spring training, hit 1.000, or pitched perfect ball, but you're no better than the next guy when the first pitch of the season starts on its way.

It usually rains, it seems to me, the night before we open the season. It did in '54, I recall, and again in '57, and '58. It's raining now, which is another good reason to go to bed at ten o'clock, to try to sleep, and then to read, and then to write a letter. Perhaps it would be better to talk it out, letting the sound of words soothe the nerves. If I was simply worried, and nervous about how badly I might bungle the job tomorrow, I

would prefer to talk it out. But I feel only a mysterious concern for the security that my successful spring has given me. Perhaps the Law of Averages will punish my pride the next time out. In this game you have to do it over and over again . . . the better you do, the more you are expected to do. Pride's price, and it is sometimes cruelly exacted by that insidious Law.

It's better to write about it. Let the sight of words console my nerves. (One reason I married my wife was to have someone to console me. She was three hundred miles away, but I could write about it as easily as I could talk about it. I took out my pen.)

Dearest Wife, And Lover, Etc.,

With the spring training season ended, and my ambitious efforts rewarded as handsomely as possible, I would not have surprised my ego had I grown peacock feathers as we flew in from Florida. [Manager Solly] Hemus, noting that I haven't given up a run in three weeks, and only three all spring, has made me No. 1—publicly hailed, or branded, me as such. Long Man, indeed!

No peacock, I though. Truthfully I'm slim-hipped, loose-armed, flat-bellied . . . and featherless. Certainly I've had a successful spring. Surely, the bell rings tomorrow, and we start from scratch. If I start to give up runs now, I'm a bum again. Success breeds a maggoty fortune that needs constant replenishment and refurbishing.

Still, there's the sun, just eight hours away. And here I am, and here's nervous bowels, and here's the issue—win, or lose everything. The prestige of my position must be upheld by the act of triumph; and every pitch must be impressive. And then, there's the next game. Success breeds also a feeling of insecurity. Where can you find a comfortable spot to relax, at the top? It's a

The first shout of "play ball!" every spring fills baseball fans with great anticipation. How will their favorite team fare? Who will emerge as the season's all-stars? From 1908 to 1957, *Baseball Magazine* kept fans informed throughout the season with stories, photos, stats, and other tidbits.

JIM BROSNAN
CINCINNATI REDS   PITCHER

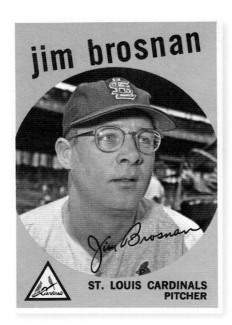

jim brosnan

ST. LOUIS CARDINALS
PITCHER

Jim Brosnan was traded from the St. Louis Cardinals to the Cincinnati Reds midway through the year while writing *The Long Season*. He appeared in 46 games in 1959, going 9-6 with a 3.79 ERA. Earning the nickname "the Professor" from his teammates, the nine-year Major Leaguer is best known for his authorial observations and insights into the life of a professional baseball player.

definite problem of balance, for there's no hand hold above, and damn little support to lean on. Besides, when you climb to the top of the ladder, the Achilles tendon is exposed, almost indefensibly. Eight other guys want this job. If the knives start to jab they may hit this heel if it's left carelessly unprotected. I'm trying to remember, here in the rain, if I made obeisance to the proper gods. Will my unguarded rear go unscathed? Let's face it, I can be had. The black forces of despair have made it with me before!

It's another year. You'll have your sorrowful, pining days as before, waiting behind, never any more sure than I am that I can do it. It's harder to sit, hopefully, on the bench than to play the game. But this man's ready to start a new season, and we're the team that can take it all . . . You and I. Not the Cardinals, probably. Hemus is optimistic about his *chances; but I'm confident about ours. So let's round those bases, and have fun, and love, for the long season ahead.*

I Love You, etc.,
MEAT

Rereading, folding, sealing, and stamping the letter took just as much energy as I had left for the night. I turned out the light and slept.

APRIL 10—OPENING DAY IN ST. LOUIS

Each and every spring, a veteran ballplayer, retired and reminiscing, reads the prologue before the curtain rises on the new season. In the spring of '59, Tommy Henrich said it:

"No matter how long a man remains in baseball he always hankers and looks forward to opening day, and believe you me, it takes a young player a long, long time to get over those opening day butterflies and discover finally that he really is an old pro."

Butterflies come in many shapes and sizes. The larger ones lie supine in the stomach most of the day—be it Opening Day, or Debut Day, or World Series time. Occasionally the younger, less experienced butterflies flutter restlessly during the first conscious stirring of the morning. As the years go by, and those days pass nervously into memory, the stomach muscles learn to tighten early on the butterfly wings. In that way the twitch is controlled, and only when the tension has mounted to its peak does that thump rattle the stomach walls. The most jaded old pro has his emotional weak spot—the first "Star-Spangled Banner" of the season; the catcher's peg to second base that signals the end of springtime playtime and the start of business; the sudden realization that from this moment on, everything goes into the record book.

I get nervous before I eat on Opening Day. Just thinking about putting something in the stomach serves to agitate my nerves. As if subconsciously I've held a tight clamp on the obvious seat of nervousness; and then to think of adding to the job! It's too much. But I eat, anyway. Proper, as it says in the book. A rare steak, a green salad, tea and a dish of ice cream. An unusual breakfast, perhaps, but then it's an unusual day . . . every year.

• • •

Four hours later I sat at a table in Thompson's cafeteria, stabbing ham and eggs, drowning my burned-up pride with cold milk, and salting, slightly, the lower lids of my angry eyes. How in hell can you get into such a sad position? How can you fall so far so fast? One minute you're a hero; four hours later you're a bum!

I can't stand to be booed. Some people say I'm being childish; most ballplayers say you get used to it. I can't believe that they really hear those boos; they turn off their ears when the ugly noise begins. Desperately, I try to do the same; inevitably I manage only to turn up the sound, and it rings and reverberates for hours after I'm gone, the crowd's gone, the game's gone.

When twenty thousand people applaud as you walk out to do your job, it should be an inspiration. It should make you feel good. (Applause is what you play for, too, as well as money.) When those same twenty thousand cry, "Ptui, you let us down," you have to feel bad. Most of the fans probably didn't open their mouths; many probably sympathized with me when the booing started; some, reasonable critics, probably said, "Guess he didn't have it tonight."

"Didn't have it! The bum blew it!"

Even in the clubhouse I could hear the final smattering of boos as Charley Jones announced the results. "Here are the summaries. Giants, 6—Cardinals, 5. Winning pitcher, Antonelli. Losing pitcher, Brosnan." Boo! Like an echo. Like the tardy, final twist of the knife. It hurts. Don't let them tell you it doesn't.

On this cold, nervous Opening Day, the Giants wasted some chances and gave us two runs, but they scored three off [starting pitcher Larry] Jackson in the first seven innings, and led by a run when Cocky was lifted for a hitter. We then scored two more runs and I was in there, ready or not.

What do you mean, ready or not? This is your job, boy. He gave you the ball, and he gave you a run to work with. What more can you want? You can't go up to him and

U.S. presidents have been throwing out the ceremonial first pitch of the baseball season ever since William H. Taft opened the 1910 season at National Park in Washington, D.C. George W. Bush, shown here ringing in the 2004 campaign at St. Louis, was the sixteenth president to throw out a first pitch on Opening Day.

say, "I haven't got it today, Solly. I don't feel up to it. I don't want that ball. It's cold and I'm shivering, and I was enjoying the game from the bench."

No, you can't back out. You take the ball and the signal for a fast ball, and you throw five straight pitches at Cepeda's fists, and he finally strikes out. The rhythm starts to beat in your mind. The winning beat—a simple co-ordination of movement. Bend for the sign, glance at the hitter, grip the ball for the selected pitch . . . whoa, now! This is Kirkland. That's a slider you called for, Smitty. I don't think I can get him with it. (Kirkland hasn't hit a slider all day. That's the pitch to throw him. Make it a good one. Try it one time.) Here it comes, then . . . up, and in . . . right on his . . . Kirkland hit it on the roof. It was gone all the way. I didn't even look. Maybe it went over the roof. I watched Willie run into the Giants' dugout, where Antonelli waited to shake his hand. The game was all tied up. Off the hook again, aren't you, John?

Spencer hit a fast ball through my legs for a single . . . I didn't get that pitch into him far enough, either. Have to go for the double play, now. Keep the slider away. And down . . .

Damn, it hung. Right in his eyes. Rodgers is a big, powerful man. His eyes lit up as he swung, and the ball went deep to center. A high fly? Maybe Cimoli can catch up to it. No, it's carrying . . . Breaking balls carry so damn much farther when they're hit well.

The Toronto Blue Jays and Texas Rangers inaugurated the 2001 baseball season at Hiram Birthorn Stadium in San Juan, Puerto Rico. Jose Feliciano performed the National Anthem in front of more than 19,000 fans. It was the second time Major League Baseball opened its season on foreign soil: In 2000, the New York Mets and Chicago Cubs played the first regular-season game in Tokyo, Japan.

Spencer scored. Rodgers had a triple. Schmidt hit a high fast ball ("He's a high-ball hitter. Keep it down") to Cimoli, who threw Rodgers out at the plate. I was backing up home, and walked quickly to the dugout when Barlick called Rodgers out to retire the side. But some alert fans spied me. "Boo!" they called. And they were so damn right.

However, Grammas tied the score a few minutes later, lining Antonelli's high fast ball ("He's a high-ball hitter," the Giants had said in their meeting, I knew) into right-center field. Antonelli was tired. Rigney came out of the Giant dugout to talk to him. Whoever was going to hit for me would face a relief pitcher. I looked down toward the Giant bullpen to see who was throwing, when Hemus, who had been standing on the dugout steps thinking to himself, suddenly decided against better judgment and said, "Come on, Jim, hit for yourself."

Good Lord, Solly, let's not carry this too far, now! I walked slowly up to the plate, barely conscious of the booing that greeted my appearance. What the hell do I look for from this guy now?

Antonelli pointed out to Rigney that I was hitting for myself, and Rigney decided to leave John in the game. There were two out and, with Antonelli the first hitter in the ninth, it would be almost a waste of pitchers to bring in someone to pitch only to me. A likely prospect considering my past record as a hitter.

But, wait now! Had I not spent hours in the cage in the springtime, learning how to hit? Hadn't it looked easy? Just breathe deep; hold it; wait till the pitch is right at the plate; belly-button; block! I grounded weakly to short and we went into the ninth.

Speake batted for Antonelli and I walked him. (No sliders this time, I decided. Be careful. Make him hit the curve.) I couldn't get the damn thing over. I watched Hemus, in the dugout, stare at his bullpen down the left field line, then stare at me on the mound. What the hell's wrong with you, Brosnan?

Davenport bunted but he hit it too hard and Speake was forced at second. There's a break. Brandt took the first slider low and just a bit outside. Good pitch if only he'd go for it. Then I hung another one.

" . . . time of game—two hours, forty-six minutes." It doesn't take very long, really, to lose your confidence. To embarrass yourself, jeopardize your position, maybe lose your job. Hemus went a long way with me. He could have taken me out. He should have taken me out! I grinned ruefully to myself.

("What the hell, man, forget it. Anybody could see you didn't have it. Hemus asked for it, the silly dope. If a pitcher hasn't got it you get him out of there before he blows it. Right?") What a second-guesser, my ego! I climbed aboard the streetcar, and went back to the hotel.

Chicagoans have been packing it in to cheer on their Cubs from the "Friendly Confines" of Wrigley Field every spring since 1916.

WAGNER. PITTSBURG

Above: Would you pay a million dollars for this card? The rare 1909 Honus Wagner T206 card from the American Tobacco Company sold at auction for $1.265 million in 2000.

Right: Allen & Ginter was one of the earliest tobacco companies to offer trading cards of the top ballplayers. This card from 1887 features Adrian "Cap" Anson of the Chicago White Stockings. Anson's Hall of Fame plaque proclaims him the "greatest hitter and greatest National League player-manager of the 19th century," and his twenty-three seasons batting over .300 and five pennants as manager support that assertion. He was the first player to collect 3,000 career hits.

ADRIAN C. ANSON.
ALLEN & GINTER'S
Cigarettes.
RICHMOND. VIRGINIA

THE COLLECTOR
J. R. BURDICK AND THE WORLD OF BASEBALL CARDS
by Mark Lamster

TEARING INTO A **pack to see if your favorite player's card is inside, checking out the stats and trivia on the back, chewing that cardboard-like gum—once an innocent childhood activity, collecting baseball cards has grown into a multimillion-dollar industry. Individual cards sell for hundreds, thousands, and in very rare cases, millions of dollars. In the days when a card collection was more hobby than investment opportunity, Jefferson R. Burdick amassed tens of thousands of cards and earned himself a place in history as the grandfather of all card collectors. This is his story.**

Author Mark Lamster is a senior editor at Princeton Architectural Press. His forthcoming book *Spalding's World Tour: A True Story of Baseball, Adventure, and Clashing Cultures in the Nineteenth Century* will appear in 2006. The author thanks George Vrechek for sharing his insight on Burdick's life, and the Metropolitan Museum of Art for generously allowing access to Burdick's collection.

On a late fall afternoon in 1947, a frail and slightly disheveled forty-seven-year-old named Jefferson R. Burdick walked into the Print Department of New York's Metropolitan Museum of Art. He had traveled to the city from his home in Syracuse on a most unlikely mission: Burdick, a quiet and unassuming man who had lived a frugal life on a salary earned assembling electrical circuits, had come to convince America's preeminent museum of fine art—repository of priceless works of genius commissioned by royalty and bequeathed by titans of industry—to accept for its own his collection of trade and souvenir cards, most worth only pennies. At its core were some thirty thousand baseball cards, every single card produced to date.

It was an audacious proposition. That the museum should take Burdick's Cobbs, Ruths, and Wagners and treat them with the same reverence as its Dürers, Rembrandts, and Renoirs seems, in retrospect, almost like heresy. But the blue-collar collector found a kindred spirit in the Met's blueblood print curator, A. Hyatt Minor. Long before the days of hundred-dollar rookie cards and high-stakes memorabilia auctions, Minor saw the value of Burdick's spectacular accumulation. So when Burdick offered what Minor called "the finest collection of American cards" ever assembled, how could he refuse?

Burdick's own story, like those found on the backs of so many of the cards he collected, is one punctuated by physical trial, drama, achievement, and pathos. It is also a story laced with irony, none more striking than the fact that Burdick, the greatest of all baseball card collectors, may never have played the game or even attended a Major League contest. Indeed, baseball cards were only a part—albeit a significant part—of the vast empire of printed ephemera he had acquired.

As with most card collectors, Burdick's habit began when he was about ten years old, prompted by his first bit of discretionary income—whether his earnings came from an allowance or a paper route or some other odd job will forever be a mystery. At that pre-adolescent time, collecting was for him, as it is for most children, a social hobby; we can imagine young Jeff, a cherubic boy with ample cheeks and a gentle smile, trading cards with his peers, flipping them against school walls, perhaps even sticking them in the spokes of a bicycle wheel. With the onset of puberty, however, Burdick put his cards aside and, by his own account, did not return to them again until his early thirties.

This scenario will sound familiar to many casual baseball-card collectors, but with Burdick, the drive to return to his erstwhile hobby was motivated by something more powerful than simple nostalgia. He was becoming an invalid. By his early thirties, Burdick had developed a severe and debilitating case of rheumatoid arthritis that would dramatically restrict his movement and eventually take his life. Imprisoned by his own body, cards became the outlet for all of his energies and

The flamboyant Mike "King" Kelly, here depicted by Goodwin's Old Judge & Gypsy Queen Cigarettes, was best known for his aggressive base running, as made famous by the poem "Slide, Kelly, Slide!" After helping lead the White Stockings to five pennants in nine years, Kelly was sold by Albert Spalding to the Boston Beaneaters for the unheard-of sum of $10,000. Kelly is also credited as the author of the first baseball autobiography, *Play Ball: Stories of the Ball Field*.

imagination. "A card collection is a magic carpet that takes you away from workaday cares to havens of relaxing quietude where you can relive the pleasures and adventures of a past day—brought to life in vivid picture and prose," he wrote in his typically elegant prose.

Burdick's trajectory as a collector also squares with psychological theories that correlate the collector's impulse with debility and a reduction in sexual activity. Freud, an avid collector of antiques in his own right, put things rather bluntly: "When an old maid keeps a dog or a bachelor collects snuff boxes, the former is finding a substitute for her need for a companion in marriage and the latter for his need for a multitude of conquests. Every collector is a substitute for a Don Juan Tenerio."

Fear for his own health was in fact what led Burdick to the Met. By 1947, he had several hundred thousand cards, and the prospect of their being dispersed in some kind of fire sale after his death must have seemed a horrifying possibility. At the time, however, they were stored at his home in a wagonload of boxes unsuitable for the museum. It was therefore agreed that Burdick would return to Syracuse to begin the arduous task of sorting through his great accumulation, which he would then send to the museum in parcels as his work progressed. A few months later, in December, the first shipment arrived: a set of large albums, each weighing nearly fifteen pounds, with card after card meticulously pasted in row after ordered row. And so, for the next thirteen years, Burdick's packages arrived on A. Hyatt Minor's desk, a bounty of impossible richness delivered in anonymous brown cartons.

But by 1960, with work still far from complete, Burdick's illness had become dramatically worse. Injections of cortisone he had begun taking in the 1950s were now barely covering his pain, and he was too ill to continue his job at the Crouse-Hines Company in Syracuse. For everyone involved with the project—most crucially Burdick himself—there was the looming specter that he might leave his great masterpiece incomplete.

Understanding the need for drastic measures, Burdick moved to New York City, taking an inexpensive apartment on lower Madison Avenue so that he might be closer to the museum. Minor, who now looked upon Burdick with a combination of affection, concern, and reverence, allowed the collector to set up a small oak desk in the Print Department. Henceforth, Burdick would come in to sort and mount his cards at the museum every Tuesday and Friday. This arrangement undoubtedly made for some odd contrasts, with Burdick, the former assembly worker, pasting down his bubble-gum cards while art historians from Harvard and Princeton examined the works of Da Vinci and Michelangelo just a few feet away.

Burdick's primary concern, however, was his rapidly deteriorating health. In a letter to his friend and fellow collector Lionel Carter in January 1961, he reported that doctors had declared him "totally disabled." Three months later, he wrote Carter that he was "definitely on the down trend" and "looked like something the cat dragged in." By May of 1962, he had checked himself into Bellevue Hospital. "My condition was getting so unbearable that I had to do something," he wrote from the hospital ward. He was released, and returned to his work at the museum in July, but he could see that the end was coming. "I may not make it," he told Minor.

But he did make it. At five o'clock on Tuesday, January 10, 1963, Burdick slowly stood up from his desk and announced that, after sixteen years, he had mounted his last card—by his count number 306,353. It was a tremendous achievement, but Burdick was in no condition for celebration. As he twisted his warped body into his overcoat, he seemed utterly exhausted. His last words, as he bade his friends goodbye, were "I shan't be back." The next morning, he walked the few blocks from his apartment to University Hospital. He never left. Two months later, on March 13, he was dead. "The will that drove him to achieve, drove him on until his work was done," wrote Minor. "And then it snapped."

If Burdick's collection, prodigious as it may be, was his only legacy, his story would be noteworthy—and certainly moving—yet of little historical consequence. But Burdick was more than just a collector, and the acquisition of more and more material was only one aspect of what became, for him, a far larger project. There is, indeed, another side to the Burdick story, and it is this aspect of his life that has rightfully secured him a place in history as the grandfather of all card collectors.

When Burdick began collecting in earnest during the early 1930s, there was no literature on the subject and only an informal group of dealers and collectors for support. Burdick set out to rectify this situation. He researched the history of trade cards with the diligence of an Ivy League professor, becoming the world's leading authority on the subject. In 1935, in his first published article, he explained to the readers of *Hobbies* magazine how nineteenth-century tobacco companies like Allen & Ginter, Goodwin, and Duke inserted trading cards featuring baseball stars like Adrian "Cap" Anson and Buck Ewing into their packaging to help sell a new product: cigarettes. Meanwhile, Burdick's inveterate collecting made him a one-man clearinghouse of information on what other collectors were looking to buy and sell. To meet the needs of this community, in 1937 he started his own newsletter, *Card Collectors Bulletin*, that brought practical information and advertising to this small group of card enthusiasts. By 1939, that two-page bulletin became a seventy-two page booklet renamed *The United States Card Collectors Bulletin*. Eventually, it would

Below, left: This interestingly posed card from Goodwin and Company's Old Judge Cigarettes features pitcher Charles "Old Hoss" Radbourn of the Boston Beaneaters. Considered the best pitcher of his era, Radbourn won 310 games in just eleven seasons, and his performance in 1884 for the Providence Grays will never be matched: 60 wins, 73 complete games, 441 strikeouts. At the end of that season, having pitched more than 678 innings, he won three complete games in the championship series.

Below: Ned Hanlon played for thirteen seasons, mostly with the Detroit Wolverines, but it was as manager of the Baltimore Orioles in the 1890s that Hanlon earned his Hall of Fame credentials. Hanlon's Orioles employed innovative strategies such as the hit-and-run, double-steal, suicide squeeze, and "Baltimore chop"—as well as general rough play and intimidation—to win three consecutive pennants in 1894–96.

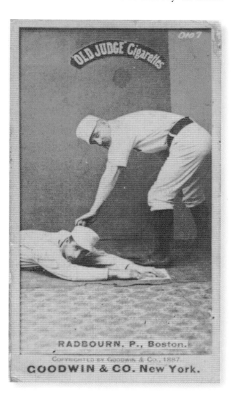

In 1887, the Buchner Gold Coin Chewing Tobacco company included Buck Ewing among the "leading base-ball players in the country." The versatile Ewing, presented here as a second baseman, had his greatest success behind the plate. He had a legendary arm for throwing out base-runners, and he was the first catcher elected to the Hall of Fame. In 1883, he became the first player to hit 10 home runs in a season.

be published (and republished and republished and republished again) as a full-fledged hardcover book, the *American Card Catalog*.

The *ACC*, as it was then and is still known, was the culmination of Burdick's endeavors as a publisher, and it remains a touchstone for card collectors and historians. It is, indeed, the foundation text of card collecting—part historical narrative, part Rosetta stone, part price guide. With the *ACC*, Burdick created the comprehensive catalog that he knew, from his own experience, other collectors so desperately needed. Inside, following brief descriptions and histories of the various card types, was a listing of every card set yet produced, each with a handy reference number and a suggested value in dollars and cents. In the words of Barry Halper, the undisputed king of modern baseball memorabilia, "What his catalog did was to transform the informal and undocumented hobby of baseball card collecting into the more elevated rank of stamp and coin collecting."

Burdick, however, rued the culture of commercialism that his *ACC* unwittingly produced. Indeed, one of his primary aims in creating it was to better educate other collectors in order to keep prices *down*. "For the good of the hobby some price schedule should be worked out," he wrote. "I am told that certain cards have changed hands at from 50 cents to $1.00 each. I doubt the justification of such prices and I think it ridiculous to expect the hobby to thrive with such ideas in effect."

Without deep pockets of his own, price escalation was a constant source of concern for Burdick, as illustrated by his reaction to the sale, in 1961, of a card featuring the great Pittsburgh shortstop Honus Wagner. The card, produced in 1909 by the American Tobacco Company and known by its *ACC* series number, T206, was already considered the ultimate prize of card collectors. According to legend, the image-conscious Wagner was not pleased that his picture was being used to sell tobacco and had the cards pulled before all but a handful were shipped. (An alternate and perhaps more likely scenario is that Wagner was simply unhappy with the financial terms offered by American Tobacco for the use of his likeness.) Whatever the case, only six of the cards were known to exist, and Burdick had one of them, given to him by a fellow collector in the 1950s as a token of admiration. Still, he was dismissive of the $150 price paid for one of the cards, which listed at $50 in the *ACC*. In a letter to a fellow collector, Burdick griped, "some kid collector asked me what it was worth in my opinion. All I can do is stick to the Catalog . . . There may be a small demand at over $50 but I don't believe it's very large." He may not have approved, but the $150 turned out to be an excellent investment. In the summer of 2000, a T206 Wagner sold at auction for $1.265 million, the highest price ever paid for a card.

The escalation in card values has placed a particular burden on Burdick's own collection, which today occupies a somewhat awkward position within the Met's archives. Burdick had assumed that the museum would make his work easily accessible to the interested public, and as long as the public was generally disinterested, the museum did just that. But in the eighties, with collecting taking on an ever more mercenary character, several valuable cards were stolen, and the museum was forced to restrict access. That Burdick's lumbering albums are exceedingly difficult to display has compounded the museum's difficulties, and complicating matters even further is the fact that Burdick actually pasted the cards down onto the album pages—a practice stupefying to condition-conscious collectors and which even he advised against. But Burdick saw the museum as a permanent home for the cards, and with duplicates provided to illustrate their backs, in this case he somehow deemed the procedure acceptable.

Today, the only hint of Burdick's great collection at the museum is a small, rotating display installed along an undistinguished corridor separating the bounty of Egypt's pharaohs from the masterworks of the American Renaissance. The balance—some four hundred albums worth—sits stacked on the shelves of a well-guarded storeroom in the darkened bowls of America's greatest museum. Meanwhile, the hobby he helped to invent flourishes. As for Burdick himself, his own final resting place is in a cemetery near his childhood home, in Central Square, New York. His tombstone reads, "Jefferson R. Budick: Greatest Card Collector Ever Known."

Below: This innovative series from Mecca cigarettes featured two players on each card. Here, the full-page figure is Johnny Evers, second baseman in Chicago's celebrated Tinker-to-Evers-to-Chance double-play combination. When the card is folded over, it reveals first baseman Frank Chance in a fielding pose. Both elected to the Hall of Fame in 1946, Evers and Chance helped the Cubs win back-to-back titles in 1907 and 1908.

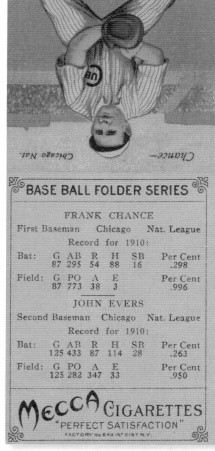

Above: The American Tobacco Company issued its gold-bordered set of cards in 1911. Cy Young was entering the final season of his career, during which he would add 7 wins to his untouchable lifetime total of 511. The durable Young also started and completed more games than any pitcher in history. Young hurled the twentieth century's first perfect game on May 5, 1905. Counting his previous two appearances (one in relief) and his next start after the perfect game, Young threw an incredible 24$\frac{1}{3}$ innings without allowing a base hit.

PART II

SEASONS OF
DREAMS, TEAMS,'
OF DESTINY

DYNASTIES: MORE THAN JUST THOSE DAMN YANKEES

by Gary Gillette and Pete Palmer

FOR ANY TEAM in any sport, the number one goal, the ultimate challenge, is winning a championship. Being able to repeat that success over several years is a truly special achievement. Then you can become a *dynasty*.

The New York Yankees have, of course, been able to assemble more dynasties than any other franchise, but in the course of the last hundred years, more than a dozen other teams have been able to lay claim to that title. In this original piece, Gary Gillette and Pete Palmer examine those "other" dynasties, how they came to be and what were the chances that each would actually reach dynasty status. Palmer and Gillette are co-editors of the 2004 edition of *The Baseball Encyclopedia*. Gillette, co-chair of the SABR Business of Baseball Committee, is also author of *Going, Going, Gone?*, as well as many other books. Among statistician Pete Palmer's other works is *The Hidden Game of Baseball*, co-written with John Thorn, and co-editor of the first seven editions of *Total Baseball*.

In the mid-1950s, the seemingly invincible Yankees continued to lay waste to the American League as the Brooklyn Dodgers won pennant after pennant in the National League. The lack of competitive balance had become a big issue by then in the provinces, where World Series berths were suddenly few and far between.

From 1947 to 1956, the three powerhouse New York teams—the Yankees, Dodgers, and Giants—combined to win all but one World Series and all but two pennants in each league. The song phrase "Willie, Mickey, and the Duke" may cause the eyes of millions of aging fans to go misty, but the trio of great New York centerfielders also dashed the dreams of millions of fans west of the Hudson and north of the Bronx.

As "Break up the Yankees!" became the rallying cry outside of New York, *Damn Yankees* became first a popular Broadway play in 1955, then a big-time Hollywood movie three years later. Both productions were based on Douglass Wallop's 1954 novel, *The Year the Yankees Lost the Pennant,* a retelling of the classic Faustian legend with a uniquely American twist.

Damn Yankees tells the story of hapless middle-aged Washington fan Joe Boyd, who sells his soul to the devil to be transformed into powerful Joe Hardy, the young slugger who will lead Boyd's beloved Senators to the World Series and vanquish the hated Yankees. (Note that the book wasn't entitled "The Year the Senators Won the Pennant," even though Washington hadn't tasted victory since 1933.)

Half a century later, is there any doubt that distraught fans in Chicago, Pittsburgh, Detroit, and a dozen other cities, would gladly sell their soul to the devil—just like Joe Boyd? How many fans whose hearts have been broken year after year could resist trading something abstract, like eternal damnation, to become their team's slugging Joe Hardy for one sweet, championship season?

THE DYNASTIC NINETEEN

One fascinating way to view baseball history is through the prism of the game's greatest teams, an overlapping string of highly talented ball clubs that, in many cases, defined their eras. Playing on the global stage of the World Series each fall has imprinted many of these fabled teams on America's collective memory. The New York Yankees have appeared in

---

The New York Yankees have accumulated far more World Series flags than any other franchise. By 1950, they had a dozen championships. Number thirteen would arrive that October, the second of five in a row for this dominating dynasty.

The New York Yankees of 1936–39 are arguably the best team ever assembled. The four-time champs outpaced their regular-season foes by an average of fifteen games and led the American League in *both* offense (runs) and defense (runs allowed) each of those years. The powerful 1938 lineup included (left to right) Frank Crosetti, Red Rolfe, Tommy Henrich, Joe DiMaggio, Lou Gehrig, Bill Dickey, George Selkirk, Myril Hoag, and Joe Gordon.

the fall classic more than twice as many times as any other franchise, and they've won more than a quarter of the championship trophies since 1903. But many other teams have been able to put together several seasons of peak success, establishing themselves as *the* dominant team in the league.

So what does it take to be a *dynasty?* When does a merely great team become dynastic? For our purposes, the minimum standard for entry into this exclusive club is winning four pennants and at least one World Series in a span of five years or winning two world championships and at least three pennants in five years. By this measure, Major League baseball has witnessed nineteen teams that can reasonably be called dynastic—five of them in Yankee pinstripes, including the unparalleled 1947–64 team that won fifteen pennants and ten world championships in eighteen years. The fourteen dynasties that didn't have the benefit of the "mystique" (or is it "luck") supposedly emanating from Yankee Stadium were able to assemble and maintain enough talent to remain at or near the top for multiple seasons.

True to the baseball adage, most dynastic teams were "built from within." Many were the result of especially fruitful periods of player development that produced a core group of teammates of a similar age. In many cases, as those homegrown stars aged, they could not be replaced from within, and the dynasty imploded. In the worst circumstances, cynical or desperate owners broke up great teams that might still have won more championships.

The dynasties can be divided into four historical categories: pre–farm system dynasties (1901–32), "classic-era" dynasties (1932–60), expansion-era dynasties (1961–75), and free-agent-era dynasties (after 1976). Championship teams in each era faced widely divergent circumstances as they attempted to sustain their winning ways.

The Fine Print

The tables accompanying this article show the scope of each Major League dynasty since 1901 (not including the Yankees), from the chances of their winning the pennant (pre-1969) or their division title to their chances of winning each postseason series. Also shown are intervening years between postseason appearances as well as years before (or after) the start (or end) of each dynasty where the team finished a strong second or third. All championships are included, with up to a two-year gap allowed.

The "RegW-L" column lists the regular-season win-loss record, and "Fin" indicates the club's finish in the standings, as well as its division (post-1968).

"PW" represents each team's probability of winning, based on simulating 1,000 seasons using their actual regular-season record. This simulation assumes that each team's regular-season record is indicative of its strength. It factors out luck while factoring in the length of each season, the number of teams in each league or division, and the strength of the opposition. For example, the 1906 Cubs could have been expected to win 97.7 percent of the time according to the results of the simulation, in which they won 977 times out of 1,000. According to the simulation, the 1909 Cubs, who actually finished second, had just a 25.3 percent chance of winning.

Casey Stengel's Yanks had plenty of reasons to celebrate. Beginning with his first campaign as the team's skipper in 1949, the "Old Perfesser" led the Bronx Bombers to a record five consecutive titles, and they added five league pennants and two more world championships before he was done. The Yanks of 1947–64 were longest-lasting dynasty of all time.

The "Diff" columns show the difference in regular-season winning percentage of the team and its postseason opponents. For, example, the 1915 Red Sox had a 77-point advantage in winning percentage over the 1915 National League champion Phillies (.669 versus .592), so the "Diff" column reads 77. The following year, the Red Sox's winning percentage (.591) was 19 points lower than that of its series foe, the Dodgers (.610), thus the entry reads -19.

"PWS" represents each team's chances of winning the World Series, based on the difference between their regular-season winning percentages and the length of the series (seven games in all years except 1903 and 1919–21, when the series was best of nine). This percentage is based on statistical analysis using each team's regular-season won-lost percentage, which shows that the one-game probability of winning is (.500 + Diff). A team with a 50-point advantage during the season would have a .550 probability of winning one game, with a .608 probability of winning a seven-game series.

"PWC" represents each team's chances of winning the League Championship Series, based on the difference between their regular-season winning percentages and the length of the series (five games from 1969 to 1984, seven games thereafter).

"PWD" represents each team's chances of winning the Division Series, based on the difference between their regular-season winning percentages and the length of the series (five games).

The "W-L" column shows the win-loss outcome of each postseason series.

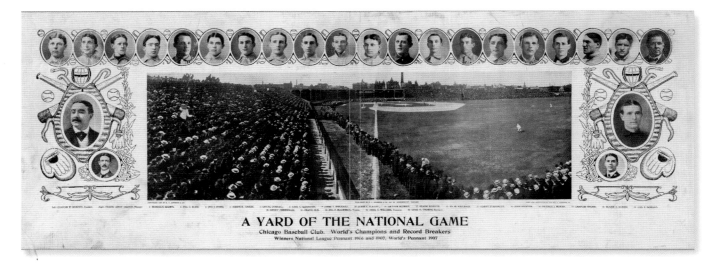

A YARD OF THE NATIONAL GAME
Chicago Baseball Club. World's Champions and Record Breakers
Winners National League Pennant 1906 and 1907, World's Pennant 1907

The Chicago Cubs won their first world championship in 1907 and followed that with a second a year later. Although Cubs fans have been waiting nearly one hundred years for championship number three, Chicago established the century's first dynasty with four pennants in five years while playing at the West Side Grounds ballpark.

PRE–FARM SYSTEM DYNASTIES

Even in an era marked by enormous differences between the best and worst players and the best and worst teams, having one great player was not always enough. The records of Ty Cobb's Tigers, Nap Lajoie's Indians, Honus Wagner's Pirates, Christy Mathewson's Giants, and Walter Johnson's Senators—three world titles among the five Hall of Famers—attest to that.

Before the development of organized farm systems, most great players were initially signed by independent minor league clubs, often a local team, and then sold to big league clubs after they stood out in that lower level competition. This system relieved the majors of paying for an extensive player development system, but it also meant that future stars could be auctioned off to the highest bidder. When the prices that minor league operators were demanding for their best prospects soared in the 1920s, Major League teams started buying minor league clubs to ensure a supply of reasonably priced talent.

Most of the early dynasties of the twentieth century were built around either a pair of all-time great players, like the 1928–31 Athletics of Lefty Grove and Jimmie Foxx, or one all-time great with a solid supporting cast, like the 1906–11 Cubs of Mordecai "Three Finger" Brown and his stellar infield. Baseball's first dynasty of the century might be virtually forgotten now if not for a few memorable lines of poetry.

Chicago Cubs, 1906–11

YEAR	REGW-L	FIN	PW	DIFF	PWS	W-L
1906	116-36	1	977	147	785	L
1907	107-45	1	951	91	693	W
1908	99-55	1	382	55	618	W
1909	104-49	2	253			
1910	104-50	1	889	-5	489	L
1911	92-62	2	238			

A good team in 1904 and '05, winning 90-plus games both years, the Cubs made the leap to first place by adding pitcher Jack Pfiester, third baseman Harry Steinfeldt, and outfielder Jimmy Sheckard—all either twenty-seven or twenty-eight years old—to an already strong core. With pitchers Brown, Ed Reulbach, Orval Overall, Jack Taylor, and Pfiester; outstanding defense up the middle in infielders Johnny Evers and Joe Tinker and catcher Johnny Kling; and several productive bats, the Cubs won back-to-back world championships in 1907 and 1908 as well as National League pennants in 1906 and 1910. They finished second in 1909 with 104 wins.

The two dynasties of the second decade of the dead-ball era—the 1909–14 Philadelphia Athletics and the 1912–18 Boston Red Sox—were built on astute player acquisitions from independent minor league clubs. Both were dispersed for financial reasons while they still were capable of winning.

Although Connie Mack's Athletics captured two pennants in the first five seasons of the American League, the groundwork for a true dynasty was laid in 1909, when Mack installed Eddie Collins at second base, Jack Barry at shortstop, and Frank "Home Run" Baker at third, improving his club offensively and defensively. With the so-called $100,000 Infield and a rotation featuring Chief Bender, Jack Coombs, and Eddie Plank, the A's won the World Series in 1910, 1911, and 1913 and another AL flag in 1914. Mack's teams sported young, inexpensive players, often college-educated. Following the shocking defeat by the Miracle Braves in the 1914 series, an angry Mack—known for squeezing his dollars so tightly that the eagles screamed—sold off most of his powerful roster to clear the salaries.

The breakup of the A's left a power vacuum that would be filled first by the Boston Red Sox and later by the New York Yankees. Tris Speaker helped lead Boston to world championships in 1912 and 1915, and the team won two more titles with an emerging young pitcher named Babe Ruth and a supporting cast. When Ruth was sold to the Yankees in 1920, New York assumed the role of American League powerhouse, winning three straight pennants in 1921–23—and dozens more to come.

Outstanding pitching, and a ballpark that was a graveyard for hitters, helped the Red Sox to contend with and ultimately overtake the A's. Outfielder Speaker and pitcher Smokey Joe Wood were the cornerstones of Boston's first championship club of 1912. The Sox then won three titles in a four-year span behind a superb mound corps—featuring Wood, Ruth, Rube Foster, Carl Mays, Dutch Leonard, and Ernie Shore—backed by an excellent defense led by Speaker and Harry Hooper. Ruth added power off the bench before converting to a semi-regular outfielder by 1918. The salary-induced trades of Speaker and Wood after 1915 and the sale of Ruth after 1919 tore apart a truly great team.

The Roaring Twenties—probably the least competitive decade of the century aside from the fifties—saw four separate dynasties make their mark. The first two, the Giants and the Yankees, shared the Polo Grounds until Yankee Stadium opened in 1923. John McGraw's Giants bested their AL tenants in the 1921 and 1922 World Series, but the tables were turned when the Yanks moved across the river to Ruth's capacious new house in the Bronx in 1923.

By 1916, John McGraw's old Giants, which had won five pennants in ten years between 1904 and 1913, were past their prime, so New York traded away stalwarts Christy Mathewson, Fred Merkle, and Larry Doyle. The following season, McGraw's revamped squad blew away the National League competition,

The "$100,000 Infield" helped carry Connie Mack's Philadelphia Athletics to four pennants and three championships between 1910 and 1914. By 1915, three-quarters of the infield and four ace pitchers had been sold or traded away by Mack, and the A's plummeted to the bottom of the standings—for seven straight years.

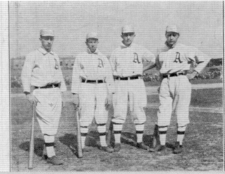

Philadelphia Athletics, 1909–14

YEAR	REGW-L	FIN	PW	DIFF	PWS	W-L
1909	95-58	2	284			
1910	102-48	1	894	5	511	W
1911	101-50	1	891	22	548	W
1912	90-62	3	44			
1913	96-57	1	671	-37	420	W
1914	99-53	1	796	37	580	L

Boston Red Sox, 1912–18

YEAR	REGW-L	FIN	PW	DIFF	PWS	W-L
1912	105-47	1	903	9	520	W
1913	79-71	4	24			
1914	91-62	2	172			
1915	101-50	1	602	77	659	W
1916	91-63	1	445	-19	465	W
1917	90-62	2	170			
1918	75-51	1	481	-56	380	W

The opening of Fenway Park in 1912 helped catapult the Boston Red Sox to dynasty status. Before the days of Fenway's ominous Green Monster and the development of the "lively" ball, Boston's talented pitching staff was able to make the most of its environs, leading the league in shutouts in three of the team's four championship seasons during the decade.

although they lost to the White Sox in six games in the World Series. After consecutive second-place finishes the next three years, New York ascended to the top for four straight seasons from 1921 to 1924. The Giants did not overwhelm the NL as the Yankees did the AL, but they managed to win two series with good and deep pitching and the strong bats of young stars like Frankie Frisch, George Kelly, and Ross Youngs, plus veteran Irish Meusel. Against the Senators in 1924, the Giants were one bad hop away from a possible third series victory.

After the Yankees franchise won its first world championship in 1923, it added a new first baseman named Lou Gehrig in 1925 and took two more World Series in the decade. The original Bronx Bombers would win their last title with the dynamic Ruth-Gehrig duo in 1932. Interrupting New York's skein was a specter from the past: Connie Mack's Athletics. Content to lose for a decade so long as he eked out a profit, Mack assembled the core of a new dynasty in the late 1920s. A virtual reprise of 1911–14 followed, with Philadelphia winning two World Series and three pennants in four years before slipping to second in 1932 and again incurring Mack's pecuniary wrath.

The emergence of outfielder Al Simmons and pitcher Lefty Grove had returned the A's to contention in 1925. Without a strong supporting cast, however, Philly couldn't rise above second until 1929, when two more youngsters—catcher Mickey Cochrane and super-slugger Jimmie Foxx—burst onto the scene, and the A's unseated the Yankees with one of the most powerful teams ever. Grove had support from a deep mound staff and strong defense. The club won World Series in 1929 and 1930. In 1932, the A's fell from the top, and Mack began unloading his stars.

New York Giants, 1921–24

YEAR	REGW-L	FIN	PW	DIFF	PWS	W-L
1921	94-59	1	552	-37	408	W
1922	93-61	1	559	-6	488	W
1923	95-58	1	582	-24	447	L
1924	93-60	1	378	11	524	L

Philadelphia Athletics, 1928–31

YEAR	REGW-L	FIN	PW	DIFF	PWS	W-L
1928	98-55	2	381			
1929	104-46	1	960	48	603	W
1930	102-52	1	812	65	650	W
1931	107-45	1	897	48	603	L

PHILADELPHIA "ATHLETICS"
AMERICAN LEAGUE PENNANT WINNERS "1929"

THE CLASSIC-ERA DYNASTIES

The dynasties of the so-called classic era span the time from the organization of strong farm systems and demise of the independent minor leagues to expansion in the 1960s. It was a period of tremendous turmoil for the game, starting with the Great Depression of the 1930s, World War II and integration in the 1940s, and finally, the abandonment of old ballparks and neighborhoods and the relocation of franchises in the 1950s.

The Depression years saw suitably depressing baseball for all but Yankees and Cardinals fans. Following the A's impressive but brief reign, the Yankees returned in 1932 to claim even greater glory, winning the first of five world championships in the decade. The Bronx Bombers of 1936 to 1939—winners of four consecutive titles while losing a total of only three World Series games during that stretch—have a legitimate claim to being the greatest team in baseball history. Even the tragic illness and retirement of Gehrig, "The Iron Horse," in 1939 did not stop the New York juggernaut, which won two more World Series in the early 1940s.

The St. Louis Cardinals of the mid-1920s through the mid-1930s were the first fruits of Branch Rickey's innovations. By creating baseball's first farm system, then pushing player development to a level no one has seen since, the pioneering Rickey took a perennial doormat and made it a perennial contender. It was a lesson that "The Mahatma" would take to Brooklyn, where he constructed another dynasty in the 1940s.

The Cardinals of the late 1920s and early 1930s were the most motley dynasty of the century, as evidenced by their six managers in nine years. Aside from "The Fordham Flash," Frankie Frisch (who came over from the Giants in a 1927 swap of Hall of Fame second basemen with Rogers Hornsby), regulars like Chick Hafey and Jim Bottomley and pitchers Jesse Haines and Wild Bill Hallahan are barely remembered today. Still, St. Louis won four pennants and two World Series between 1926 and 1931. With the addition of John "Pepper" Martin, Joe "Ducky" Medwick, and Jay "Dizzy" Dean, the Redbirds coalesced into the famous Gas House Gang—a colorful, combative, and competitive team that took another world championship in 1934.

Above: Connie Mack and his A's were back on top in 1929. This collection of all-stars was able to unseat the powerful Yankees, winning over 100 games three years running (1929–31). By the end of the decade, however, Philadelphia was back at the bottom. Shipping Al Simmons to Chicago in 1933, Mickey Cochrane to Detroit in 1934, Lefty Grove to Boston in 1934 and Jimmie Foxx in 1936, the Athletics finished dead last nine times between 1935 and 1946.

St. Louis Cardinals, 1926–35

YEAR	REGW-L	FIN	PW	DIFF	PWS	W-L
1926	89-65	1	363	-13	471	W
1927	92-61	2	261			
1928	95-59	1	427	-39	414	L
1929	78-74	4	11			
1930	92-62	1	374	-65	350	L
1931	101-53	1	843	-48	397	W
1932	72-82	6	6			
1933	82-71	4	33			
1934	95-58	1	479	-35	423	W
1935	96-58	2	276			

Pitching brothers Jay "Dizzy" Dean and Paul "Daffy" Dean won all four games for the Gas House Gang in the 1934 World Series. It was the Cardinals' third title since 1926. In its previous championships, St. Louis bested two other dynasties: the New York Yankees in 1926 and the Philadelphia Athletics in 1931. (Their 1934 opponent, the Detroit Tigers, won the title a year later.)

The war years of the 1940s saw a second dynasty take shape in St. Louis, aided by the fact that the Cardinals used draft deferments to retain many of their regulars through the 1944 season—notably Stan "The Man" Musial, the National League's best player. The St. Louis club that Rickey built dominated the game until 1947, when Rickey's next rehab project—the once-bankrupt Bridegrooms of Brooklyn—burst upon the league.

St. Louis's extensive farm system produced more than enough talent to outclass the NL during World War II, capturing four pennants and three World Series in five years. Infielders Marty Marion and Whitey Kurowski were draft-exempt; it was only when Musial and catcher Walker Cooper were finally called up in 1945 that the Cards fell to second. They returned to the top in 1946, and Musial and company remained contenders into the 1950s, but the team's failure to integrate left them in the wake of the Dodgers and Giants.

Unlike in St. Louis, Branch Rickey's Brooklyn club was not purely the product of his extensive farm system: Brooklyn's signing of Jackie Robinson caused a permanent paradigm shift in baseball. The Dodgers gained their critical edge by virtue of their trailblazing integration in 1947, when they won the first of six pennants in ten years. Aside from the haughty Yankees, whose vast resources allowed them to continue winning even while spurning black talent, no other team would become a dynasty after 1947 without being truly integrated.

While Rickey built the great Dodgers teams of the 1940s and 1950s with his farm system and by signing Negro League players, Walter O'Malley kept the Dodgers at the top even after pushing Rickey out in 1950, though the hated Yankees continued to vex Brooklyn in the World Series until 1955.

The Dodgers of the late 1940s won with speed and disciplined hitters like Robinson, Pee Wee Reese, Pete Reiser, and Eddie Stanky. By the early 1950s, farm products Gil Hodges and Duke Snider, along with Negro Leaguers Roy Campanella and Don Newcombe, added power to the attack and a powerful ace to an otherwise undistinguished pitching staff. In contrast to their bitter rivals in the Bronx, the

Dodgers rarely made midseason deals to strengthen the club, relying instead on homegrown stars and further farm products like Jim Gilliam, Carl Erskine, and Johnny Podres. After moving to Los Angeles in 1958, it took the Dodgers a few years to find the right combination again. They did win a second world championship in 1959 with a weak team that included many Brooklyn holdovers at the end of their careers. However, Los Angeles barely scraped by Milwaukee, and it wasn't until 1961 that the West Coast Dodgers really hit their stride.

THE EXPANSION-ERA DYNASTIES

The addition of four new teams at the start of the 1960s, and four more at the end, completely changed the landscape of the national game. Two relocated teams, the Dodgers and the Athletics, established the first dynasties on the West Coast. The Orioles, another relocated team, established a dynasty thirteen years after it moved to Baltimore from St. Louis, where the Browns had won only one pennant in fifty-two years.

Not even Charlie Dressen, Brooklyn's manager from 1951 to 1953, could have predicted the team's dominance over the National League in the late 1940s and 1950s. Shown here before the 1951 season with coaches Clyde Sukeforth, Jake Pitler, and Cookie Lavagetto, Dressen led Brooklyn to pennants in 1952 and '53, only to fall at the hands of the Yankees both times. The Dodgers finally got over the hurdle in 1955 under manager Walter Alston.

St. Louis Cardinals, 1941–46

YEAR	REGW-L	FIN	PW	DIFF	PWS	W-L
1941	97-56	2	351			
1942	106-48	1	589	19	542	W
1943	105-49	1	943	46	600	L
1944	105-49	1	883	104	720	W
1945	95-59	2	325			
1946	98-58	1	519	-47	398	W

Brooklyn/Los Angeles Dodgers, 1946–59

YEAR	REGW-L	FIN	PW	DIFF	PWS	W-L
1946	96-60	2	425			
1947	94-60	1	597	-20	456	L
1948	84-70	3	118			
1949	97-57	1	548	0	500	L
1950	89-65	2	321			
1951	97-60	2	481			
1952	96-57	1	580	10	522	L
1953	105-49	1	902	26	557	L
1954	92-62	2	247			
1955	98-55	1	867	18	540	W
1956	93-61	1	382	-26	443	L
1957	84-70	3	86			
1958	71-83	7	3			
1959	88-68	1	417	-46	400	W

After moving to spacious Dodger Stadium in Chavez Ravine, Los Angeles assumed the mantle of supremacy from its Brooklyn predecessor. The Dodgers hosted the defending-champion Cincinnati Reds in the stadium opener on April 10, 1962, and they went on to lead the league in attendance in every season during their 1962–66 dynasty.

After two second-place finishes, Los Angeles won three pennants and two World Series as Sandy Koufax, Don Drysdale, and their supporting cast (including Dodger Stadium) completely stifled opposing hitters. The Dodgers were the first dynasty of the expansion era, thriving during the offensive crash of the mid-1960s as power pitching ruled the game.

The patchwork 1959 Dodgers—one of the worst world championship teams ever—only became *The Dodgers* of the 1960s when outfielders Willie and Tommie Davis came aboard in 1961. Aided by pitcher-friendly Chavez Ravine, Koufax and Drysdale became a fearless and fearsome 1-2 starting duo. As in Brooklyn, more homegrown players, including Ron Fairly, John Roseboro, Frank Howard, Jim Lefebvre, and Wes Parker, arrived to contribute. Longtime minor league knockabout Maury Wills performed well for a decade after being promoted to the bigs in 1959. The 1960s Dodgers narrowly missed a fourth pennant, losing in 1962 to San Francisco in a three-game playoff series after the teams finished with identical regular-season records. When Koufax retired and Wills and Tommie Davis were traded following the 1966 World Series sweep at the hands of the Baltimore Orioles, the team crumbled immediately.

Los Angeles Dodgers, 1961–66

YEAR	REGW-L	FIN	PW	DIFF	PWS	W-L
1961	89-65	2	273			
1962	102-63	2	358			
1963	99-63	1	590	-35	424	W
1964	80-82	6	15			
1965	97-65	1	449	-31	434	W
1966	95-67	1	385	-20	456	L

Left: Built on speed, pitching, and defense, Walter Alston's Dodgers benefited from young homegrown talent and veteran leadership. In 1965, they won their second World Series in three years, defeating the Minnesota Twins in a seven-game classic. Los Angeles hit a league-low 78 home runs during the season, but their team ERA of 2.81 was enough to edge out rival San Francisco for the pennant.

Below: The Cardinals didn't win their first pennant until 1926—becoming the last National League franchise to reach the World Series—but over the next five decades, they established three different dynasties. To date, St. Louis has won more world championships than any other NL team.

The Cardinals finally returned to power in the mid-sixties, after nearly a two-decade absence from the fall classic. They won world championships in 1964 and '67, and they were within a few outs of another in 1968. The fact that the Redbirds' dynasty of the 1960s featured black stars Bob Gibson, Lou Brock, and Curt Flood showed how the team's refusal to embrace integration had doomed Stan Musial and his mates to also-ran status for fifteen years. (St. Louis waited seven years after Robinson's debut to integrate.)

The Cards posted their winningest season in thirteen years in 1963, and they reached the top a year later after the midseason acquisition of Lou Brock. Following their 1964 World Series win, the aging club collapsed. St. Louis quickly retooled, though, adding veterans Orlando Cepeda and

St. Louis Cardinals, 1963–68

YEAR	REGW-L	FIN	PW	DIFF	PWS	W-L
1963	93-69	2	204			
1964	93-69	1	241	-37	420	W
1965	80-81	7	7			
1966	83-79	6	23			
1967	101-60	1	720	59	627	W
1968	97-65	1	672	-37	420	L

Baltimore Orioles, 1966–74

YEAR	REGW-L	FIN	PW	DIFF	PWC	W-L	DIFF	PWS	W-L
1966	97-63	1	644				16	535	W
1967	76-85	6	4						
1968	91-71	2	98						
1969	109-53	1e	934	74	636	W	56	621	L
1970	108-54	1e	887	62	615	W	47	602	W
1971	101-57	1e	841	12	523	W	40	587	L
1972	80-74	3e	143						
1973	97-65	1e	687	19	535	L			
1974	91-71	1e	467	6	511	L			

Brooks Robinson jumps for joy after Baltimore swept Los Angeles in the 1966 World Series. In the clincher, Dave McNally pitched the third straight shutout for the Orioles, who kept the Dodger hitters scoreless for thirty-three consecutive innings. Robinson, McNally, and catcher Andy Etchebarren were among the seven O's who remained with the team throughout their nine-year dynasty.

Roger Maris and farm-system hurlers Nelson Briles and Steve Carlton to the core of peerless Gibson, catcher Tim McCarver, Brock and Flood in the outfield, and infielders Julian Javier and Dal Maxvill. They won the 1967 series and came within a whisker in 1968. Owner Gussie Busch then petulantly broke up his high-salaried club, dealing away Cepeda, Flood, and Carlton.

The last dynasty of the 1960s, the Baltimore Orioles, lasted into the mid-1970s and straddled the advent of divisional play in 1969. Hank Bauer's powerful 1966 team and Earl Weaver's 1969–74 squads were built upon a hitting philosophy that prevails in the AL to this day: Eschew "little-ball" tactics like running and bunting, stack the lineup with disciplined hitters who can get on base, and wait for a three-run homer to break the game open. The O's also boasted top-notch pitching with Jim Palmer, Mike Cuellar, Dave McNally, and others.

Following a heartbreaking loss to the Yankees in 1964, Baltimore promoted youngsters Davey Johnson, Boog Powell, Paul Blair, and Jim Palmer. Adding power-hitting veteran Frank Robinson in 1966 led the "Baby Birds" to an easy pennant and a four-game sweep of the favored Dodgers. Baltimore followed the classic pattern—solid starting pitching, strong defense up the middle, and power at the infield and outfield corners. Injuries ravaged the young staff, but by 1969, Palmer, McNally, and Tom Phoebus formed a new nucleus for manager Earl Weaver. Trades for veterans Cuellar and outfielder Don Buford completed a club that won three consecutive pennants. After being stunned by the Miracle Mets in the memorable 1969 fall classic, the Birds topped the mighty Cincinnati Reds in 1970 for another world championship.

Cincinnati's Big Red Machine of the 1970s may have been the most arrogant modern dynasty, though its achievements ultimately fell short of the Reds' perennial self-assessment as the best team around. Despite a truly awesome starting lineup that made Cincy the team to beat for a decade, mediocre pitching kept them from doing much more than breaking even in October. The Reds racked up six divisional titles and four pennants but only two world championships, as the team peaked in 1975–76.

By 1970, most of the pieces were in place for a decade-long run in Cincinnati, with farm products Johnny Bench, Tony Perez, Pete Rose, Bobby Tolan, Dave Concepcion, and Gary Nolan. Trades brought in the incomparable Joe Morgan, as well as Tom Hall, Pedro Borbon, George Foster, Cesar Geronimo, and Jack Billingham; the Cincy system added Ken Griffey, Dan Driessen, Don Gullett, and Ross Grimsley. After three postseason losses in the early 1970s, Sparky Anderson's club beat the Red Sox in the heart-stopping 1975 World Series, then swept the Yankees in 1976. The last hurrah of the Big Red Machine came in 1981, when Cincinnati compiled the best record in the National League but was excluded from the postseason since it didn't finish first in the West in either "half" of the strike-marred campaign.

While the Reds dominated the "senior circuit," two bare-knuckled dynasties succeeded the Orioles in the American League. Oakland won three consecutive world

Manager Sparky Anderson was on top of the world after leading his Big Red Machine to back-to-back titles in 1975 and '76. With future Hall of Famers Tony Perez, Pete Rose, Joe Morgan, and Johnny Bench, the Reds of the 1970s featured one of the most potent lineups ever assembled. Morgan won the league MVP award in each of Cincinnati's championship seasons.

championships from 1972 to 1974 despite friction in the clubhouse and the players' hatred of the team's owner. The eccentric and meddlesome tightwad Charley Finley saw his A's become the first dynasty dismantled by having its stars leave via free agency. The fractious 1976–81 Yankees, under an equally meddlesome and controversial owner, became the first dynasty built through free agency.

A tremendous burst of talent from the Kansas City–Oakland system from the mid-1960s through the early 1970s produced such stars as Bert Campaneris, Reggie Jackson, Catfish Hunter, Rollie Fingers, Blue Moon Odom, Gene Tenace, Joe Rudi, Vida Blue, and Sal Bando. Add 1972 acquisition Ken Holtzman, and Oakland had a dynamo. Gruff Dick Williams was a brilliant manager for the club, keeping the team's bumptious star egos in check and constructing productive lineups and solid bullpens. After five consecutive division titles and three straight World Series wins, most of the stars either left via free agency or were dealt by Finley as he cut his payroll to the bone.

Cincinnati Reds, 1969–81

YEAR	REGW-L	FIN	PW	DIFF	PWC	W-L	DIFF	PWS	W-L
1969	89-73	3w	209						
1970	102-60	1w	862	81	649	W	-47	397	L
1971	79-83	4w	62						
1972	95-59	1w	763	-2	496	W	17	537	L
1973	99-63	1w	557	102	687	L			
1974	98-64	2w	307						
1975	108-54	1w	966	96	676	W	73	657	W
1976	102-60	1w	820	7	514	W	20	544	W
1977	88-74	2w	147						
1978	92-69	2w	301						
1979	90-71	1w	558	-36	432	L			
1980	89-73	2w	204						
1981	66-42	2w	627						

Oakland Athletics, 1971–76

YEAR	REGW-L	FIN	PW	DIFF	PWC	W-L	DIFF	PWS	W-L
1971	101-60	1w	918	-12	477	L			
1972	93-62	1w	658	49	595	W	-17	463	W
1973	94-68	1w	648	-19	465	W	71	652	W
1974	90-72	1w	520	-6	489	W	-74	341	W
1975	98-64	1w	730	11	522	L			
1976	87-74	2w	328						

THE FREE-AGENT–ERA DYNASTIES

The Yankees of the 1970s were the first dynasty built largely upon big spending for free agents, as George Steinbrenner spent millions outbidding other teams for Goose Gossage, former A's stars Catfish Hunter and Reggie Jackson, and numerous others. Succeeding Oakland, New York won three pennants and two world championships from 1976 to 1978 despite fisticuffs in the clubhouse and an imperious, intrusive owner in Steinbrenner.

Facing page: Eccentric owner Charles O. Finley was both a master of promotion and a great judge of talent. Though Charley O. the Mule, the A's mascot, contributed little to the team's success, Charley O. the owner turned around a franchise that had not posted a winning season since 1952. His Oakland A's of 1972–74 are the only non-Yankee team ever to win three consecutive championships.

The strategy that had returned the Yanks to the top of the heap also hastened the franchise's longest postseason drought since 1920. Unwise and pricey free-agent acquisitions by "King George" opened the door for other teams, and a new level of parity emerged. In stark contrast to the 1970s, when the top two teams combined to win eight or nine divisional titles in each of the four divisions, the 1980s were a free-for-all. Five or more teams from each division went to the postseason at least once. Only the Dodgers and Athletics managed to win more than three divisional titles in the decade. The closest anyone came to a dynasty was Oakland, where Tony La Russa's 1988–90 A's won three AL pennants in a row but were upset twice in the fall classic.

In the 1990s, revenue and payroll disparity between the haves and the have-nots increased dramatically as huge cable TV contracts exacerbated the disparity

by fattening the coffers of many large-market teams. In addition, new retro-style ballparks opened in many cities, bringing in fresh streams of fans and lucrative stadium sponsorships. The result was a complex picture where small-market clubs like Cleveland could compete financially with the wealthy clubs by virtue of selling out Jacobs Field every game for years. Atlanta, in a mid-size but rapidly growing market, prospered with revenue from the national broadcasts of Braves games on superstation WTBS, as well as from its new ballpark. A few contending clubs in large markets, like Boston, became even richer by setting up their own regional sports networks.

As a result of this financial revolution and the damage wrought by the strike-induced "nuclear winter" of 1994–95, many small-market and poor clubs cut payroll to the bone. The accepted wisdom was that it was better to keep expenses and risk low, thus guaranteeing a profit, even if that meant fielding losing teams year after year.

The first dynastic team to arise in the 1990s was Atlanta. General manager John Schuerholz and field manager Bobby Cox took the Braves from worst to first in 1991, and their club hasn't relinquished its hold on the NL East since. The organization produced a plethora of young talent on which to build, while the ability to spend hundreds of millions of Ted Turner's money allowed Atlanta to fill any needs with quality free agents. The Braves fared less well in October, however, showing both the blessings of the new postseason format, where the best teams almost always qualify, along with the curse of the new format—it's damn hard to win three postseason series in a row, no matter how good a team is.

Pitching has been the name of Atlanta's game throughout their unprecedented run. When twenty-one-year-old Steve Avery blossomed in 1991, he combined with Tom Glavine and John Smoltz to form the best rotation in the NL; farm products Ron Gant, Jeff Blauser, Dave Justice, and Mark Lemke bolstered the lineup. Starting in 1992, the Braves led the National League in fewest runs allowed for eleven straight

Bobby Cox gets into a heated argument with umpire Tim Welke during the 1996 fall classic—but few can argue that Atlanta doesn't belong among baseball's dynastic teams. Although the Braves have been able to collect only one World Series trophy, Cox is the only manager ever to lead a team to the postseason thirteen years in a row—and counting.

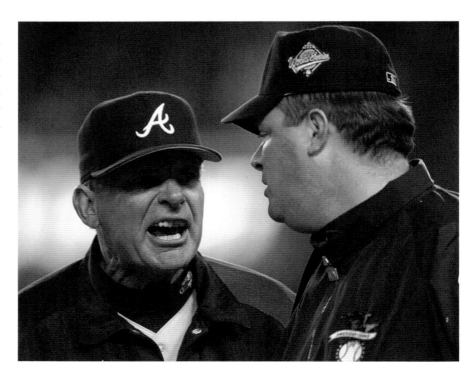

Atlanta Braves, 1991–2003

YEAR	REGW-L	FIN	PW	DIFF	PWD	W-L	DIFF	PWC	W-L	DIFF	PWS	W-L
1991	94-68	1w	523				-25	454	W	-6	487	L
1992	98-64	1w	745				12	526	W	-12	474	L
1993	104-58	1w	503				43	593	L			
1994	68-46	2e	723									
1995	90-54	1e	981	90	665	W	35	576	W	-69	352	W
1996	96-66	1e	884	37	570	W	50	608	W	25	554	L
1997	101-61	1e	916	104	690	W	55	618	L			
1998	106-56	1e	928	102	687	W	49	606	L			
1999	103-59	1e	644	37	570	W	41	589	W	31	567	L
2000	95-67	1e	445	0	500	L						
2001	88-74	1e	411	-31	442	W	-25	454	L			
2002	101-59	1e	879	32	560	L						
2003	101-61	1e	730	80	647	L						

years. When free agent Greg Maddux signed on in 1993, a devastating and durable rotation was born. Homegrown Javy Lopez, Ryan Klesko, Chipper Jones, Mark Wohlers, Kevin Millwood, Andruw Jones, and Rafael Furcal blended into a roster filled out with transitory veterans. Despite this sustained level of excellence, Atlanta experienced repeated frustration in the postseason, winning only one World Series out of five in twelve consecutive October forays.

At the opposing end of two of Atlanta's October losses were none other than the New York Yankees. Just as Atlanta was forming its dynasty in the National League, the Yankees re-emerged in the mid-1990s as the American League superpower. After being cut short by the strike in 1994 and the Seattle Mariners in 1995, the Yanks brought in skipper Joe Torre, who led New York to six World Series in eight years, yielding four world championships. Wheeling and dealing and spending hundreds of millions of dollars, Steinbrenner's Yankees brought in high-profile free agents and other stars through salary-dump trades. Hated by some, feared by everyone, and loved by their legions of fans worldwide, the damn Yankees were back as the new century dawned.

ALL OTHER THINGS ARE NOT EQUAL

Only one team since the dawn of free agency in 1976 has won more than two world championships: The Yankees, of course, with six. Sixteen other teams experienced the glory of "that championship year," but none of those could repeat its feat more than once. Even granting New York's built-in advantage, the three-layer postseason format should have put an end to that kind of dynastic dominance.

The 1994–2003 Yankees are the fifth dynasty in the team's history, and they may not be finished yet. Joe Boyd is by no means the only fan out there who cries out every October, "Just how do those damn Yankees do it?"

FIRST NINE OF THE

CINCINNATI

(RED STOCKINGS) BASE BALL CLUB.

THE RED STOCKINGS
BASEBALL'S FIRST PROFESSIONAL TEAM

IN 1869, HARRY Wright made the revolutionary decision to pay the players on his Cincinnati ball club—or at least the Red Stockings were the first to admit openly that the players received financial compensation. With player salaries ranging from $600 to $1,400, the team traveled the country, competing in fifty-seven official matches as well as many exhibition contests during the year—without losing a single one. It took until June of the following year for the Red Stockings to lose their first game, ending their phenomenal eighty-one-game winning streak.

The first article reprinted here, from the *Brooklyn Eagle,* offers a recap of the 1869 season and reflects on the resourcefulness of this Cincinnati juggernaut. The second piece is the *New York Times*'s coverage of the first defeat of the Red Stockings.

SPORTS AND PASTIMES—BASE BALL

The Season Just Passed.— The season for playing is drawing to a close, and we are enabled to see how matters stand. The season was commenced with a new feature, and it was almost in the light of an experiment to be tried, in recognizing professional players. It has been tried and to all appearances has worked well. The Cincinnati Club of Cincinnati has been the first club to take up professionalism in a thoroughly systematic way. They placed their players upon salary, bound them down by contract, to observe certain agreements, placed them under a captain who was given absolute control over them in matters appertaining to the playing of the game. What has been the result? Simply that it has been the most successful club in the country. The nine has played nearly sixty games, and lost none at all. Is there not a lesson here to be learned from the season's play? Can we not profit by what has shown to be the result of temperate habits, systematic and intelligent practice. Here in the city of Brooklyn, where the clubs have so long borne the palm of excellence, we have allowed a comparatively new club to carry off the honors of the season. This in a great measure is our own fault, and next season we should look to it, that it does not occur again.

It seemed to be the general impression in the early part of the season that the Atlantic Club would carry everything before it, but the terrible onslaught that the Cincinnati Club made upon the clubs of the East rudely dispelled our hopes. True, the "Red Stockings" were very shrewd in coming on at such an early date, before our clubs were in practice and it may be that in another contest with the Atlantics, the result might have been entirely different. Such a contest, the Atlantics have endeavored to bring about. They could not go to Cincinnati, for they probably were never so badly placed as during the present season. Three of their players occupied such positions, that it was a matter of simple impossibility to leave so long a time, as to go to Cincinnati and back. They proposed in August that the Cincinnati Club should come here and play the return game, but that club standing upon its undoubted right to have the return game upon their ground, refused as it had a right to do. So the matter ended. The Atlantics however, stand next in order of the Cincinnati Club having won the championship and lost fewer games than any. Yet for this club it has not been a successful season. They lost a series of games with the Haymakers which should not have been. A greater and steadier amount of practice will place them on their old footing.

— *Brooklyn Eagle,* November 11, 1869

This lithograph features the first nine of the 1869 Cincinnati Red Stockings (clockwise from upper left): Fred Waterman, third base; Calvin A. McVey, right field; George Wright, shortstop; Douglas Allison, catcher; Harry Wright, center field/pitcher; Charlie Gould, first base; Andrew J. Leonard, left field; Charles J. Sweasy, second base; Asa Brainard, pitcher.

THE RED STOCKINGS DEFEATED!
THE MOST EXCITING GAME ON RECORD—Eleven Innings Played with a Score of 8 to 7

Fully 20,000 people must have been in and around the Capitoline Ball Grounds in Brooklyn yesterday, on the occasion of the match between the Atlantics and Red Stockings, and though the weather was excessively warm, the immense assemblage bore the heat of the sun patiently for three hours, rather than forego a single inning's play of the contest, so absorbing an interest was the contest from first to last.

The general anticipation was that, in the half-demoralized condition of the Atlantic Club, which followed their defeat by the Forest City nine, the Red Stockings, flushed with their victory over the Mutuals, would have little difficulty in winning the game of yesterday; but the Atlantic managers surprised everybody by doing two things which no one thought they would do, and these things were their playing Pearce in their nine and using a dead ball in the game. To the latter they unquestionably owe their victory, as by using such a ball they afforded their players a chance for skillful fielding; and they greatly strengthened their nine by replacing Pearce in his old position.

The game opened in favor of the Cincinnatis by a score of 2 to 0, and at the close of the third innings the tally stood at 3 to 1 in their favor. In the fourth innings the Atlantics first began to score, and at the close of the sixth innings they had secured a lead of 4 to 3, small figures to look at, but a single run is an important advantage in a match such as this was. In the seventh innings the Cincinnatis rallied at the bat, and regained their lost lead, the tally at the close standing at 5 to 4 in their favor. In the next innings,

CHAMPIONS OF AMERICA.

Above: The Brooklyn Atlantics were undefeated for two years running in 1864 and 1865, enough to earn them the title of "Champions of America." By the end of the decade, the Atlantics had been supplanted by the Red Stockings as baseball's elite team. Brooklyn got the last word, though, handing the seemingly invincible Cincinnati club their first defeat.

Right: As baseball in Cincinnati entered a new century, the city was home to one of the nation's grandest ballparks. The temple-like structure known as the Palace of the Fans opened in 1902. The grandstand, which provided seating for some 3,000 fans, featured classical columns and a pediment behind home plate.

12,000 People at the Ball Park, Cincinnati, O.

however, the Atlantics scored one run after "whitewashing" their opponents, the game now standing at 5 to 5. The last innings was now commenced, amid great excitement, and when the Cincinnatis were put out for a blank, the game was considered sure for the Atlantics, and the yelling, partisan crowd present rejoiced in proportion as they thought they saw a sure ending in store for their pet club. The Red Stockings, however, disposed of the Atlantics without their being able to add a run to their score, and thereby left the game a tie. Henry, one of the Atlantic directors, now came on the field and wanted the game to stand at a draw, but to this the Cincinnatis would not consent. Just at this time Chapman, another of the directors of the Atlantic Club, as well as a player of the nine, took up their hats and began to go off the field as if the game was finished, and seeing this the crowd ran in upon the players and for a time confusion reigned supreme. The majority of the assemblage called for the game to be played out, and finally, after the Atlantics had all gone in to dress, the umpire decided to call "play," and if the Atlantics did not respond to give the game to the Cincinnatis. Seeing this the Atlantics came out on the field again, and resuming their places the contest went on again and the tenth innings was commenced. Once more the Cincinnatis were put out without scoring, and again the Atlantics went in to win, and but for a strategic piece of play by George Wright they would have done so, but Wright, by dropping a fly ball, made a double play and put the side out for a blank. This necessitated the playing of the eleventh innings, and this time the Cincinnatis scored two runs, and the game was booked for them as certain. By important fielding errors, however, the Atlantics managed to secure three runs for their share of the score, and amid the greatest excitement they closed the eleventh innings with the score in their favor by the totals of 8 to 7, Smith making the hit which saved them, Pearce the base running which tied the game, and Ferguson the winning run. The umpiring was the best of the season, Mr. Mills being thoroughly impartial and strict in keeping the players up to the rules.

The fielding was a model display on both sides, the errors being few and far between. The only drawback was the miserable partisan character of the assemblage which was the most discreditable gathering we have seen on the Capitoline Grounds for many years.

— *The New York Times*, June 15, 1870

Teams honored baseball's centennial year in 1969, acknowledging the 1869 Cincinnati Red Stockings as the pioneers of the professional game. The first organized league was established later, in 1871, as the National Association of Professional Baseball Players, which was succeeded by the National League in 1876.

GOLDEN JUBILEE
CINCINNATI REDS
Champions 1869-1919
OFFICIAL SOUVENIR SCORE CARD.

WORLD'S SERIES
GAMES

REDLAND FIELD
1919

THE BLACK SOX SCANDAL

from *Eight Men Out* by Eliot Asinof

THE 1919 CHICAGO **White Sox were, in the words of Eliot Asinof, "a mighty ball club with a history of triumphs." Those triumphs, however, soon gave way to disgrace when news broke that eight Sox players had done the unthinkable: They agreed to throw the World Series in exchange for cash.**

Asinof's *Eight Men Out* examines the full story of the scandal, from the earliest planning through the investigation and its aftermath. Asinof, who was born in the year of the scandal, is the author of several books, including *1919: America's Loss of Innocence* and the novels *Man on Spikes* and *Off-Season*.

On this Wednesday morning [October 1, 1919], 30,511 people paid their way into Redland Park. To the Cincinnati fans, there was a throbbing nervous excitement and a secret foreboding. For all their enthusiasm, few could realistically anticipate a World's Championship. Deep down inside, they foresaw the adversary walking all over them. Not even Miracle Men could be expected to stop the all-powerful colossus from the West.

For they were the Chicago White Sox, a mighty ball club with a history of triumphs. It was said that Chicago fans did not come to see them win: they came to see *how* . . . There was a growing mythology about this great team; the public had placed a stamp of invincibility on it. To Cincinnati fans who had never seen the White Sox play the image seemed frightening. These were the big-city boys coming down to show the small-towners how the game should be played. There was no other way for any real fan to see it.

There was, however, one incredible circumstance that would have a bearing on the outcome: eight members of the Chicago White Sox had agreed to throw the World Series . . .

• • •

On September 21, the eight ballplayers assembled after dinner in Chick Gandil's room at the Ansonia. In the history of American

---

The 1919 World Series opened at Redland Field in Cincinnati on October 1. Although the Reds won 96 games that year and had strong pitching and hitting, it took some dubious behind-the-scenes activity to stop the heavily favored Chicago White Sox.

sport, it would be difficult to find another meeting that led to events so shattering. The ballplayers, however, appeared to have treated it all lightly. There was none of the conspiratorial somberness that might normally be attached to such occasions. Several of them made a joke out of it all, suggesting special bonuses to the guys who could make the most errors or leave the most men on bases. Happy Felsch lapped it up: he recalled—aptly—that when he was a kid, he used to get hit on the head by fly balls that seemed to slip through his glove.

Gandil, however, made sure that the terms were clearly specified. He recounted how he had demanded $80,000—in advance—at his meeting with Sport Sullivan, who had agreed to get it. The ballplayers would be paid off in full before the opening game. Details on how the games were to be thrown would be worked out with Sullivan and his backers, depending on how they wished to manipulate the odds—and how Kid Gleason chose to work the pitchers.

With hindsight, this meeting looms as a macabre opening to a tragedy. No doubt a wiser man than any of these eight players would have known it then and there. Here were eight men at the peak of their careers, playing on a pennant-winning club that might well be rated as one of the great teams in baseball history. They were idols to millions of fans, especially in Chicago, perhaps the best baseball town in America. With the exception of [pitcher Eddie] Cicotte, they could look forward to six to ten years of continuing triumphs and rising incomes. Instead, they chose to risk all this for a sleazy promise of dirty money.

Here was Shoeless Joe Jackson, commonly rated as the greatest natural hitter the game had ever seen. At thirty, he had

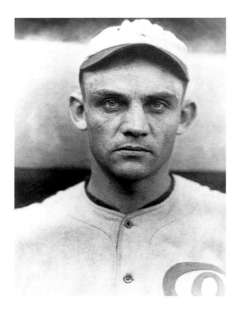

Above: Arnold "Chick" Gandil was the ringleader of the plot to throw the 1919 World Series. He and several of his teammates were fed up with the tightfisted ways of White Sox owner Charles Comiskey. Gandil was a weak-hitting, solid-fielding first baseman, but his career came to an abrupt end when the scandal broke.

Above, right: Widely considered one of the greatest players of his day, Joe Jackson batted .356 for his career, good enough for third best of all time (behind Ty Cobb and Rogers Hornsby). Even though he hit .375 and drove in a team-high six runs during the 1919 series, "Shoeless Joe" received a lifetime ban for his role in throwing the series. He played out his remaining days in semi-pro leagues.

passed ten sensational years in big-league ball, compiling a remarkable batting average of .356. His tremendous skill as a hitter kept improving with each passing year. He was a superb outfielder with a rifle for an arm.

Here was George "Buck" Weaver, smiling, boyish, not quite thirty, already heralded as the classiest third baseman in the game. Agile as a cat, defiant of all hitters, the only man Ty Cobb refused to bunt against. He had become a steady .300 hitter, climbing each year. He was an indomitable lover of baseball.

Here was Charles "Swede" Risberg, twenty-five years old, and in his third season in the majors. A big, rangy, brilliant shortstop, who could throw bullets to first base, who played ball like a man on fire.

Here was Oscar "Happy" Felsch, a warm, smiling, fast-moving outfielder, also under thirty. He was rapidly becoming a leading power hitter. As a centerfielder, he was among the best.

Here was Claude "Lefty" Williams, number two pitcher for the Sox. A quiet, soft-spoken Southerner with a highly skilled left arm. He had won 23 games, could boast of the finest control in baseball. On the mound, he always knew exactly what he was doing.

Then why . . . ?

Or, perhaps more significantly, why not?

It never entered their minds that they could not get away with their plan. There was almost no discussion of its dangers. They didn't even care about the men who would back it. The only security measure they ever took was to leave the hotel room one or two at a time.

For this was the world of baseball in 1919. Every one of them knew of thrown ball games. Two years before, they had participated in a strange manipulation that helped them win the American League pennant: almost the entire club had been openly assessed $45 each, ostensibly to reward two Detroit Tiger pitchers for beating Boston in a crucial series, but actually to bribe them to throw a double header to the

In the wake of the Black Sox Scandal, Kenesaw Mountain Landis was hired by the league's owners to serve as baseball's first commissioner. Here, Landis presides over an inquiry in his Chicago office. Although the eight players were acquitted of all criminal conspiracy charges in Cook County Supreme Court, Landis proclaimed, "Regardless of the verdict of juries, no player who throws a ballgame, no player that undertakes or promises to throw a ballgame, no player that sits in conference with a bunch of crooked players and gamblers where the ways and means of throwing a game are discussed and does not promptly tell his club about it, will ever play professional baseball."

Sox. Their own experience, as well as the existing corruption in baseball, made their participation in the fix all too easy.

Money was the goal, to be leaped at from a springboard of bitterness. These were eight bitter men with a common enemy: Charles Albert Comiskey. Whatever his stature in professional baseball, however many his notable contributions to its turbulent history, to his employees he was a cheap, stingy tyrant. All baseball salaries suffered in 1919, as noted, but even before that a skimpy paycheck was nothing new to a Chicago White Sox ballplayer. Joe Jackson, one of the greatest sluggers of his time, had never earned more than $6,000. Buck Weaver, the same. Gandil and Felsch were paid $4,000. Lefty Williams and Swede Risberg got less than $3,000. No players of comparable talent on other teams were paid as little. Compared with their 1919 World Series rivals from Cincinnati, these figures seemed pitiful. Outfielder Edd Roush, leading Reds hitter, though some 40 or 50 percentage points below Jackson, made $10,000. Heinie Groh, at third base, topped Weaver's salary by almost $2,000. First baseman Jake Daubert, recently acquired from Brooklyn, earned $9,000. It was the same all around the leagues. Many second-rate ballplayers on second-division ball clubs made more than the White Sox. It had been that way for years.

Eddie Cicotte was one of the top pitchers of his era, winning 28 and 29 games in Chicago's pennant-winning seasons of 1917 and 1919, respectively. During his tearful testimony about the scandal before the grand jury, Cicotte said that he needed the money to pay the mortgage on his farm: "I was thinking of the wife and kids."

The White Sox would receive their annual contracts and stare glumly at the figures. In the face of Comiskey's famous intransigeance, their protests were always feeble. Harry Grabiner, who, as club secretary, handled the contracts, would repeat the timeworn threat: Take it or leave it! The threat had absolute impact, backed by the rules and contracts of professional baseball itself. For each of them was owned by the club, totally and incontrovertibly. If they refused to accept the terms offered them, they could not play baseball anywhere else in the professional world. No one could hire them. This was the famous reserve clause, included in every contract, the rock upon which professional baseball rested. It said, in effect, that the club owner would employ the player's services for one year, holding in reserve the right to renew his contract the following year. And so on, in perpetuity.

But there was more to their grievances. Comiskey's penuriousness went beyond their salaries. It was his habit to squeeze them in petty ways as well. They resented his $3-a-day meal allowance while on the road. It was a kind of joke among other clubs, almost all of whom received a minimum of $4. Even the poorer clubs that finished in the second division did not cut such corners. This was all the more an irritant since Comiskey seemed inordinately concerned about the newspapermen who hung around. For them, he had a special room in Comiskey Park, with a huge table laden with succulent roasts and salads, a chef to serve them, and a bottomless supply of fine bourbon to liven their spirits. His generosity here was unmatched. Yet his great ball club might run out on the field in the filthiest uniforms the fans had ever seen: Comiskey had given orders to cut down on the cleaning bills.

There were betrayals, too. Like Comiskey's promise to give Cicotte a $10,000-bonus in 1917 if he won 30 games. When the great pitcher threatened to reach that figure, it was said that Comiskey had him benched. The excuse, of course, was to rest him for the World Series. There had also been talk that Comiskey had promised all the players a bonus if they won the 1917 pennant. They won it—and the world's championship. The bonus was a case of champagne at the victory celebration.

A monetary frustration hung over them all. If the public looked up to them, admired them, chased after them, this very prominence served to exacerbate their sense of helplessness. Their taste of fame whetted their appetites, but there was no meat and potatoes to satisfy them. All they'd been eating was Charles Comiskey's garbage. They wanted to shout to everyone: "Look, it's not the way you think it is!" The obvious outlet for their complaints was cut off from them, for newspapermen were Comiskey's boys. Their bread was buttered on the other side. They rode in the Pullmans as guests of the club owner, all expenses paid and then some. Officially they were on the staff of their respective papers, but Comiskey always made them feel as if they were working for him. And in the process, he made the ballplayers feel like dirt.

It was foreboding that Gandil's meeting broke up without any real resolution. The players could rationalize that the next move was not theirs anyway: it was up to Sport Sullivan to come up with the money. Even now Lefty Williams didn't particularly go for the idea. Happy Felsch covered a growing uneasiness.

They would all wait and see.

Hall of Fame catcher Gabby Hartnett autographs a baseball for a loyal Cubs fan—in this case it's Sonny Capone, son of noted gangster Al Capone, who sits beside him. Notwithstanding the occasional crossing of baseball and criminal elements such as this, the game was largely cleaned up in the years following the 1919 World Series scandal.

1941: AN UNMATCHABLE SUMMER

by Ray Robinson

IF THE 1919 **World Series was a dark blot in the history of Major League baseball, 1941 is seen by many as the last truly pure season. The final baseball campaign before the United States was thrust fully into World War II saw unsurpassed achievements by legends Joe DiMaggio and Ted Williams and great postseason drama.**

On the fiftieth anniversary of that memorable season, longtime sportswriter Ray Robinson reflected on the events that took place on the ball fields of pre–Pearl Harbor America. Robinson has written biographies of Lou Gehrig and Christy Mathewson and co-authored histories of the New York Giants and New York Yankees.

On a gleaming spring day in Florida 50 years ago, Joe DiMaggio, eager as usual to get to work, received a traffic ticket for speeding. As things turned out, so the exaggeration goes, it was the only time that the New York Yankees' centerfielder was stopped during that enchanted year.

DiMaggio's elegant presence and 56-game hitting streak were hardly the only reasons that 1941 merits inclusion in any baseball time capsule. That summer, as the United States edged toward entry into World War II, the game produced a blend of grand-scale heroics from Ted Williams and his .406 batting average, Bob Feller, Lefty Grove, Bucky Walters, Pete Reiser, Tommy Henrich, Whitlow Wyatt, Cecil Travis, Country Slaughter, Johnny Vander Meer, Leo Durocher and Dixie Walker.

That summer, in the waning days of the Great Depression when more than nine million remained unemployed, baseball seemed to provide a cocoon for many Americans amid lingering economic woes of the past and Hitler's ominous conquests in Europe. The basic nourishment at ballparks was the nickel hot dog, and, after the game, a full-course dinner at a good restaurant could be eaten for half a dollar. Tickets to the ballpark ranged from 50 cents for a perch in the bleachers to $1.10 for general admission to $3 for the best seat in the house.

Joe DiMaggio's historic 56-game hitting streak in 1941 captured the attention of the nation, with songs written in his honor and people everywhere tuning in to see how "Joltin' Joe" fared each day. DiMaggio's grace at bat and in the field—and his later marriage, albeit brief, to Marilyn Monroe—made him a true American icon.

On the field, New York boasted 3 of the 16 Major League ball clubs. The Yankees, under Joe McCarthy, were set to scale the heights again, after losing to Detroit in 1940. The Brooklyn Dodgers, pennant-less since 1920, played under the strident lash of the former pool hall hustler from Massachusetts, Leo Durocher. At the rusty old Polo Grounds, the Giants were being managed by Bill Terry, who had hit .400 in 1930, something no one had done since then.

It was DiMaggio, however, who set the tone for the season. After winning batting titles in 1939 and 1940, the 26-year-old outfielder had become the acclaimed successor to Babe Ruth and Lou Gehrig. In 1941, he was playing for $37,500 (the average big league salary that year was $7,300), but only after being forced to stage a holdout against a hardened Yankee front office.

As the 1941 season began, DiMaggio had already hit in 19 straight games in spring training. He added eight games at the beginning of the regular season before drifting into a brief slump. On May 15, a day sticky as flypaper at Yankee Stadium, DiMaggio singled against Chicago's Edgar Smith. Baseball's most sustained skein of batting brilliance had begun.

The tapestry of consistency continued through May, days that were cluttered with speculation about Rudolf Hess's unscheduled aerial adventure in a stolen plane from Augsberg to Scotland, apparently attempting to arrange peace with the British. There were also fallacious reports that the German boxer Max Schmeling had been killed by the British in Crete while trying to escape capture.

And the news of war intersected with the news of sports. Hank Greenberg, a bachelor with no dependents and runner-up for the most valuable player award in the American League in 1940, played the first three weeks of the 1941 season, then became the first star player to be drafted into the Army. His salary went from $55,000 a year down to $21 a month. By the end of the year, four other big leaguers had gone into the service.

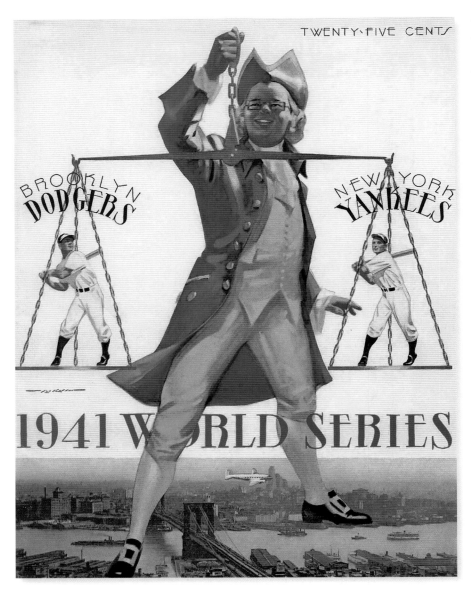

TWENTY·FIVE CENTS

BROOKLYN DODGERS

NEW YORK YANKEES

1941 WORLD SERIES

New York was the center of the baseball world in October 1941, when the Dodgers of Brooklyn challenged the Yankees of the Bronx for the world championship.

By June 2, DiMaggio was one-third of the way through a record that was captivating America (soon Alan Courtney's lyrics—"Joe, Joe DiMaggio, we want you on our side"—were composed in tribute). That night, baseball lost Lou Gehrig, the mighty oak, whose consecutive game streak of 2,130 games had endured through Prohibition, the Roaring Twenties, the Great Depression and F.D.R.'s New Deal. The first basemen died in the Riverdale section of the Bronx three weeks short of his 38th birthday after a two-year battle against amyotrophic lateral sclerosis, an affliction since named after him.

DiMaggio's streak went to 30 games on June 17, an all-time Yankee mark. That night, Joe Louis retained his heavyweight boxing crown when he knocked out the converted light heavyweight, Billy Conn, in the 13th round. A spectator at the Polo Grounds fight, DiMaggio drew thunderous applause as he entered the park.

DiMaggio raised his number to 54 with a lucky infield hit on July 13. The same day, the movie producer Samuel Goldwyn said he intended to film Gehrig's life story. Mentioned as a candidate to play the ill-fated player was a former baseball broadcaster and actor named Ronald Reagan. Gary Cooper eventually won the part.

DiMaggio's streak went to 55 on July 15, against Ed Smith, who had fed him the pitch on May 15 that started the historic barrage. On the same afternoon, the Secretary of the Interior, Harold Ickes, blasted Charles Lindbergh, the heroic Lone Eagle of the '20s, for his isolationist policies. War was creeping closer.

The next day the streak reached 56 as DiMaggio collected three hits in four trips in Cleveland.

A crowd of 68,000 showed up in Cleveland on July 17, but ill fortune finally caught up with DiMaggio, as third baseman Kenny Keltner snared two vicious ground balls and threw him out. In his last time at bat, DiMaggio hit Jim Bagby's pitch into a double play. The streak was ended.

Meanwhile, in Boston, Williams, whose eyesight was reputed to be keen enough to spot a poor dry cleaning job from 30,000 feet up, was on a season-long tear. On Sept. 27, the 23-year-old Red Sox slugger went to bed in Philadelphia with a batting average of .3996, enough to grant him entry into the pantheon of .400 hitters. The last player in the American League to hit .400 had been Harry Heilmann of Detroit, at .403 in 1923.

Joe Cronin, the Red Sox manager, assured Williams on Sunday morning that nobody would hold it against him if he chose to sit it out in that afternoon's doubleheader with a Philadelphia club that was 37 games behind the flag-winning Yankees. The Red Sox, in second place, were 17 games out. Nothing was at stake in the games.

"It's entirely up to you," said Cronin. "You've got .400 in the bank now. What do you say: play or sit it out?"

Williams needed only seconds to respond.

"A man is a .400 hitter or he isn't," Williams said. "I'm going to play. I don't want anyone to say I walked in through the back door. I'm going to prove it."

On a damp day, 10,628 fans came out. Facing three pitchers in the first game, Williams went four for five, including his 37th homer. In the second game he continued his bravura display, with two hits in three times at bat. When the curtain came down, Williams was at .406.

Marveling at what his protégé had accomplished, Eddie Collins, the general manager of the Red Sox, said, "All Ted has ever lived for is his next turn at bat."

Below: On the list of "unbreakable records," Johnny Vander Meer's back-to-back no-hitters in June 1938 stand alongside DiMaggio's amazing streak of '41. Vander Meer tossed his second no-no for the Reds during the first night game at Brooklyn's Ebbets Field. He led the National League in strikeouts three years running (1941–43) before entering the military and losing two prime seasons in 1944 and 1945.

Left: Pitcher Hugh Casey's would-be game-ending third strike to Tommy Henrich gets by catcher Mickey Owen in the fourth game of the 1941 World Series. Owen's passed ball allowed the Yankees to rally for four runs in the ninth inning and take a commanding three-games-to-one lead in the series. New York wrapped up the championship the following day—and Mickey Owen was forever enshrined in baseball's "Hall of Shame."

But there was still more to come in this wonderful season. The Dodgers won the National League pennant, clawing and scratching to defeat the Cardinals, even though a young player who hit out of an unorthodox corkscrew stance was brought up from Rochester in September to help the Cards. His name was Stan (the Man) Musial, and his measly .426 average in 12 games was not enough to sidetrack Durocher's team. But it was the first of many years in which Musial would never fail to hit at least .300.

In the World Series, the Yankees won two of the first three games. But it was the fourth at Ebbets Field that long-suffering Dodger fans remember.

Pete Reiser's two-run homer had given the Dodgers a 4-3 lead into the ninth. With Hugh Casey, Brooklyn's most rugged relief pitcher, snarling down at the Yankees, it seemed a good bet that the Series was on the verge of a two-all deadlock. When Johnny Sturm and Red Rolfe were retired, the Yanks were down to their last out.

With a count of three balls and two strikes on the Yankees' Old Reliable,

Above: Even in the distant military camps of northern Africa, American GIs kept the national pastime going strong during World War II. This makeshift Yankee Stadium was one of seven ball fields at Camp Marshall near Lyautey, Morocco.

Facing page: "Hammerin' Hank" Greenberg was a powerhouse hitter for the Detroit Tigers in the 1930s and '40s. A Jewish-American, Greenberg was chasing Babe Ruth's home run record at a time when Jews in Germany were being chased from their homes. Missing nearly four seasons in his prime, Greenberg was the first star to leave the game for active duty in World War II.

Tommy Henrich, Casey unleashed a pitch—could it have been a spitter?—that Henrich swung at and missed. But the Dodgers' catcher, Mickey Owen, who hadn't committed an error in a year, also missed. The ball tore through his grasp and rolled to the grandstand as Henrich sped to first base.

Already on their way to take their post-game showers, the Yankees returned to the playing field. A game beyond recall had taken on a new life. In quick succession, a despondent Casey gave up a single to DiMaggio, a double to Charlie Keller, a walk to Bill Dickey, a double to Joe Gordon and a walk to Phil Rizzuto. When the slaughter ended, the Yankees had won, 7-4, and they won the next day, too.

"I'm only sorry about one thing," Owen said later. "I should have called time and stopped the game, giving Casey and myself a chance to get over the shock. I've always kicked myself for not doing that."

Less than two months later, on Dec. 7, the Japanese navy rained bombs down on the Hawaiian island of Oahu. The attack on Pearl Harbor, a place unknown to most Americans, cost 2,280 American lives and wounded more than 1,000.

In recalling that time, the author William Manchester would write: "It had been a fine, golden autumn, a lovely farewell to those who would lose their youth, and some of them their lives, before leaves turned again in a peace-time fall."

BROOKLYN DODGERS

vs.

NEW YORK YANKEES

★ ★ ★ **1955** ★ ★ ★

WORLD SERIES

GAME 1 PITCHERS: NEWCOMBE vs. FORD

SEPT. 28, 1955 - 1:30pm

NEXT YEAR ARRIVES
THE 1955 BROOKLYN DODGERS
from *Wait Till Next Year* by Doris Kearns Goodwin

For decades, "wait till next year" was the rallying cry for the Brooklyn faithful, who watched their beloved Dodgers fall short season after season. For Doris Kearns Goodwin, the fortunes and misfortunes of "dem Bums" provide the backdrop for her memoirs of growing up in suburban New York in the 1950s, with the climax coming on Brooklyn's much-anticipated victory over the Yankees in the 1955 World Series.

Goodwin is an historian and Pulitzer Prize–winning author of *No Ordinary Time*, *Lyndon Johnson and the American Dream*, and *The Fitzgeralds and the Kennedys.* She now cheers for the Boston Red Sox.

Although our school principal, Dr. Richard Byers, refused our request to pipe the first game over the PA system, we managed to follow the action at Yankee Stadium through portable radios, with notes passed from desk to desk, and by observing the reactions of classmates. When I saw a look of pain cross the face of my friend Moose Fastov, a devoted Yankee fan, I knew that something good must have happened. Paul Greenberg, who was listening via earphones to a radio surreptitiously tucked under his desk, had just signaled him that Jackie Robinson had tripled to left and scored on a single by Don Zimmer. The Dodgers were ahead 2-0. Barely ten minutes later, however, Moose's fist shot triumphantly into the air when Elston Howard's home run off Newcombe tied the score, 2-2. During the break between classes, Duke Snider homered off Whitey Ford to put the Dodgers up 3-2, but by the time French class had begun, the Yankees had tied it again. When the bell signaled the end of school, it was already the seventh inning and the Yankees led 6-3. Afraid of missing the decisive action if we dashed for home, we gathered on the outside steps of the school building to listen to the final innings. Liberated from the constraints of the classroom, I screamed when the ever-amazing Robinson

The National League–champion Brooklyn Dodgers were headed for their sixth postseason battle with the crosstown-rival New York Yankees as the 1955 World Series got underway. Although they would lose the series opener (as they had four times before) and the second game as well, the Dodgers bounced back to sweep Games 3, 4, and 5 in Brooklyn and take the series lead.

stole home in the eighth. But in the end, the Yanks held on to win the game, 6-5.

Even though the Series had just begun, the voice of doubt now entered into confrontation with the voice of hope. "They've lost the first game," said doubt. "It looks bad. They're going to lose the Series again, just as they always have."

"It's only one game," countered hope, "and it was in Yankee Stadium. It was a close game, they played well. Tomorrow is another day."

But by the end of the following day, doubt, swollen by fear, was in the ascendancy. The Dodgers had lost again, by a score of 4-2, on a five-hitter by Tommy Byrne. Was the Series already gone? For the past thirty-four years, no team had ever come back to win a Series after being down two games to none. And Dodger history did not encourage dreams of a historic comeback. There's more to life than baseball, I told myself, with the wisdom my twelve years had given me. There was the Sadie Hawkins dance, for instance, and my choice of a date. And there was my paper on Reconstruction.

"Don't give up now," my father admonished me. "They'll be coming back to Brooklyn. Home-field advantage is a big thing, and nowhere is it bigger than at Ebbets Field." And he was right. The Dodgers roared to life in the third game, banging out eight runs and fourteen hits. Surprise starter Johnny Podres pitched a complete game to celebrate his twenty-third birthday; Campanella hit a home run, double, and single; and Jackie Robinson ignited the crowd and his teammates when he unnerved Yankee pitcher Bob Turley with his daring on the bases.

My pleasure over Robinson's virtuoso performance and the Dodgers' victory was cut short that night when Elaine called to me from her window. She was so overwrought I could barely understand her and feared that something catastrophic had happened in her house. "Just meet me outside," she said tearfully. I ran down the stairs and met her under the maple tree. She threw her arms around me and told me she had just heard on the radio that James Dean had been killed. His Porsche Spyder had careened off the road between Los Angeles and Salinas. His neck had been broken and he had died instantly.

For a long while we barely talked at all. Then we talked half the night. No one was awake in either of our houses, and soon all the lights on our block were out. There was no banter about that afternoon's game. We were two twelve-year-olds lying on our backs, surrounded by darkness, looking up at the autumn sky and talking fiercely about death and James Dean, who was not so much older than we were, grieving as perhaps only two teenage girls can grieve. Above us, the leaves of the maple tree rustled, and as we looked up at the night stars, the spirit of James Dean seemed very close.

I was exhausted the following day and watched drowsily as the Yankees jumped ahead with two quick runs off Carl Erskine. But when home runs by Campanella, Hodges, and Snider put the Dodgers ahead 7-3 in the fifth, my suddenly revived spirits dissolved all fatigue. In the next inning, the Yankees reduced the Dodger lead to 7-5, scoring two runs on a double by Billy Martin. But in the eighth, Campanella scored an insurance run and the Dodgers held on to win 8-5. The Series was now tied at two games apiece.

Overcoming the disaster of the first two games, the Dodgers had captured the momentum. They won the fifth game on Sunday afternoon as rookie Roger Craig and reliever Clem Labine held the Yankees to three runs while Brooklyn scored five times. "This could be both the day and the year," the *New York Post* predicted in a front-page story Monday morning. "This better be 'next year,'" one fan was quoted as saying. "If the Bums blow this one, the cops better close the Brooklyn Bridge. There'll be more people taking long dives than in 1929."

The sixth game began on Monday, while we sat in Mrs. Brown's geography class. The boys who had the portable radios with earphones sat against the back wall and sent messages forward as each inning progressed. We were studying Mongolia that day, and Mrs. Brown asked us to name Mongolia's three main products. "Yaks, yurts, and yogurt," my friend Marjorie answered. Suddenly there was a muffled roar from the back of the room. Bill Skowron had just hit a three-run homer, putting the Yankees ahead of the Dodgers 5-0. "Well, class," Mrs. Brown said, with a knowing smile, "I'm glad you find the three products of Mongolia as thrilling as I do." Then, to our amazement, she put a radio on the front desk and let us listen to the game. Unfortunately, the Dodgers never got started, and the Yankees won easily by a score of 5-1, tying the Series at three games apiece.

Before my father left for the Williamsburg Savings Bank the Tuesday morning of Game Seven, he promised to call as soon as the game was over. "I feel good about our chances today," he said, as he kissed me goodbye. "I've been waiting for a championship since I was a lot younger than you, and today it's going to happen at last."

"Do you really think so?"

"I really feel it." He winked at me and was off to work.

The Giants win the pennant! Bobby Thomson's home run in the third game of the 1951 playoff between the New York Giants and Brooklyn Dodgers ranks among the most memorable moments in sports history. The three-run blast at the Polo Grounds gave the Giants a come-from-behind win over their number-one rival.

My morning classes stretched out endlessly before game time finally arrived. At noon, we were astonished to hear Principal Byers's voice telling us to report at one o'clock to our homerooms. We would be allowed to listen to the deciding game over the PA system.

When the lineups were announced, I was dismayed to learn that Jackie Robinson was not starting. Hobbled by a strained Achilles tendon, he was replaced by rookie Don Hoak. My only compensation was the not unwelcome news that an injury to Mickey Mantle would keep him from the Yankee lineup. Young Johnny Podres was on the mound, trying to post his second victory of the Series and win it all for the Dodgers; Tommy Byrne was pitching for the Yankees. In the early innings the classroom was tense, as neither team was able to score. Then, in the fourth, Campanella doubled, moved to third on a groundout, and reached home on a single by Hodges. The Dodgers were ahead, 1-0. In the sixth, they scored again on a sacrifice fly by Hodges.

Even though the Dodgers held a 2-0 lead, there were no sounds of celebration, no blustering talk from the Dodger fans in our class. We were a generation that had been nurtured on tales of tragedy, and memories of defeat: 1941, 1949, 1950, 1951, 1952, 1953. The prideful Yankee fans among us were composed, waiting for Berra or Martin or some other hero to overcome the Brooklyn chokers and transform looming defeat into victory. In the bottom of the sixth, it seemed that their time had come. Billy Martin walked on four straight pitches. Gil McDougald followed with a perfect bunt single. With two on and no outs, Berra came to the plate. Had I been home, this was the moment I would have fled the room, hopeful that when I returned Berra would be out. As it was, I had no choice but to remain at my desk, sandwiched between Michael Karp and Kenny Kemper, certain that trouble was brewing.

It was a little after three in the afternoon when Berra came to bat. The bell ending the school day had just rung, but we sat immobile in our seats, heard the portentous crack of the bat, and listened as the ball sailed toward the distant corner of left field. Some 150 feet away, leftfielder Sandy Amoros, having shifted toward center anticipating that Yogi would pull the ball, turned and began his long chase. The Yankee runners, Martin and McDougald, rounded the bases, their faces turned toward the outfield, watching for the ball to drop for a certain double. But Sandy Amoros, fleet of foot, gallant of will, raced to within inches of the concrete left-field wall, stretched out his gloved hand, and snatched the ball from the air. For a moment he held his glove aloft, then, steadying himself with one hand against the wall, wheeled and rocketed the ball to Reese, the cutoff man, who, in turn, threw to first to double up McDougald.

We were going to win. At that moment, I knew we were going to win. Amoros's spectacular catch augured victory just as surely as Mickey Owen's dropped third strike in '41 had foretold defeat. The gods of baseball had spoken. I ran the mile to my home, anxious to see the end of the game with my mother in familiar surroundings. When I reached home, the score was still 2-0, and it was the bottom of the ninth. Give us three more outs, I prayed. Please, God, only three more outs. I sat cross-legged on the floor, my back leaning against my mother's knees as she sat on the edge of her chair. She edged forward as the first batter, Bill Skowron, hit a one-hopper to the mound. Two more outs. Bob Cerv followed with an easy fly to left. One more out. Elston Howard stepped to the plate. After the count reached two and two, Howard fouled off one fast ball after another, then sent a routine ground ball to Reese at shortstop, who threw to Hodges at first for the third and final out.

Brooklyn leftfielder Andy Pafko can only look up in vain as Thomson's "Shot Heard 'Round the World" lands in the Polo Grounds seats. It was a moment of pure elation for the Giants and their fans, while marking yet another hardship for the long-suffering Brooklyn faithful.

There was a moment of frozen silence. Then Vin Scully spoke the words I had waited most of my life to hear: "Ladies and gentlemen, the Brooklyn Dodgers are the champions of the world." Later, Scully was asked how he had remained so calm at such a dramatic moment. "Well, I wasn't," he said. "I could not have said another word without breaking down in tears." Just as Campanella leaped up on Podres, I jumped up and threw my arms around my mother. We danced around the porch, tears streaming down our cheeks, as we watched Campanella, Reese, Hodges, Robinson, and all the Dodgers converge on the mound, with thousands of delirious fans in pursuit.

"We did it! What did I tell you, we did it!" my father bellowed merrily when he reached us minutes later. His call was one of tens of thousands made between 3:44 p.m. and 4:01 p.m., as parents, children, friends, and lovers exchanged screams, shouts, and expressions of joy. Trading on the New York Stock Exchange virtually came to a halt. On that afternoon, the phone company later estimated, it had put through the largest volume of calls since VJ day a decade earlier. "Listen," my father said, holding the phone to the open window of the Williamsburg Bank. "Do you hear the horns, the church bells, the factory whistles? It's absolute pandemonium. There's going to be one grand celebration here tonight. You two have got to come in. Take the next train and meet me at the bank as soon as you can."

My mother paused only to change her clothes, and the two of us were on the train heading for Brooklyn. We emerged from the subway into a crowd of hundreds, then thousands of people dancing in the streets to the music of a small band that had occupied the steps of the Williamsburg Bank. Bunting and banners flew from the windows, pinstriped effigies of Yankee players hung from the lampposts, confetti sifted down onto the sidewalks. The traffic was at a complete standstill, but no one seemed to mind. Finding his bus trapped at an intersection, a bus driver abandoned his vehicle and joined the revelers on the street.

My father suggested dinner at Junior's, a landmark delicatessen on Flatbush Avenue, just two long blocks north of the bank. The place was packed: eight or ten people crowded every booth. Some leaned against posts, many laughed, shouting and jumping ecstatically. We stood happily for an hour or more, hugging each new

This young Dodger booster couldn't quite make it through this early-season game at Ebbets Field in 1955, but you can be sure he was fully awake when October rolled around. This painting by Earl Mayan appeared on the cover of the *Saturday Evening Post* in April 1955. The scoreboard in the background shows the Dodgers and Phillies knotted in a 6-6 tie in the ninth.

Brooklynites came to storied Ebbets Field for more than forty years, until the Dodgers moved west to Los Angeles in 1958. The ballpark was a centerpiece of its neighborhood, and it was renowned for its devoted and colorful fans.

celebrant who walked in the door, until we finally found seats. In the booth next to ours, an old man boisterously announced that if he died the next morning he would go happily to his grave. We ordered corned-beef sandwiches, topped off by Junior's famous cheesecake.

Someone at Junior's said that the official celebration was taking place at the Bossert Hotel, where the Dodgers were scheduled to hold their victory dinner and dance that night. With scores of others, we took the subway to Brooklyn Heights and got off at Montague Street. There, standing behind police barricades, we joined tens of thousands of Dodger fans hoping to catch a glimpse of our heroes as they made their way into the old-fashioned hotel with its marble pillars and ornate ceilings. As the players walked in, they greeted the crowd. Even after their dinner began, they kept returning outside to wave to us again. Walt Alston posed with a group of teenagers while the crowd serenaded him with "For he's a jolly good fellow." A grayhaired woman in a wheelchair reached up to Johnny Podres and he bent down to kiss her. Even the reticent Carl Furillo was caught up in the exuberance of the night. "Oh, God, that was the thrill of all thrills," he later said. "I never in my life ever seen a town go so wild. I never seen people so goddamn happy." At last, Robinson appeared and spoke to the crowd. "The whole team knows it was the fans that made it for us," he told us. "It was your support that made this great day possible. We thank you from the bottom of our hearts."

No one wanted the night to end. When my father turned to ask my mother how she was holding up, she replied she felt twenty again. He led us to the foot of Montague Street, where a promenade overlooking the East River offered a view of the Statue of Liberty and the lights of Manhattan. Ever since the day in 1898 when Brooklyn had given up its proud history and independent status to merge with New York City, Brooklynites had lived in the shadow of Manhattan. Each new slight—including the demise of the famed *Brooklyn Eagle* earlier that year—only reinforced the perception of second-class citizenship. But this night was Brooklyn's night. This night, Brooklyn, not Manhattan, was the center of the world.

Never again would Dodger fans have to wait till next year. The world championship was theirs. As the *Daily News* proclaimed in the next morning's banner headline: "This IS next year!"

Jubilation at last! Pandemonium broke out on the Yankee Stadium field on October 4, 1955, when the Dodgers secured the first championship in franchise history. Celebrations extended for days throughout the borough of Brooklyn.

In Game 6 of the 1975 World Series, Carlton Fisk broke a 6-6 tie in the bottom of the twelfth inning to win the game for Boston. The thrilling home run barely stayed in play, bouncing off Fenway Park's left-field foul pole—perhaps persuaded by Fisk's body language.

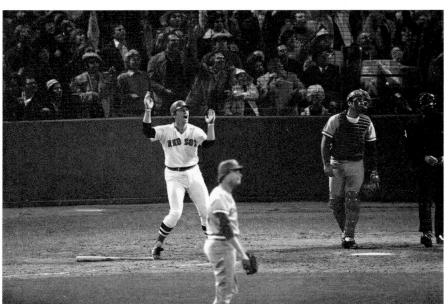

THE 1975 WORLD SERIES
AN OCTOBER CLASSIC
from *The Wrong Stuff* by Bill Lee with Dick Lally

As the sixth game of the 1975 World Series headed into extra innings, Cincinnati's Pete Rose came to the plate and, turning to Boston catcher Carlton Fisk, commented, "This is some kind of game, isn't it?" Even the players in the midst of the excitement knew they were involved in one of the greatest games and series of all time.

Bill Lee was in the heart of the action, as starting pitcher for Boston in the second and seventh games, and he recounts the memorable series in his autobiography, *The Wrong Stuff.* Lee pitched for Boston for ten seasons before finishing out his career with four seasons on the Montreal Expos. His antics and humor earned him the nickname "Spaceman."

Baltimore started to make their move in the final weeks of the season. In early September we could feel their crab breath on our necks. A Baltimore disk jockey traveled to Kenya, seeking a witch doctor who would cast a spell on us on behalf of the Orioles. The doc did cast the spell, but warned that it would be useless unless the Orioles refrained from consuming meat, candy, and alcohol for the rest of the season. They also had to vow that they would refrain from having sex for twelve hours prior to each game. No wonder they couldn't catch us. We held them off and clinched the division with a September 27 win over New York. I didn't have much to do with our stretch drive. My elbow had almost expired, a victim of the designated-hitter rule.

On August 24, I beat the White Sox for my seventeenth win of the season. I didn't get another victory the rest of the year. Obviously, I wasn't destined to win twenty. If I had been, I would have done it that year. Shortly after that win, our pitchers started taking batting practice in preparation for the World Series. There was no d.h. in the Series back then, and Johnson wanted us to be ready to face live pitching. I loved it. The first time out in the cage, I hit a few home runs and really started hot-dogging it, trying to hit each successive shot a little bit farther. After being held out of the batter's box for so long, I did not want to leave. The next day my muscles were sore from overswinging, but I paid no attention. I took batting practice again, got jammed by a pitch, and swung too hard. I had hyperextended my arm, tearing a small tendon in my

elbow. I was useless for the next six weeks and didn't completely heal until the World Series started. The injury kept me out of the playoffs against Oakland.

We took the A's in three straight, clinching the pennant in Oakland with a 5-3 win. As soon as that game's final out was made, we went berserk. [Red Sox owner] Mr. Yawkey made his way into our jammed clubhouse and invited all of us to a victory celebration he had already scheduled for that evening. I attended, but I don't remember very much of it. I got blitzed forty-five minutes after it started and stayed in that condition until we met Cincinnati.

I was up for the Series. I liked the idea of competing against the best in a forum that allowed small margin for error. That Cincinnati team was the Big Red Machine. The scouting report on them was amazing: "Pitch around Rose, pitch around Morgan, pitch around Perez, etc." According to our scouts, the best strategy to use against the Reds was to start the game with the bases loaded, five runs in, and their pitcher at the plate. Then you had a chance.

The Reds should have had Jack Webb as a manager. I had never seen a team so well-schooled in basics as they were. They were the third most fundamentally sound team I had ever seen. Only the USC Trojans of 1968 and any one of the Taiwanese Little League champions would rate higher. The Reds were a club that took its personality from one individual: Pete Rose. Pete and his club were always battling you. Rose is extremely carnivorous, an obvious flesh-eater. Meat diets tend to bring out

Above: Bill Lee delivers the first pitch of the crucial seventh game of the 1975 series. The "Spaceman" spent fourteen years in the majors, but he may be best remembered for his irreverent attitude and unique perspective on the game of baseball. Lee started two games for Boston in the '75 series, posting a solid 3.14 ERA, but left with two no-decisions, as both games he started were decided in the final inning.

Facing page: Although Carlton Fisk's homer in Game 6 provided incredible drama and is the most memorable moment from the series, Cincinnati captured the championship on Joe Morgan's run-scoring single in the ninth inning of Game 7. It was the Big Red Machine's first of two straight World Series titles.

man's competitive nature, while robbing him of the ability to show compassion for his fellow human beings. Carnivores are not concerned with problems outside of baseball. All they care about is scoring the winning run and having the opposing shortstop placed on the dinner menu.

I had no anxiety before the American League playoffs. I knew I wouldn't be pitching, and, like the rest of the club, I figured Oakland was ready to be taken. I did experience some anxious moments before the Series started. I was afraid we'd be swept out of the Series without winning a game. I was fearful not because a sweep would have been embarrassing; I didn't want to beat the Reds four in a row, either. I knew that these games would be our last chances to play ball for the rest of the year, and I was afraid it would be over too quickly. I wanted to string out the fun and excitement for as long as it could last.

[Pitcher Luis] Tiant's seventy-year-old father, a former pitching star in Cuba, threw out the ball for the first game in Boston. The Red Sox and the State Department had been able to bring Luis's mother and father over from Cuba, allowing them the privilege of watching their son pitch in a World Series. During the pre-game festivities, the elder *El Tiante* walked out to the mound and threw the ceremonial first ball to Fisk. He threw a strike. Then he threw another strike, followed by still another. I'll tell you something, he was in great shape. Every pitch he threw had mustard on it and he probably would have kept throwing if someone hadn't led him off the mound. I swear, he could have gone nine.

His son pitched the opener for us against Don Gullett. It was a close duel for a while, but then we blew them away. Tiant threw a five-hit shutout. I started Game Two. While warming up, I noticed the Reds watching me from their dugout. They couldn't believe what they were seeing, I was throwing so much junk. Most of them were laughing, and I thought they were going to knock each other over, racing to the plate to hit against me. Pete Rose was their lead-off hitter, and I struck him out. I didn't hear too many peeps out of them for the rest of the afternoon.

It was a weird game. The day was drizzly and the basepaths were sloppy. We put six men on in the first two innings, but scored only one run. The Reds tied the score in the fourth, and then we got a run in the sixth to take the lead, 2-1. That's where matters stood when the sky opened up and the umpires called a rain delay. As we waited in our clubhouse for the game's resumption, we were joined by Mr. and Mrs. Henry Kissinger and about three hundred Secret Service men. Kissinger sat on a table, signing autographs for the writers and players. At one point he informed one of his agents that he had to go to the bathroom. The Secret Service men had to check out our john before he used it, making sure that no revolutionaries were coming up through

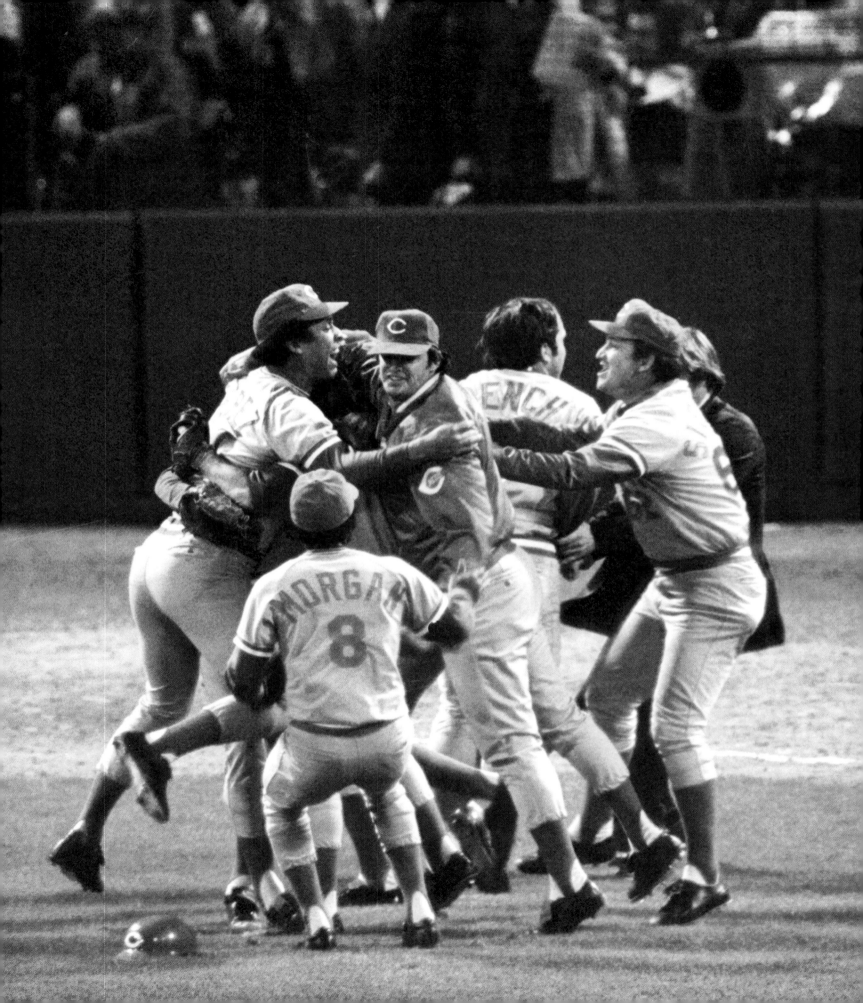

the plumbing. All they found was the Tidy Bowl Man. They frisked him for hidden weapons, but he was clean.

During that delay, unbeknownst to yours truly, Johnny Bench was being interviewed for television in the Reds clubhouse. When asked what he'd be looking to do against me when play resumed, John replied that he was going to try to hit me to the opposite field. He had been trying to pull me all afternoon, and I had gotten him out by pitching him away. Bench was now telling sixty-five million Americans that he was going to take the ball to right, and not one of them thought to call me with a warning. Did that piss me off later! I don't watch much TV, and when Bench and I faced each other after the rains let up, I was unaware of his strategy. John led off the ninth with the score still 2-1. My first pitch to him was a sinker low and away that he hammered to right for a double. Johnson came out to yank me, replacing me with Dick Drago. Dick retired the next two hitters and needed only one more out to give us the win. Davey Concepcion was the next batter. He broke our hearts with a seeing-eye single up the middle that knotted the game up. Then he stole second and scored what proved to be the winning run on a double by Ken Griffey. At the press conference afterward, a writer asked me to sum up the Series so far. I told him it was tied.

Pete Rose shows how he got the nickname "Charlie Hustle." A cornerstone of the Big Red Machine of the 1970s, Rose's aggressive play and clutch hitting (and .485 on-base percentage) helped win him the World Series MVP in 1975. He would eventually become baseball's all-time hit leader, amassing a record 4,256 hits in twenty-four seasons.

We lost Game Three in Cincinnati, 6-5. That was the Armbrister Game. With the score tied 5-5 in the bottom of the tenth, Ed Armbrister, a backup outfielder, was pinch-hitting for the Reds with Cesar Geronimo on first. While attempting to sacrifice, he bounced the ball high in the air in front of home plate. Armbrister, batting from the right side, was very slow getting out of the batter's box. Though clean-shaven when the pitch had first been delivered, he had grown a beard by the time he took his initial step in the direction of first base. Fisk crashed into him as he was in the process of fielding the ball. Pushing Armbrister out of the way, Carlton gunned a throw to second in an attempt to get Geronimo. The ball sailed past the second baseman and out to Lynn in center field. Geronimo tried to take an extra base, but Freddy came up with the ball and fired it to third. Catching the ball on one clean bounce, Petrocelli made a perfect tag to nail Cesar for the out. But the umpire blew the call. Geronimo was ruled safe, and the game was as good as over. In looking back on that game, everybody focuses on that brief collision at the plate, not realizing that it was the blown call at third that would eventually kill us. Geronimo scored the winning run on a base hit by Joe Morgan, and yet that's the play that nobody talks about. Instead, everybody chooses to argue whether or not Armbrister should have been called out for blocking Fisk at the plate. He wasn't, but he sure should have been. His interference was blatant. Larry Barnett, the home-plate umpire, made the wrong call, and [manager] Darrell Johnson didn't negotiate properly in an attempt to get

Above: Bill Mazeroski's home run for Pittsburgh in the 1960 World Series is perhaps the greatest World Series moment, if not the greatest in all of baseball history. It's every kid's fantasy—bottom of the ninth, seventh game of the World Series, tie ballgame, a home run to win it all. Maz is the only player ever to bring such a moment to life.

Left: In 1993, Toronto's Joe Carter became the only player to bring his team from behind to win a World Series with a home run. His three-run, walk-off homer gave the Blue Jays a 6-5 win in Game 6 against the Philadelphia Phillies, clinching the series. A year after defeating the Atlanta Braves, Toronto became the first back-to-back champions since the Yankees of 1977–78.

him to reverse it. He didn't argue vociferously enough. An energetic display won't get an umpire to change his call, but it might lend you some protection for the next close play. Many umpires will tread lightly if you intimidate them with enough bluster. Darrell didn't give it his all. If it had been me, I would have climbed up Barnett's back and bit his ear off. I would have Van Goghed him.

A loss like that could have hung us, but, if anything, it only made us play harder in Game Four. An exhausted Tiant had just enough to win that game, 5-4. Luis could hardly lift his arm over his head, and the Reds hit rockets off of him, but it didn't matter. He had guts, brains, and Fred Lynn in center field. Freddy made more great catches in that one game than I had seen in my entire career. The Reds won the fifth game, 6-2, taking a 3-2 lead in games won. We went back to Fenway, needing to win two.

Game Six was delayed by three days of rain. When the Series was resumed, Darrell made his fatal error. For the last two years, I had been unhappy with the way Johnson had handled our pitching staff. He left starters in too long and never really established any sort of order in the bullpen. Nobody out there knew what their job was supposed to be. There was no official short man, because Darrell just went with whoever had the hot hand at the moment. When he managed us to the pennant, I attributed it to his talent for falling out of trees, but landing on his feet. He still managed to land on his feet in this game, but he also stubbed all his toes.

The mistake he made was in starting Tiant in Game Six, instead of me. That's not my conceit talking, it's just common sense. Those rains had been a godsend, giving our tired pitching staff some much needed rest. Luis found it especially beneficial, but he still needed one more day. On the other hand, too much rest was hazardous to me. I was primed and ready to go on what would have been my normal starting day. But Darrell passed over me to go with his best.

For pure fairy-tale drama, it's hard to beat Kirk Gibson's blast in the 1988 World Series. Barely able to walk due to an injured knee, the gimpy Gibson smacked a two-out, pinch-hit homer in the bottom of the ninth inning in the series opener, setting the stage for an improbable upset victory by the Los Angeles Dodgers over the Oakland A's. It was Gibson's only appearance of the series, and it came against baseball's most dominant reliever, Dennis Eckersley.

The choice, wrong as it was, did result in setting up the dramatic events of the magic sixth game. Unable to stay in one place, I divided my time that evening between the bullpen and the dugout. We scored three runs in the first inning, but the Reds got to Luis for three in the fifth and two in the seventh. By the bottom of the eighth, the Reds had a 6-3 lead. Lynn led off with a walk, Petrocelli singled. Cincinnati's relief ace Rawley Eastwick was brought in, and he struck out Evans and then got Burleson on a fly ball. Carbo was sent up as a pinch hitter. As he walked to the plate, I knew he was going to hit a home run. Eastwick was a fastball pitcher, facing a dead fastball hitter with a strong wind blowing out. It was a scene written for Bernie. I stood up in the dugout and tried to get his attention, pointing to the wall and imploring him to hit it out. Bernie jolted Eastwick's second pitch, hitting it into the center-field bleachers. When he made contact, everyone in our dugout went crazy; we all knew the ball was gone when he hit it, and that it was now just a matter of time before we would win this game.

I was in the trainer's room when Fisk hit his famous twelfth-inning homer off Pat Darcy that ended the game and gave us the victory. It was getting late, and I knew I was going to be starting the next day, so I was stretching out, trying to get some rest. I saw the shot on TV. Carlton golfed the crap out of a fastball. He used a six iron, drawing from right to left and putting a shade of English on the ball. It landed on the left digit of a local green. The drive almost went foul, but Fisk used his body language, ordering it to stay fair, and it obeyed.

I felt I would pitch well in the seventh game. I had crazy rushes of energy surging through my body, but my mind was mellow and in complete control of the rest of me. I would be starting against Don Gullett. Prior to the game, Sparky Anderson, the Reds' manager, had announced, "I don't know about that fellah for the Red Sox, but, sometime after this game, my boy's going to the Hall of Fame." Upon hearing that remark, I replied, "I don't care where Gullett's going, because after this game, I'm going to the Eliot Lounge."

Scoring three runs in the third, we had Sparky's Hall-of-Famer out of there by the sixth inning. When we scored those three runs, the crowd went wild. But, after we failed to score again, I could feel the paranoia creeping through the stands. It was as if everyone was thinking, Okay, how are we going to fuck this one up?

You can't discuss World Series heroics without mentioning "Mr. October" himself, Reggie Jackson. His record-tying three home runs in Game 6 of the 1977 World Series each came on the first pitch of the at-bat, against three different Dodger pitchers. The Yankee star also homered in Games 4 and 5 to set the record for a six-game series with five round-trippers.

We carried that 3-0 lead into the sixth. Rose led off that inning with a base hit. I got the next hitter on a pop-up and then faced Johnny Bench. Swinging at a fastball low and away, John hit a nice two-hopper to Burleson. It was a sure double play. But before I had thrown the pitch, the coaches had moved our second baseman, Denny Doyle, over to the hole, away from second. Rick was ready with the throw, but Denny had to come a long way to get to the bag. Flying across second, Doyle took the toss and fired the ball to first before he had a chance to get set. The throw went sailing into the stands. Instead of being out of the inning, I had Bench on second with two men out. And Tony Perez at the plate.

I had been having good success with Tony, throwing him my slow, arching curveball, so I thought it would be a good idea to throw it to him again. Unfortunately, so did Tony, who timed it beautifully. He counted the seams of the ball as it floated up to the plate, checked to see if Lee MacPhail's signature was on it, signed his own name to it, and then jumped all over it. He hit the ball over the left field screen and several small buildings. The score was 3-2. Pitching with a broken blister in the top of the seventh, I put the potential tying run on. When I walked that lead-off hitter, I was sick with myself. I did not want to come out of that ballgame, but Darrell was right in bringing in Roger Moret. That busted blister had made it impossible for me to get the ball over the plate. The moment it popped, I knew I was finished for the season. Now, all I could do was watch. When Roger allowed that tying run to score, I wanted to dash out and buy some razor blades. For my wrists.

Jim Willoughby relieved Moret and got us out of the seventh. He pitched great through the eighth, but in the bottom of that inning, we were done in by the d.h. rule. Since there was no designated hitter for this Series, Johnson felt forced to lift Willoughby in favor of a pinch hitter. It was a tough decision to make. We either had to take our best shot for a possible run or leave in a guy who had been our best pitcher over the last two months. I thought we should have left Jim in. Willoughby was a good-hitting pitcher, and, by taking him out, we were forced to insert a rookie, Jim Burton, who hadn't been used much all year. Willoughby was a veteran who had possessed great karma since August. We should have gone with the hot hand.

Jim Burton, though, came on in the ninth and pitched well. He just had bad luck. After walking Griffey, who was sacrificed to second, he retired Driessen, and then walked Rose. Joe Morgan was the next batter. Burton threw him a hell of a pitch—a slider down and away—but Morgan was just able to fight it off, blooping it into short center field in front of Lynn. Griffey scored the tie-breaking run. We went down in order in the bottom of the ninth, and the Series was over.

I was upset, at first, about the loss. I was even more upset that I hadn't started Game Six, allowing Luis his rest. Luis would have won that seventh game; I'm certain he would have blown them away. But I eventually realized that, if it had gone that way, the Series wouldn't have been as great as it was. That sixth game was something else. I wish I had been in it, but if I had been, I might have gotten jocked worse than Luis—or I might have pitched a shutout. Then we wouldn't have had Carbo's and Fisk's home runs to remember. We didn't win the Series, but we didn't lose it either. Baseball won. We were part of an event that we could tell our grandchildren about. I want to win as much as anybody. I felt our loss deep in my guts. But, if we had to lose, we couldn't have picked a better way. We gave it everything we had from the first pitch to the last.

Facing page: The World Series is not all about hitting the long ball. In 1956, Yankee Don Larsen delivered an unprecedented and unmatched no-run, no-hit, no-error perfect game in the fall classic. In fact, there have been only five one-hitters in series history. Brooklyn's Jim Gilliam, at bat, waits for the game's opening pitch—in vain.

BOSTON		1	2	3	4	5	6	7	8	9	10	AB	R	1B	TB	SH	PO	A	E
Dougherty	lf																		
Collins	3b																		
Stahl	cf																		
Freeman	rf																		
Parent	ss																		
Lachance	1b																		
Ferris	2b																		
Criger Farrell J Stahl	c																		
Hughes, Young Dineen	p																		
TOTAL																			

PITTSBURG		1	2	3	4	5	6	7	8	9	10	AB	R	1B	TB	SH	PO	A	E
Beaumont	cf																		
Clarke	lf																		
Leach	3b																		
Wagner	ss																		
Bransfield	1b																		
Ritchey	2b																		
Sebring	rf																		
Smith Phelps	c																		
Seever Phillippe	p																		
TOTAL																			

THE GREATEST WORLD SERIES

by Josh Leventhal

EVERY OCTOBER, AT the end of a long summer of baseball, one team is left standing as the champion of the sport. The pennant winners from the National and American Leagues compete to decide which one shall lay claim to the title of world's best. In the course of its first century, this annual competition has emerged as an American institution, the pinnacle of the sport's year—the World Series.

No matter who is involved and whatever the outcome, every World Series has moments of excitement and drama. Some go down to the wire, only to be decided in the final at bat of the final inning of the final game. Others see individuals shine with record-breaking feats. But which series stand out as the *most* exciting, the *most* dramatic? Here's one opinion.

1975—CINCINNATI REDS 4, BOSTON RED SOX 3

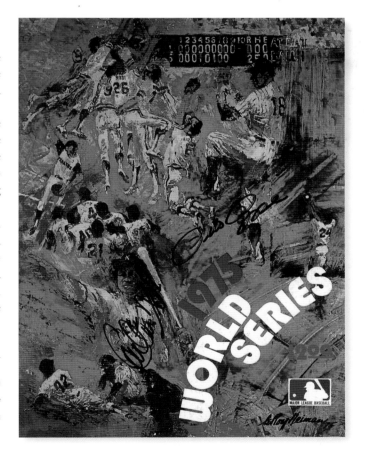

The 1975 World Series between the Boston Red Sox and the Cincinnati Reds was undoubtedly one of the best ever. In five of the seven games, the winning team edged out victory by a single run, and four of those were decided in the final inning, including two in extra innings. Carlton Fisk's memorable twelfth-inning homer to win Game 6 was made possible thanks to a game-tying, three-run, pinch-hit blast by Bernie Carbo four innings earlier. The Reds' Joe Morgan won two games with base hits in the final inning, including the deciding seventh game. The series was not without its controversy, either. Ed Armbrister's collision with Fisk in Game 3 (described in detail in the previous piece by Bill Lee) was hotly contested by Fisk but in the end opened the door for Morgan's game-winning single two batters later. Capping off what had been a hard-fought series from the start, the Reds rallied from down three runs to claim the clinching game, scoring four runs in the final four innings.

Facing page: The very first official World Series opened in Boston on October 1, 1903. Cy Young started for the Pilgrims (as they were then unofficially known) and got the loss, but his Boston club won the series.

1991—MINNESOTA TWINS 4, ATLANTA BRAVES 3

Another series offering a plethora of one-run ballgames (five), extra-inning tilts (three), clutch hitting, masterful pitching, superb fielding, and even some controversy, the "Worst to First" series of 1991 pitted two teams that had finished in last place a year earlier: the Minnesota Twins and the Atlanta Braves. After dropping the first two games in Minnesota, the Braves came back to win the next two in dramatic fashion, pulling out walk-off wins on consecutive nights. The lone blowout of the series was Game 5 (Atlanta won 14-5), but the teams bounced back with tense extra-inning affairs in the final two games—the only time in history that has happened. In Game 6, Kirby Puckett provided the glove work and bat power for Minnesota. He robbed Ron Gant of a fifth-inning home run with a leaping catch at the wall, and he drove in three of Minnesota's four runs, including a game-winning homer in the eleventh inning to send the series to a seventh game. Jack Morris's complete-game, ten-inning shutout in Game 7 is simply one of the best pitching performances in World Series history.

2001—ARIZONA DIAMONDBACKS 4, NEW YORK YANKEES 3

The Yankees were coming off three consecutive World Series titles, and the city of New York was recovering from the terrorist attacks of September 11 just six weeks earlier, but the Arizona Diamondbacks took baseball's ultimate prize in 2001. With ace hurlers Randy Johnson and Curt Schilling holding the Yanks to six hits and no runs in the first two games, the D'Backs silenced the Yankee bats with a .183 team average for the series. New York took the series lead after two remarkable come-from-behind wins in Games 4 and 5. Down two runs in the ninth inning in both games, they twice rallied against Arizona's star reliever, Byung-Hyun Kim, who yielded clutch homers to Tino Martinez and Derek Jeter in Game 4 and to Scott Brosius in Game 5. In the end, though it was the lefty-righty duo of Johnson and Schilling that closed the door on the Bombers. Johnson got the win in the last two games, starting Game 6 and closing out Game 7 in relief the next night. In the final game, Luis Gonzalez's blooping, bases-loaded single over a drawn-in infield produced just the tenth walk-off clinching hit in series history.

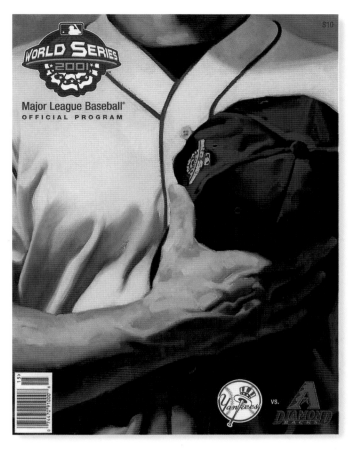

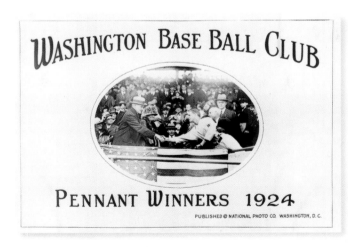

1924—WASHINGTON SENATORS 4, NEW YORK GIANTS 3

In 1924, the New York Giants were headed to their ninth World Series under veteran skipper John McGraw. The Washington Senators, under the guidance of twenty-seven-year-old player-manager Bucky Harris, were looking at their first. But the Senators did boast one of the game's greatest pitchers in Walter Johnson, who was nearing the end of his career and was the sympathetic favorite. In the only series ever to begin and end with extra-inning games, the Giants and Senators battled through four games decided by a single run. Johnson went the distance in Game 1 and struck out a then-record 12 batters, but lost the game in twelve innings. The teams alternated wins the rest of the way. In the finale, the Giants held a two-run lead in the eighth inning, but with the bases loaded for Washington, a routine groundball took a bad hop and bounced over the head of third baseman Fred Lindstrom, tying the game. Four innings later, with two Senators on base, a grounder *again* bounced over Lindstrom's head, and the series-winning run came home. Johnson, pitching in relief, earned his first World Series win.

1947—NEW YORK YANKEES 4, BROOKLYN DODGERS 3

The Yankee-Dodger matchups of the 1940s and '50s were filled with memorable moments—Mickey Owen's passed ball in 1941, Billy Martin's lunging catch in 1952, Brooklyn finally winning in 1955, Don Larsen's perfect game in 1956. But it was the surprise heroes of 1947 that make this Subway Series stand out. Bill Bevens, the fourth pitcher in the Yankee rotation, took a no-hitter into the ninth inning in Game 4. Despite walking two batters in the inning, Bevens found himself one out away from the first postseason no-no. Then, up came Brooklyn reserve Cookie Lavagetto, who knocked a two-out, pinch-hit double that not only ended the no-hitter but won the game for Brooklyn. In Game 6, backup outfielder Al Gionfriddo preserved a Brooklyn lead by robbing the immortal Joe DiMaggio of a home run with a lunging catch in the left-field corner, 415 feet from home plate. After three one-run games in the series, the Yanks pulled out the win in Game 7. Although New York and Brooklyn would meet five more times in the next ten years, near-heroes Bevens, Lavagetto, and Gionfriddo never played another game of Major League ball.

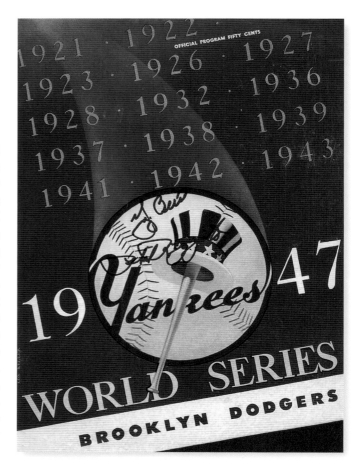

1986—NEW YORK METS 4, BOSTON RED SOX 3

The 1986 World Series is best remembered for a single play—a play that to Red Sox fans represents all that is wrong with the world. For Mets fans, it's another autumn miracle. When Sox first baseman Bill Buckner let Mookie Wilson's groundball roll through his legs, not only did the Mets win Game 6 and stay alive for another day, but the momentum seemed to turn in New York's favor heading into Game 7. In fact, the Red Sox got on board first in the deciding game with three runs, and they held New York scoreless through five innings. But then the bottom dropped out, and the Mets ran off eight runs in their last three times at bat.

While Buckner gets most of the blame for the Game 6 fiasco, Boston reliever Calvin Schiraldi gave up three consecutive hits in that game to put New York within a run after bringing his team one strike away from the title. Schiraldi also earned the loss in Game 7. A wild pitch by Red Sox closer Bob Stanley let the tying run score in Game 6 and moved the go-ahead run to scoring position. Then Wilson and Buckner took center stage.

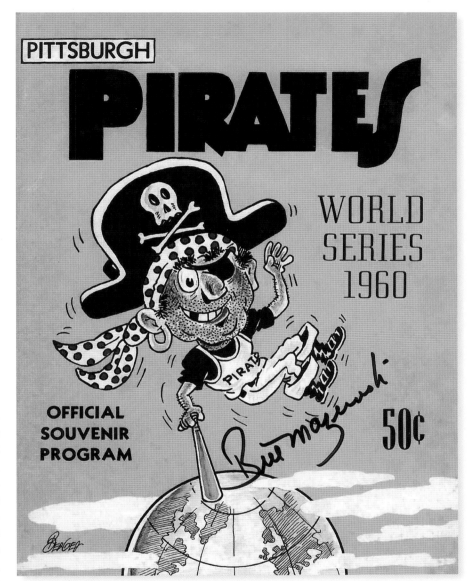

1960—PITTSBURGH PIRATES 4, NEW YORK YANKEES 3

The 1960 World Series was a blowout. One team set multiple records for a seven-game series: most runs (55), most hits (91), highest average (.338), highest slugging percentage (.528). That team won games by scores of 16-3, 10-0, and 12-0. That team was the New York Yankees. That team lost the 1960 series. Although the Yankees dominated the games they won, and the Pittsburgh Pirates eked out victories by one, two, or three runs in the other games, the thrilling conclusion to the series and the improbable outcome make this one for the ages. After being outscored 46-17 through the first six games, the Pirates jumped out to a 4-0 lead in the deciding game. New York twice came from behind, including two Yankee runs in the top of the ninth that brought the teams even. It seemed that the fates were once again on the side of the "Damn Yankees." But in baseball's most dramatic moment, Bill Mazeroski delivered the blow that toppled the Yanks in the final inning of the final game. He is the only player in series history to decide a winner-take-all Game 7 on one swing of the bat with a home run.

1912—BOSTON RED SOX 4, NEW YORK GIANTS 3 (1 TIE)

In 1912, John McGraw's New York Giants, participants in nine series between 1903 and 1924, went the distance and beyond against the Boston Red Sox, owners of the first World Series trophy from 1903 and four more from 1912 to 1918. The teams battled through four one-run games, plus another that ended in a tie after eleven innings. New York's Hall of Fame pitching tandem of Christy Mathewson and Rube Marquard posted a combined ERA of 0.79, but Mathewson had two losses to show for his effort, including the heartbreaking final game. In the first extra-inning Game 7 in history, New York gained a 2-1 lead in the top of the tenth, but a fielding error in the bottom of the inning by outfielder Fred Snodgrass and another Giants misplay on an infield foul popup gave Boston extra lives. The Sox took advantage and scored two runs off Mathewson to win the series, and "Snodgrass's muff" would go down in World Series annals as one of the great goats.

1969—NEW YORK METS 4, BALTIMORE ORIOLES 1

It wasn't the closest World Series ever. Some might argue that it wasn't even the greatest upset. But when the New York Mets defeated the Baltimore Orioles in the 1969 World Series, it was unlike anything seen before. The Mets were not merely underdogs. Over the previous seven seasons, they were one of the worst teams the sport had ever seen, never finishing higher than ninth place in a ten-team league. The Orioles, by contrast, were just three years removed from a world championship, and 1969 was the first of three straight pennants. After Baltimore predictably won the series opener, the "Amazin' Mets" rattled off four straight victories, holding Baltimore to a total of five runs in those four games. New York broke a 1-1 tie in the ninth to win Game 2. They shut Baltimore out 5-0 in Game 3, aided by two spectacular catches by Mets outfielder Tommie Agee. Another 1-1 squeaker in Game 4 was won by New York in extra innings, with more stellar fielding, this time by Ron Swoboda, helping to secure the victory. The Miracle Mets then rallied from down by 3-0 in Game 5 to win the series. Behind clutch hitting, near-untouchable pitching, and awe-inspiring fielding, the 1969 Mets shocked the baseball world.

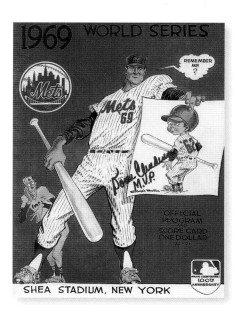

1972—OAKLAND A'S 4, CINCINNATI REDS 3

The 1972 World Series was a clash of titans of the early seventies: Charley Finley's Oakland A's versus Cincinnati's Big Red Machine. Between them, the teams claimed all the championship trophies handed out from 1972 to 1976. When the two went head to head, it was about as close as you can get. After seven games, they finished with identical batting averages (.209) and slugging averages (.295). Each of Oakland's four wins came by a one-run margin; two of Cincinnati's wins were decided by one. In a series filled with future Hall of Famers, the unlikely hero was Oakland's Gene Tenace, a backup catcher who homered in each of his first two World Series at bats and added two more before it was all over. Tenace also drove in two runs in Oakland's 3-2 victory in the deciding game.

1998: THE YEAR BASEBALL CAME "BACK"... BUT DID IT EVER REALLY LEAVE?

by Alan Schwarz

JUST FOUR YEARS removed from Major League Baseball's eighth work stoppage—and the first cancelled World Series in ninety years—baseball fans gradually and in some cases begrudgingly were returning to the ballpark. In 1998, the league and the nation were electrified by Mark McGwire and Sammy Sosa's historic chase of Roger Maris's single-season home run record. In the words of the baseball pundits, baseball was "back."

But as Alan Schwarz explained in *Baseball America* in September of 1998, baseball never really left, and the game always remained in the forefront of the national psyche. Schwarz is author of *The Numbers Game: Baseball's Lifelong Fascination with Statistics*. He also is the Senior Writer of *Baseball America*, a weekly columnist for ESPN.com, and a regular contributor to the *New York Times*.

St. Louis—I feel a little out of place, because you know just as much as I do, maybe more.

Sure, I was there in the press box when Mark McGwire blasted home run No. 61 and himself into American folklore. I watched as Busch Stadium erupted with ovation after ovation for its bulging-bicep, spinach-eating hero. All my friends are envious that I could be on site for such a moment, and would be there for No. 62, with the privilege of reporting and interpreting the event for fans across the nation.

The thing is, you already understand. Better than me. As I stood in the antiseptic press box as McGwire rounded the bases, the crowd around the stoic writers roaring like a jet engine, I smiled not for my undeniably good fortune—but for how much fans everywhere were enjoying themselves. Moments later, as I started typing, I wondered: What could I possibly tell them from this vantage point?

Frankly, to not listen. As thick as the St. Louis air was throughout the magical stretch of games that led up to McGwire's moment, thicker was the talk of how baseball is "back." The

announcers announced it. Writers wrote it. Mark McGwire exclaimed it, and no one was about to argue with him.

And it was all so silly. Baseball never went anywhere.

A PULSE BEATS ON

As far as that strike thing goes, granted, it was one hell of a speed bump. Yet there's no way fans would have been nearly as resentful at the players' walkout and the owners' bumbling stubbornness had they not had beaten into their skulls every day for a year that baseball was dead, slain by its reckless leaders.

"There was a game called baseball. You would have loved it," the late Jim Murray eulogized in the *Los Angeles Times* the day after the 1994 World Series was cancelled. But as sincere as Murray and countless others may have been, they were wrong. This game will carry on long past those who claim to monitor its pulse, and whose daily vagaries stir public opinion. I'm reminded of something Gloria Steinem once said: "Being a writer keeps me from believing everything I read."

Of course, baseball is enjoying a summer of resurgence. McGwire and Sammy Sosa, Kerry Wood and David Wells, the Yankees, Turner Ward running through a fence, they're all ingredients in this delectable soup of a season. But they thrill us on their own merits, not just in comparison to the down times.

Now other sports are feeling baseball nipping at their heels. At a Fox luncheon in New York, designed to kick off their

---

Mark McGwire belted his way into the record books with home run number 62, which came off Chicago's Steve Trachsel on September 8 at St. Louis's Busch Stadium. Although his record stood for just three years (Ruth held the mark for thirty-four years, Maris for thirty-seven), McGwire's feat symbolized the resurgence of baseball in the hearts and minds of Americans.

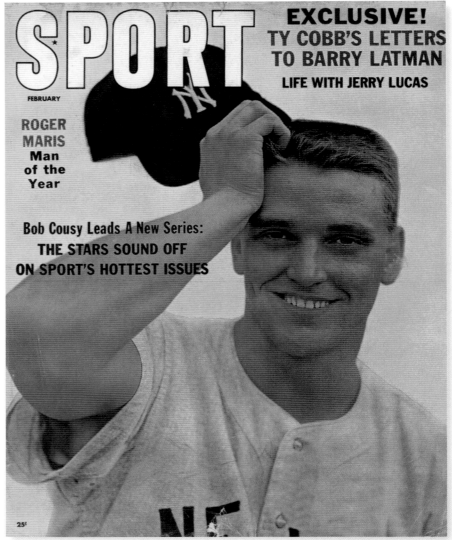

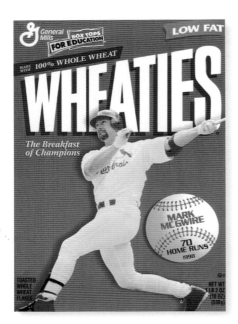

In contrast to the support and celebration surrounding Mark McGwire and Sammy Sosa in 1998, Roger Maris endured immense pressure during his chase of Babe Ruth's record thirty-seven years earlier. Although *Sport* magazine did not hesitate to label Maris "Man of the Year" for 1961, the new record was given an asterisk by commissioner Ford Frick, since Maris's 61 homers came in a 162-game season, while the Babe got his 60 in 154 games.

in-your-face NFL coverage, topic No. 1 was the home run chase. "Baseball?" Terry Bradshaw yelped. "Is that why we're here?" And basketball's impending implosion will do wonders for a sport that gradually is losing its media-darling status.

That label seems to have been placed on baseball again, and it's such a crock. Three years ago, in these pages during the throes of the strike, I wrote that baseball would be the hot sport again by the end of the decade. I'm not some genius. Baseball simply has too much of a hold on the nation, too much momentum, to fall off the sine curve of popularity.

And with so many column inches and airtime minutes to fill, heck, we gotta say *something*.

FANS CALL THE SHOTS

It seems so long ago, but remember when we were debating about whether Cal Ripken's streak would end if teams used replacement players? Another ridiculous question. What the record-keepers didn't understand, and many fans didn't realize, is that Ripken's feat could not be diminished if the public wouldn't let it. Even if some nut ruled that Ripken's 2,131st weren't official, there's no way the fans of Baltimore would have stood for it. They would have planned a celebration, the media would have picked up on it, and before baseball would know what was happening, Ripken would have broken Lou Gehrig's record.

What such a scene would have demonstrated is that the caretakers of baseball's popularity are not the owners, or the players, but the fans. You are the ones ultimately responsible for cradling the game's meaning and importance down the time line. And you seem to have done a pretty good job so far.

Baseball was "back" the minute games resumed on April 25, 1995, because it was then that the game had no choice but to begin regenerating itself day after metronomic day. We got to watch Ken Griffey hit and field. Alex Rodriguez blossom. The Yankees win the World Series. Roger Clemens. Pedro Martinez.

And now, Mark McGwire, who gave us one of those "Where were you when …?" moments that we'll remember forever. We'll remember even when baseball goes through a down period again, which it surely will in the next five or ten years. But who cares?

Baseball doesn't have to be the "greatest" game anymore. It's a great game.

But you already knew that.

Three years before the great home run chase of '98, and in the immediate aftermath of the players' strike of 1994–95, Cal Ripken gripped the nation with his chase of another seemingly immortal record: Lou Gehrig's "Iron Man" streak of 2,130 consecutive games played. Ripken broke the record on September 6, 1995, and then extended it for another 502 games before sitting out a tilt at Baltimore's Camden Yards on September 20, 1998.

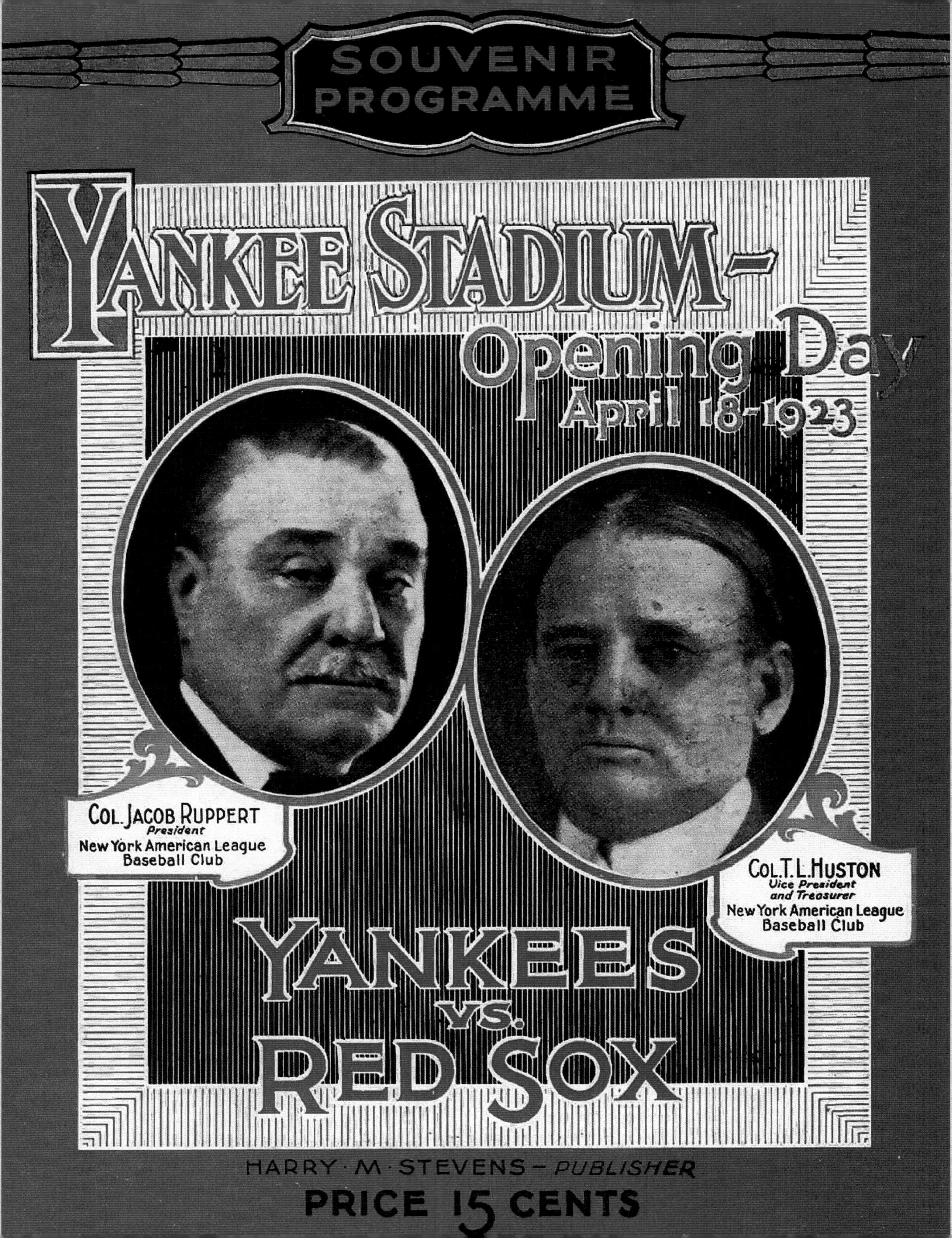

SOUVENIR PROGRAMME

YANKEE STADIUM –
Opening Day
April 18-1923

COL. JACOB RUPPERT
President
New York American League
Baseball Club

COL. T. L. HUSTON
Vice President
and Treasurer
New York American League
Baseball Club

YANKEES
VS.
RED SOX

HARRY · M · STEVENS – PUBLISHER
PRICE 15 CENTS

THE GREATEST RIVALRY
YANKEES VS. RED SOX
by Harvey Frommer

THE LONGSTANDING RIVALRY between the New York Yankees and the Boston Red Sox is the most storied and passionate in all of sports. From bench-clearing brawls to dramatic comebacks and heartbreaking collapses, the Boston–New York matchup has seen it all. The 2004 postseason, addressed at the end of this article, is only the most recent spectacle.

In his book *Red Sox vs. Yankees: The Great Rivalry*, Harvey Frommer takes an in-depth look at this intense rivalry. The following original essay provides an overview of the most significant moments. Frommer is a sports historian, journalist, and author of thirty-four sports books.

I was a lifelong New Yorker until about eight years ago, when I moved on to teach and write and live in New England. Back in the Big Apple, I had always been a keenly interested onlooker to the rivalry between the New York Yankees and the Boston Red Sox. But it wasn't until I was living in the mountains of New Hampshire that I realized via conversations at the gas pumps, the town dump, and the general store just how important THE RIVALRY is—especially to the Red Sox Nation.

As the story up here goes, there was a get-together in the woods of a Red Sox fan, a Cub fan, and a Pirate fan. They all wondered when their team would make it to the World Series again and decided to call on God for advice.

The Pirate fan asked first: "When will my team return to the World Series?"

And God replied: "Not in your lifetime."

The fan of the Cubs popped the same question.

And God replied: "Not in your children's lifetime."

The Red Sox fan, who had listened quietly, finally worked up the nerve to ask: "When will my beloved Red Sox return to the World Series?"

God thought for a moment and then answered: "Not in My lifetime."

The cities of Boston and New York have been bitter baseball rivals for more than a century. Both franchises inaugurated their new ballparks by hosting the other. The Red Sox came to the Bronx for the opening game at Yankee Stadium on April 18, 1923, eleven years after Boston bested New York in the first game at Fenway Park.

For fans of the old Brooklyn Dodgers, the slogan was, "Wait till next year." That team, talented as it was and try as it may, just could not beat the New York Yankees in the World Series. And then came the magical year of 1955.

"Wait till next year" could also have been the mantra for the long-suffering fans of the Boston Red Sox. All told, there have been fourteen years of Boston runner-up finishes to New York in the regular-season standings: 1938, 1939, 1941, 1942, 1949, 1977, 1978, 1998, 1999, 2000, 2001, 2002, 2003, 2004. The second-place blues have long frustrated the Red Sox Nation, stoking the coals of the always hot Boston-New York rivalry.

The roots of the rivalry extend all the way back to the first time the teams faced off, on May 7, 1903, at the Huntington Avenue Grounds in Boston. They weren't the Yankees and Red Sox then but instead had more geographically correct names: the New York Highlanders—they played on the high terrain of upper Manhattan at Hilltop Park—and the Boston Pilgrims—in tribute to their New England heritage. Boston won that first game, 6-2, as well as baseball's inaugural World Series later that year. New York finished in fourth place, seventeen games off the pace. Over the next fifteen years, the Red Sox were one of baseball's most successful franchises, winning five championships in five trips to the fall classic.

The New York Highlanders—they became the Yankees in 1913—finished under .500 eight times in their first sixteen years of existence. They ended up in last place twice. But things would change.

After the Red Sox won the 1916 World Series, Harry Frazee, a former billposter from Peoria, Illinois, who had become a show business wheeler-dealer, purchased the club. A good friend of Yankee owners Colonel Jacob Ruppert and Colonel Tillinghast l'Hommedieu Hutson, Frazee was eager to wheel and deal with wealthy New Yorkers.

He had a home in Boston, but his main residence was on Manhattan's Park Avenue. He liked to quip, "The best thing about Boston is the train ride back to New York."

On January 9, 1920, "Harry Frazee's Crime" was committed. At a cold morning press conference, a very happy Jake Ruppert announced: "Gentlemen, we have just bought Babe Ruth from Harry Frazee of the Boston Red Sox. I can't give exact figures, but it was a pretty check—six figures. No players are involved. It was strictly a cash deal."

Harry Frazee said, "No other club could afford to give the amount the Yankees have paid for Babe Ruth. And I do not mind saying I think they are taking a gamble."

Boston general manager Ed Barrow saw it differently, telling Frazee, "You ought to know that you're making a mistake."

The fallout from Frazee's infamous deed has come to be known as the "Curse of the Bambino." In Boston, more colorful, if less family-friendly, phrases describe the act.

From 1919 through 1933, the BoSox endured a stretch of losing campaigns, dropping at least one hundred games in a season five times, and at least ninety games five more times. Last-place finishers on nine occasions during that era, they had become a sorry excuse for a big league baseball team. The Red Sox failed to win a single American League pennant from 1919 to 1945 (the only one of the league's eight teams never to finish first during that span), finishing an average of thirty games back in the standings.

In 1915, a twenty-year-old lefty named Babe Ruth (far left) was in his first full season as a pitcher for Boston. He is shown here with fellow hurlers Ernie Shore and Rube Foster and first baseman Bill Gainer. Although Ruth made only a brief appearance as a pinch hitter in the World Series (he grounded out in his one at bat), the Red Sox captured the franchise's third title that year.

The shipping of Ruth to New York has been followed by all sorts of Red Sox misfortunes: losing the seventh game of the World Series four times, in 1946 ("Slaughter's Mad Dash"), 1967, 1975, 1986 (one word: Buckner); losing one-game playoffs in 1948 and 1978; and most recently, coming within five outs of winning the 2003 American League Championship Series, only to lose 6-5 in eleven innings in Game 7—to the Yankees, no less.

In sharp contrast, the longstanding golden age of Yankee baseball can be traced directly to the arrival of George Herman Ruth. The team has captured twenty-six world titles since 1920. The Yankees roll on, rolling over teams, especially the Red Sox. They are the champions, the front runners, the crème de la crème of Major League Baseball.

Through it all, the rivalry has seen its share of historic, auspicious, ridiculous, odd, dramatic, poignant, bizarre, and amazing moments, as exhibited by the following timeline:

April 20, 1912 – The first game at Fenway Park, New York versus Boston, was finally played after being rained out for two straight days. The home team prevailed 7-6 in eleven innings.

May 6, 1915 – Red Sox pitcher Babe Ruth hammered his first Major League home run. It came against the Yankees when they still called the Polo Grounds

home. The twenty-year-old Ruth's dinger and his two other hits notwithstanding, the Yankees eked out a 4-3 triumph in thirteen innings over the Red Sox, who committed four errors. The Babe earned the loss.

April 24, 1917 – Yankee George Mogridge hurled the first no-hitter in franchise history. It was against the Red Sox at Fenway.

May 1, 1920 – Babe Ruth slugged his first home run as a Yankee. It cleared the roof of the Polo Grounds, capping a 6-0 Yankee romp over the Red Sox.

April 18, 1923 – Yankee Stadium opened before a reported crowd of 74,200. Babe Ruth hit the first home run as the Yankees defeated the Boston Red Sox.

Spring 1925 – The Yanks were most anxious to trade a first baseman to the Red Sox for Phil Todt. Boston blinked, then passed on the trade. The first baseman, Lou Gehrig, would become one of the greatest players of all time. Todt batted .258 lifetime with 57 home runs.

Familial relationships were at stake in the heated Boston–New York competition. Brothers Dom and Joe DiMaggio were on opposite sides of the battlefield for nine seasons. Despite playing in the shadow of older brother Joe (and teammate Ted Williams), Dom DiMaggio was a seven-time all-star with the Red Sox. He was a temporary teammate of Joe's in the 1941 All-Star Game, Dom's first.

August 12, 1934 – In what was to that point the largest crowd in Fenway Park history, the Yankees and Red Sox split a doubleheader. It was Babe Ruth's final game at the ballpark where his professional career had begun.

March 29, 1948 – The Yankees and Red Sox played through four hours and two minutes to a 2-2 tie in a spring training game in which thirty-three players were used.

October 2, 1949 – The Yankees clinched another pennant in a 5-3 victory over the Red Sox.

April 14, 1955 – Elston Howard, the first black player on the Yankees, singled in his first Major League at bat in a game against the Red Sox.

August 7, 1956 – A crowd of 36,350 watched the Sox defeat the Yankees, 1-0, in eleven innings. Ted Williams walked with the bases loaded to drive in the winning run.

October 1, 1961 – In the last game of the season, Roger Maris hit his 61st home run, breaking Babe Ruth's single-season record. The shot came off Boston pitcher Tracy Stallard.

August 29, 1967 – Both clubs struggled through nineteen innings until the Yankees won the game, 4-3, in the twentieth inning. It was the longest game (in innings) ever played at Yankee Stadium.

October 2, 1978 – After coming back from trailing Boston by fourteen games in July, the Yankees nipped the Red Sox, 5-4, to win the division in just the second playoff game in league history. Bucky Dent's wind-blown homer in the seventh inning was the game winner, and led to his name being forever changed in New England to "Bucky F—ing Dent."

Elston Howard is one of nearly three hundred Major Leaguers who have donned both Yankee and Red Sox uniforms. Howard, the first African-American player signed by the Yankees, spent twelve-and-a-half seasons with New York before closing out his career in Boston. He was also the first black player to win the Most Valuable Player award in the American League (1963).

July 4, 1983 – Yankee stalwart Dave Righetti pitched a no-hitter against the Red Sox, winning 4-0 before 41,077 at the Stadium.

June 19, 2000 – The Red Sox suffered their most lopsided loss ever at home, a 22-1 drubbing by the Yankees.

October 16, 2003 – Five outs away from earning a trip to the World Series, Boston ace Pedro Martinez gave up three runs in the eighth inning to allow the Yankees to tie the deciding game of the American League Championship Series. New York's stunning come-from-behind victory was secured on Aaron Boone's eleventh-inning homer in a sold-out Yankee Stadium.

October 20, 2004 – Boston completes the greatest comeback in postseason history by defeating the Yankees for the fourth night in a row after falling behind three games to none in the ALCS. They would win the World Series one week later.

• • •

The Yankees of New York versus the Red Sox of Boston is the greatest, grandest, strongest rivalry in baseball history—perhaps in all of sports. History, style, culture, dreams, bragging rights—all are mixed in, mixed up with this storied battle of franchises.

The competition is so much more than a baseball team from Boston going against a baseball team from New York. It is a competition of images, cities, styles, ballparks, fans, and media. It is, at its heart, a competition between the provincial capital of New England and the mega-municipality of New York City—the different lifestyles, accents, slogans, and symbols. It's the Charles River versus the East River, Boston Common against Central Park, the Green Monster versus Monument Park, WFAN versus WEEI, the *New York Daily News* matched up with the *Boston Herald*.

The rivalry is reflected in the starkly contrasting images of the teams. The New York Yankees are the glitz and glamour that comes with being the most successful franchise in baseball history. The Bronx Bombers boast an impressive legacy of stars: Yogi Berra, Bill Dickey, Joe DiMaggio, Whitey Ford, Lou Gehrig, Goose Gossage, Ron Guidry, Reggie Jackson, Derek Jeter, Mickey Mantle, Roger Maris, Don Mattingly, Thurman Munson, Vic Raschi, Allie Reynolds, Mariano Rivera, Phil Rizzuto, Babe Ruth. Winning has been as much a part of Yankee baseball as the monuments and plaques in deep center field at the Stadium, as much as the pinstriped uniforms, the intertwined N and Y on the baseball caps.

Less successful, more human, more vulnerable, the Bostons have seemed like the rest of us. But they, too, have had their share of superstars: Cy Young, Joe Cronin, Jimmie Foxx, Ted Williams, Dom DiMaggio, Bobby Doerr, Mel Parnell, Carl Yastrzemski, Carlton Fisk, Dwight Evans, Jim Rice, Nomar Garciaparra, Pedro Martinez, Wade Boggs, Roger Clemens, and of course, Babe Ruth.

"Regardless of where either team is in the standings," notes former Yankee and Red Sox player Mike Stanley, "people mark off the Yankee-Red Sox playing dates on their calendars."

In Boston, fans scream, "Yankees suck! Yankees suck!" even when the Yankees are not playing in Boston. You can hear the chant (and worse) at Fenway Park during a Tampa Bay or Toronto, Mets or Baltimore game.

Bumper stickers throughout New England proclaim: "I Love New York, Too. It's the Yankees I Hate." Two hundred miles to the southwest, it's: "Boston Chokes. Boston Sucks. Boston Does It In Style."

Bucky "F—ing" Dent hit only 40 home runs in his twelve-year career, but few homers are as clearly etched in the minds of New Englanders as the light-hitting shortstop's shot over the Green Monster on October 2, 1978, which proved to be the game- and pennant-winning hit for the Yanks.

The rivalry is Mickey Mantle slugging a 440-foot double at Yankee Stadium in 1958 and tipping his cap to the Red Sox bench. It is Carl Yastrzemski trotting out to left field at Fenway with cotton in his ears to shut out the boos of disheartened Sox fans. It's Mickey Rivers jumping out of the way of an exploding firecracker thrown into the visitors' dugout at Fenway. It's Ted Williams spitting, Reggie Jackson gesturing, Billy Martin punching, Roger Clemens and Pedro Martinez throwing high and tight. It is Carlton Fisk's tension headaches on coming into Yankee Stadium.

"I was always aware of the mix at Fenway Park," said Lou Piniella, who spent fourteen years in a Yankee uniform as player and manager. "There was always a lot of excitement in that small park that made it special. You might have 20,000 Red Sox fans at Fenway and 15,000 Yankee fans. Their rivalry helped our rivalry. It excited the players, who had to respond to it."

Former Red Sox star Dwight Evans was not nearly as enamored with the atmosphere at Yankee Stadium. "When you have a coke bottle go by your head from the third deck, and they miss you by six inches, you wonder what kind of people these are," he said. "When you have cherry bombs thrown at you or thrown into crowds, that's not fun and those are not fans. Don't get me wrong, but I think the people that are crazy in New York are more crazy than the ones in Boston, and you have crazy people there, too. I had to wear helmets out there in the outfield many times. It's a great ballpark to play in, yet you have to watch out for things. When they throw a penny or a dime from the third deck and it hits you, it's going to put a knot on your head."

"In all my years of covering the New York Yankees," notes *Daily News* sportswriter Bill Madden, "I can hardly remember a game at Fenway Park that was a normal game. I'm sure there were some, but it seems like they have been low-scoring, tension-filled, white-knuckle games or these 10-9 barn burners where no lead was safe. Players will never admit it, but the intensity level is up whenever the Yankees and Red Sox meet."

Intensity, for sure. The rivalry intermittently has flared into rage, occasionally into violence. Sometimes it has been triggered by personality clashes, at other times the trigger has simply been the "bad blood" that characterizes the mood and climate whenever the longtime rivals compete head to head.

In 1938, players from both teams stormed the mound at Yankee Stadium when New York's Jake Powell and Boston's Joe Cronin came to blows. The flash point for the incident was Powell's rush to the mound to throttle Sox southpaw Archie McKain. Cronin was ejected from the game. Moments later, he was assaulted by several Yankee players under the stands.

During a game in 1952, Boston's rookie outfielder, Jimmy Piersall, shouted to Yankee infielder Billy Martin, "Hey, Pinocchio!" (an overt reference to the size and contours of the second baseman's nose). "Too damn yellow to fight?"

Martin snarled back, "Put up, or shut up your damn ass. Let's settle this under the stands right now!"

Martin was trailed by Yankee coach Bill Dickey. Ellis Kinder, a Boston hurler, ran after Piersall. The two fury-filled players faced off. Unprintable words spewed forth from Martin and Piersall before Martin jabbed two powerful shots to Piersall's face. Bleeding profusely from the nose, the Boston outfielder dropped quickly to the ground. The one-sided battle ended as Dickey and Kinder stepped between the two.

In the Yankee dugout, manager Casey Stengel was informed of what had taken place. "That was all right, all right," said the wizened pilot, who had seen everything

The Red Sox were one out away from winning the 1986 World Series against the "other" New York team, the Mets, when it all unraveled before their eyes—and between their legs. Bill Buckner's failure to field Mookie Wilson's groundball in the tenth inning of Game 6 is the moment that best symbolized "the Curse," but Buckner must share the goat label with pitchers Calvin Schiraldi and Bob Stanley, who failed to hold the lead for Boston.

in his many years in the game. "I'm happy as long as Billy starts with players on the other teams and doesn't start with any players on the Yankees."

That moment in Yankee-Red Sox history underscored the bad blood between the teams. But it was not the most famous of the on-field altercations. One that qualifies for the title took place on August 1, 1973.

At the time, debate raged over the relative abilities of two young, up-and-coming catchers: Boston's Carlton Fisk and New York's Thurman Munson. Fisk led the American League all-star balloting for the position that year. Munson was runner-up. "That was part of the conflict," explained Yankee broadcaster Frank Messer. "And there was even some personality conflict between the two of them."

"Fisk hated Munson," recalled Don Zimmer, who managed the BoSox from 1976 to 1980. "Munson hated Fisk."

On that August day in 1973, the teams were deadlocked 2-2 in the ninth inning at Fenway. With John Curtis on the mound for Boston, Munson doubled down the left-field line. An infield groundout by Graig Nettles moved him to third base. Gene

The intensity of the rivalry went up a notch in 1973 when Thurman Munson collided with Carlton Fisk at home plate in Boston. The two all-star catchers—both born in 1947, both making their Major League debut in 1969—clashed for eleven seasons before Munson's untimely death in a plane crash in 1979.

Right: Something special was sure to happen when the Yankees and Red Sox met in the American League Championship Series in 2003, though few could have expected this: a seventy-two-year-old coach attacking the game's best pitcher during a brawl and being thrown to the ground. Later in the same game, two Yankee players scuffled with a Fenway Park groundskeeper in the bullpen.

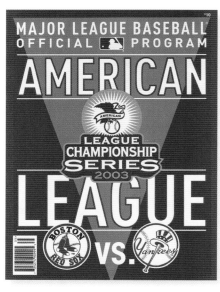

Michael missed on an attempted squeeze bunt, but the solidly built Munson came tearing down the line anyway. Fisk had the ball and was blocking the plate. Munson slammed hard into Fisk. Fisk held onto the baseball. Munson was out. Fisk shoved the Yankee catcher off of him and Munson retaliated with a punch to the opposing catcher's face, bruising his left eye.

The two got into clinching and clawing. Michael managed to get in a few punches of his own. Next thing, the field was swarming with players—pushing, shoving, cursing—more than sixty players and coaches, even those from the bullpen 350 feet away, in the mix. When order was finally restored, Fisk and Munson were ejected from the game, and another exclamation point was added to the rivalry.

Thirty years later, the intensity had not waned a bit. During the third game of the 2003 League Championship Series, the benches cleared after one too many hit batters and inside pitches. In the midst of the melee, Don Zimmer, then a bench coach with the Yankees, charged Boston's Pedro Martinez. Martinez, grasping Zimmer by the head, tossed the seventy-two-year-old coach to the ground, sending him tumbling end-over-end on the Fenway Park grass.

When it comes to Red Sox–Yankees baseball, there is never a dull moment, and every Yankee loyalist or Red Sox rooter has a story to tell, a memory to share of heartbreak or jubilation from this most emotional rivalry.

Dan Mackie, a feature writer and columnist for a New Hampshire newspaper and a die-hard Red Sox fan, remembers a special rivalry moment. "By 1978," he says, "I was a grown person and could have chosen another path. But I read the box scores, listened to the radio, watched games on TV. I got in deeper and deeper.

"Anyway, this is all history, like the fall of the Roman Empire, or Enron. Despite being fourteen games behind the Sox in July of '78, the Yankees, who had a terrific team of their own that year, caught up, fell behind, caught up again, and forced a one-game playoff. Bucky Dent won it with a wind-assisted popup that barely got out of the infield, and through a harmonic convergence—the Jet Stream, Babe Ruth in heaven, a minor earthquake in the Philippines, gravity from Mars and Pluto, a kid stomping his foot in the Bronx, high pressure over the Northeast, a jet landing at Logan Airport, a pigeon flapping its wings, a whale spouting off the coast of Finland, a heavy lady in the third row waving her program and yelling 'Get out, get out,' all these forces and more aligned—a little white ball floated farther and farther, up and over the Green Monster, light as a feather, then fell like a stone into the net, the home run net.

"I hit bottom," Mackie continues. "I swore them off. I said I'd turn my life over to a higher power. Unfortunately, the higher power turned out to be Roger Clemens. He was a false god."

Through it all, Mackie remains an avid Red Sox fan. "I hate the Yankees. A Yankee loss is as good as a Red Sox victory. That's sweet bile, I know, but it's all I have. And I mainline optimism, addictive as opium, every spring."

Sherwood Boehlert, a Republican congressman from Cooperstown, New York, offers his own musings. "I'm glad I turned out a Yankees fan, because I've had a lot fewer disappointments in my life," he observes. "You might think it's silly for a twenty-year veteran of Congress, who is a committee chairman, who serves on the Intelligence Committee, who deals with big issues, to say that baseball's important to him. But it is. It adds an extra dimension to my life."

Above: Fenway Park is just one of Boston's many historic monuments. It has been the site of plenty of battles in the Yankee–Red Sox baseball war.

Left: The fireworks continued in 2004, when New York's latest megastar, Alex Rodriguez, took exception to being hit by a pitch from Boston's Bronson Arroyo. Words were exchanged, things got heated, and fisticuffs ensued. A-Rod and Boston catcher Jason Varitek were at the center of the brouhaha.

"My wife and I have a fifty-three-inch-screen TV—only because of baseball. We wear our Yankees hats, and we get sunflower seeds and a bowl, we spit 'em in there, we have a couple of beers, and we have fun."

So does former three-term governor of New York, Mario Cuomo, a very longtime Yankees fan. "The Red Sox start ahead and cave in August," Cuomo says. "That's the myth. And that's the myth I don't want to go away. Having experienced both the glory of victory and the anguish of defeat, I've learned to enjoy winning. And that creates a decided advantage for the Yankees in my mind. The dominance of the Yankees over the Red Sox makes it fun to be a Yankees fan. It's nice to win."

Equal time must go to Michael Dukakis, former governor of Massachusetts, rabid Red Sox fan. "By 1978," Dukakis recalls, "I was governor of Massachusetts. I could identify with the Red Sox that year. They had blown a fourteen-game lead, and I lost the Democratic primary to Ed King after leading by forty points with five weeks to go. Not only was I feeling very upset about that, but then I had to watch Dent hit that pop fly into the screen. Dukakis and the Red Sox both went down the tubes together.

"The games between the Yankees and Red Sox are always intense. I get a sense that the players feel it too. No matter who they are, or where they come from, how long or little they've been with the team, there's something about those series."

• • •

The Saturday Evening POST
April 20, 1957 – 15¢

You Can't Afford a Divorce

Warren Spahn Says,
Milwaukee Will Win the Pennant

Singer Harry Belafonte

Mayan

Any time the Yankees and Red Sox meet up, it captures the attention of all baseball fans—not just in New York and Boston. This *Saturday Evening Post* cover from April 20, 1957, painted by Earl Mayan, depicts Yankee catcher Yogi Berra waiting to field a foul pop-up as the Fenway faithful give him an earful from the stands.

Perhaps no two players symbolize the Yankee-Red Sox rivalry more than Joe DiMaggio and Ted Williams. Both Californians, they found stardom in the East. Both bigger than life, they seemed sculpted into their respective superstar roles. One was an outspoken iconoclast, the other a soft-spoken team man.

Born November 25, 1914, in Martinez, California, Joseph Paul DiMaggio was one of nine children of a fisherman father who had immigrated from Sicily. The plan was for Joe to become a fisherman like his father. His real passion was playing baseball. Rosalie, the mother, would cover for the DiMaggio boys when they arrived home with torn pants, and she encouraged them to play.

"I began playing baseball on a vacant lot in San Francisco with the other kids in my neighborhood when I was about ten years old," recalled the man they would call the Yankee Clipper. "In those days, I preferred almost anything to working on my father's fishing boat or cleaning it up when the fishing day was over. I hated the smell. My father looked on baseball in much the same way as I did on fishing."

DiMaggio's first foray into professional baseball was with the San Francisco Seals of the Pacific Coast League, which at the time was the closest thing to Major League baseball on the West Coast. In 1934, the Yankees purchased DiMaggio's contract from the Seals. "Getting him," general manager George Weiss was fond of saying, "was the greatest thing I ever did for the Yankees." The price for DiMaggio was $25,000 and five players. The deal also held the condition that the graceful outfielder be permitted to play one more season for the Seals. DiMaggio gave the city of San

Francisco something to remember, batting .398 with 270 hits and 154 RBIs.

In early 1936, DiMaggio was told to drive cross-country with fellow San Franciscans Tony Lazzeri and Frank Crosetti to join the Yankees at their spring training camp in St. Petersburg, Florida. Reportedly, after completing the first day of driving, Lazzeri turned to the young DiMaggio and said, "You take over, Joe."

DiMaggio supposedly replied, "I don't drive"—the only words he uttered during the three-day journey from California to Florida.

"Joe DiMaggio was a guy who didn't graduate from high school," noted Jerry Coleman, a one-time teammate of DiMaggio's. "He went to about the 10th grade. He was totally insecure, and consequently his quietness came from his preferring to say nothing rather than say something that would make him look bad."

Joe's father sent him a telegram during that first spring training with the Yankees: "Come home, Joe. The fish are running. Give up this game of baseball. It is for loafers."

He played in his first Major League game on May 3, 1936, at Yankee Stadium against the St. Louis Browns. In his first time at bat, he hit the second pitch into left field for a single. He had another single and then a triple to left. Joe DiMaggio played 138 games in his rookie season, batting .323 with 29 home runs and 125 runs batted in. And he never let up.

Ted Williams was four years younger than DiMaggio, born on August 30, 1918, in San Diego. In 1935, as a pitcher-outfielder at Herbert Hoover High School in his hometown, Williams hit .586. His mother, an ardent Salvation Army worker, thought he was worth a $1,000 bonus for signing with a Major League team. Bill Essick, a scout for the Yankees, listened, thought, and finally decided that Williams was not worth that much money.

"I don't know whether $1,000 stood between me being a Yank or not," Williams later recalled. "There were those who said years later, 'You will regret not having been a Yankee. You would be a great hero in New York. Yankee Stadium was built for a left-handed hitter.'"

Williams signed with the San Diego Padres of the Pacific Coast League before he was even eighteen years old. He played in just 42 games in 1936, but he hit .291 with 23 home runs and 98 RBIs the following season. The manager of the National League's Boston Bees, a humorous but baseball-wise gent named Casey Stengel, observed Williams playing for San Diego. He recommended that Boston sign the youngster. The Bees' management decided that the asking price was too high. The other Boston team, the Red Sox, thought the price was right and signed Williams.

The six-foot-three-inch, curly-haired Williams arrived at the Red Sox training camp in early spring 1938. "Ted," said Bobby Doerr, a friend of Williams's from their

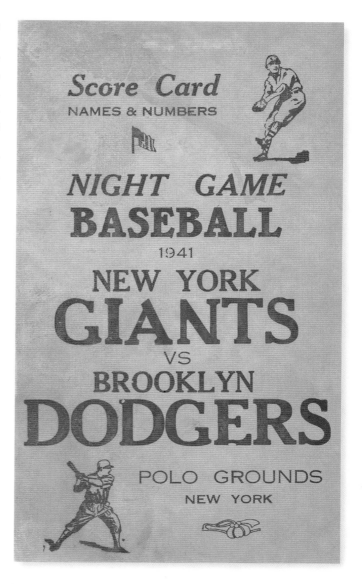

The only rivalry that might rival that of the Yankees and Red Sox is that between the Giants and Dodgers, which goes back earlier and has thrived on two coasts. Since Brooklyn joined the National League in 1890, the teams have finished first and second in the standings thirteen times. In 1951 and 1962, the teams ended the regular season with identical records and required playoff games to decide the pennant. (The Giants won both times.)

PCL days, "wait till you see this guy Jimmie Foxx hit," referring to a future Hall of Famer.

"Bobby," Williams retorted, "wait till Foxx sees *me* hit."

Williams did not hit very well in spring training that year, however, and to the delight of some of the Red Sox stars whom he had alienated with his bombast, he was sent down to Minneapolis of the American Association for more seasoning. "I'll be back," he snarled at some of the Boston stars, "and I'll be greater than you guys."

Williams's first year with the Red Sox, 1939, was DiMaggio's fourth with the Yankees. In his first three seasons, the Yankee Clipper had batted .323, .346, and .324 and glided about the center-field pastureland of Yankee Stadium with a quiet ease and grace. The Red Sox and Yankees went head-to-head for the pennant in 1939, and Williams and DiMaggio went head-to-head in the first of many seasons in which they would vie for the attention and admiration of fans. They were rivals, but they always had mutual respect for each other.

Joe DiMaggio and Ted Williams both passed away as the twentieth century turned to the twenty-first—DiMaggio on March 8, 1999, four months past his eighty-fourth birthday, and Williams on July 2, 2002, two months shy of his eighty-fourth. The accolades for these two ballplayers came from all corners. Former Dodgers manager Tommy Lasorda said of Joe D., "He was to people all over the world what a baseball player was supposed to be like. If you said to God, 'Create someone who was what a baseball player should be,' God would have created Joe DiMaggio." In the words of sportswriter Robert Lipsyte, "Ted Williams was what John Wayne would have liked us to think he was. Williams was so big, and handsome, and laconic, and direct, and unafraid in that uniquely American cowboy way."

Any discussion of these baseball icons must address the rumored trade of Ted Williams for Joe DiMaggio. As the story goes, Red Sox owner Tom Yawkey and Yankee boss Dan Topping were at the famous New York nightspot Toots Shor's one night bantering about how much better Ted Williams would hit at Yankee Stadium and how much better Joe DiMaggio would hit at Fenway Park. The night concluded with the two owners exchanging a handshake and agreeing to make a DiMaggio-Williams trade.

Reportedly, when Topping arrived home at four o'clock in the morning and realized what he had agreed to, he picked up the phone and called Yawkey in a panic.

"Tom," he began, "I'm sorry but I can't go through with the deal."

"Thank God," was Yawkey's reported reply.

Another version of the purported DiMaggio-Williams deal has Yawkey the one who made the phone call. "Dan, I know it's very, very late, and I still want to make that trade we discussed. However, if you still want to make it you'll have to throw in that left-handed hitting outfielder. You know who I mean, that little odd-looking rookie."

"I can't," Topping said. "We're thinking of making him a catcher. I guess we'll have to call off the deal."

So Joe DiMaggio remained a Yankee, and Ted Williams played out his career with the Red Sox. And that little odd-looking rookie? He stayed with the Yankees, became a catcher, and won a record ten World Series rings with New York. His name was Yogi Berra.

· · ·

Facing page: Throughout their careers, Boston's Ted Williams and New York's Joe DiMaggio were pitted head-to-head in the debate over who was the game's greatest player. In 1948, *Sport* magazine asked Yankee broadcaster Mel Allen and Red Sox broadcaster Jim Britt to make a case in support of their respective hometown heroes. While Williams was tops in the league in batting and slugging that year and DiMaggio led in homers and RBIs, Cleveland's Lou Boudreau snuck away with the American League MVP trophy.

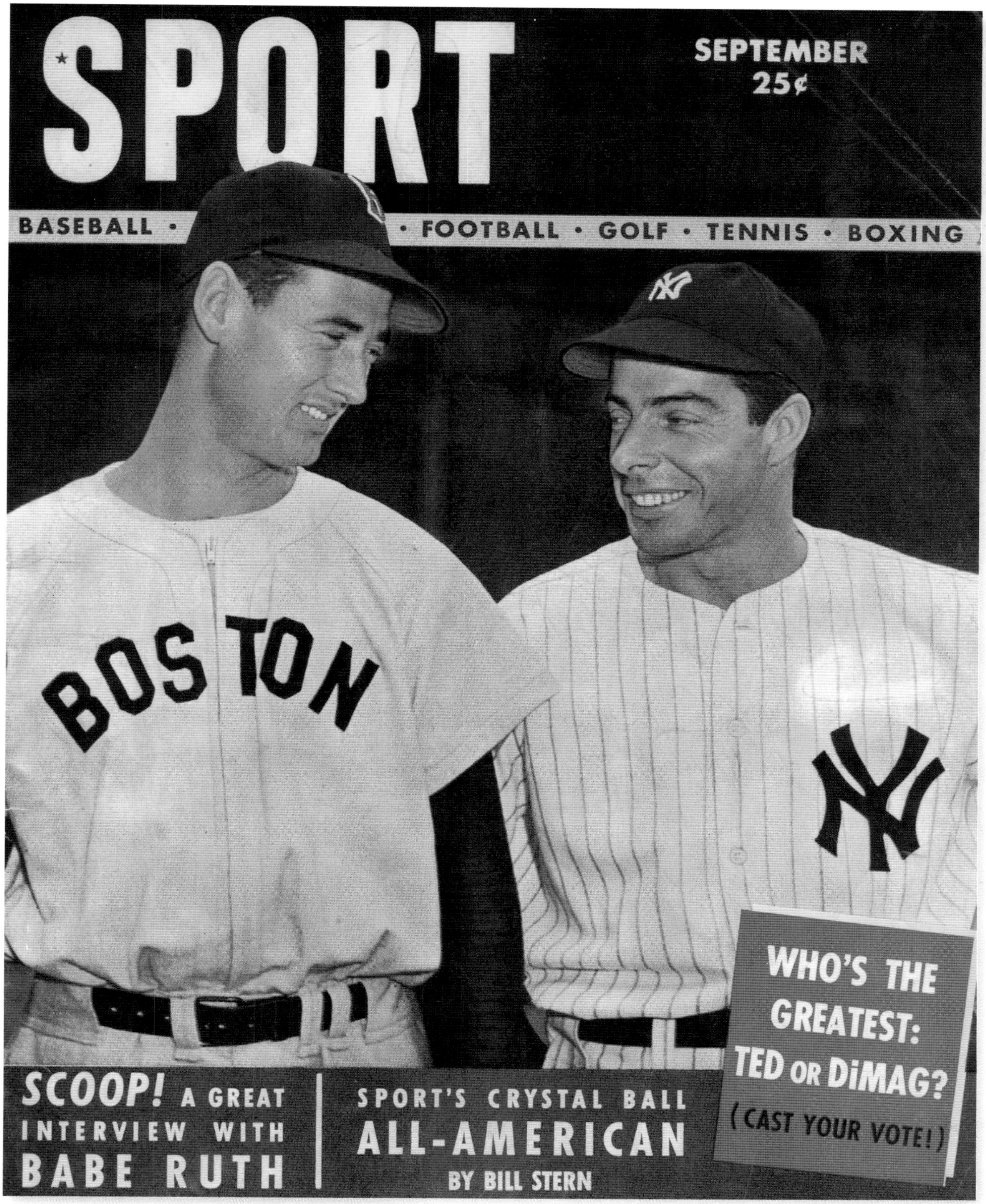
SPORT
SEPTEMBER
25¢
BASEBALL • • FOOTBALL • GOLF • TENNIS • BOXING
BOSTON
WHO'S THE GREATEST: TED OR DiMAG?
(CAST YOUR VOTE!)
SCOOP! A GREAT INTERVIEW WITH BABE RUTH
SPORT'S CRYSTAL BALL
ALL-AMERICAN
BY BILL STERN

Just as this book was going to press, a new chapter was unfolding in the storied Red Sox–Yankees rivalry. The "Curse" was finally broken.

The "Curse" lasted 31,457 days. For the first time since 1918, the Boston Red Sox held the title of world champions. No longer would the names Bill Buckner, Bucky "F—ing" Dent, and Aaron Boone have the pain for Boston fans they once had.

To become 2004 kings of the hill, the Red Sox had a long, tough climb. Boston became the first team in Major League history to finish in second place for seven straight years. In the American League Championship Series, the Red Sox once again came up against their age-old nemesis, the Yankees, who had recorded their seventh consecutive division title with a new group of high-priced free agents—including the highest of the high-priced, Alex Rodriguez. He had been actively pursued by Boston in the off-season before being snatched up by "King George" Steinbrenner. While the wild card–winning BoSox did make some significant acquisitions of their own before the 2004 season, most notably pitchers Curt Schilling and Keith Foulke, the lineup appeared as a ragtag bunch, many of them unshaven or badly shaven and sporting shaggy locks. They even embraced the self-proclaimed nickname "the Idiots."

Three straight wins by New York opened the ALCS. The Red Sox Nation seemed to be headed for another heart-wrenching defeat at the hands of the "Evil Empire." The Yankees disposed of Boston aces Schilling and Pedro

Boston slugger David Ortiz came through with clutch, game-winning hits on back-to-back nights during the 2004 ALCS. His fourteenth-inning RBI single in Game 5 brought the Red Sox one game closer to ending "the Curse." Ortiz drove in 11 runs in the series and went home with MVP honors.

Martinez in Games 1 and 2 and then unloaded on Boston, 19-8, in Game 3. Things were looking grim in Beantown.

No team in the history of postseason baseball had rallied to win a seven-game series after losing the first three games. The Red Sox were going to have to defy history, logic, and the "Curse" in order to make their first World Series appearance since 1986.

Incredibly, unbelievably, the team from Boston prevailed in Games 4 and 5 in extra innings. The game-winning hits in each contest were courtesy of DH David "Papi" Ortiz, a player George Steinbrenner had ached to sign before the 2003 season.

Game 6 was surreal. The umpires reversed two calls—one that gave Boston a run and another that took a run away from New York—and it seemed that the stars might finally be aligned for the Red Sox. Curt Schilling hurled a nearly flawless game despite being afflicted by a ruptured ankle tendon held together by sutures stitched in by team doctors just the day before.

The arch rivals were deadlocked in the series, winners of three games each. It came down to a winner-take-all seventh game to decide who would go on to the World Series.

Boston's epic comeback was sealed early in Game 7. Johnny Damon, who had managed only 3 hits in 29 times at bat in the first six games, delivered a grand slam in the second inning. When the Red Sox shelling was finally—and mercifully, for Yankee fans—over, the Stadium scoreboard read, Boston 10, New York 3.

The city of Boston erupted in celebration as soon as the game ended. While many saw the defeat of the Evil Empire as the ultimate triumph, there was still business to attend to—namely, the World Series. Matched up against the same opponent that had denied them glory in 1946 and 1967, the Red Sox made quick work of the National League champion St. Louis Cardinals, taking the series in four straight games.

At precisely 10:40 P.M. on Wednesday, October 27, 2004, at Busch Stadium in St. Louis, Boston Red Sox closer Keith Foulke fielded Edgar Renteria's grounder and made an underhand toss to first baseman Doug Mientkiewicz. It was the final exclamation point in the Red Sox sweep of the Cardinals, a team that had won 105 regular-season games.

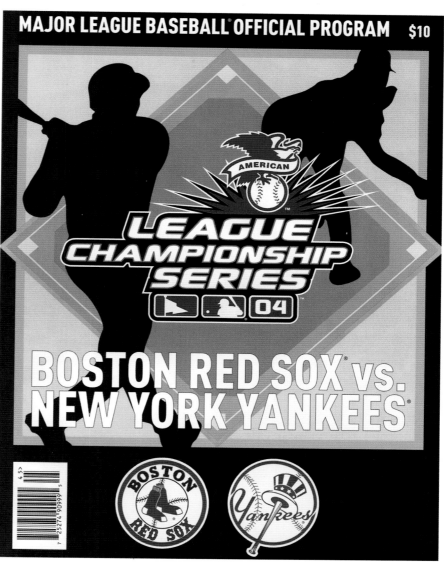

Showering each other with champagne and digging plugs of dirt from the mound at Busch Stadium, several Red Sox players remained on the field for more than an hour.

"Being world champion is by far the best," said Sox manager Terry Francona. "I didn't do this for any other reason. We can't reverse what was long ago. I'm sure there are a lot of people in New England dancing in the streets right now. For that, I am thrilled."

As the World Series games played out in Boston and St. Louis, Yankee owner George Steinbrenner met his team executives in Tampa, plotting big Yankee moves for 2005.

Two years in a row, these historic rivals battled through dramatic seven-game series to decide the league pennant. Both the 2003 and 2004 American League Championship Series rank among the greatest postseason series of all time.

PART III

PENNANT MADNESS— AND A BOY GROWS UP

from *My Life in Baseball* by Ty Cobb with Al Stump

UNDOUBTEDLY ONE OF baseball's all-time great players, Ty Cobb was also one of its all-time cantankerous characters. His combative style produced record-setting achievements on the field as well as countless skirmishes with players, managers, owners, and fans alike throughout his twenty-four-year career.

In his colorful if self-sanitized autobiography, ghostwritten by sportswriter Al Stump, Cobb shares his views on his life experiences and his take on the state of baseball in the early 1960s. Three decades later, Stump penned a more revealing biography of Cobb, detailing the harrowing experience of collaborating with this aged, dying, and troubled baseball legend.

Soon after the long trip up from Georgia to the biggest burg I'd yet seen (Detroit population: about 300,000 in 1905), I began to suspect that I had worse troubles than earning my spurs with manager Bill Armour's collection of hard-nosed athletes.

Like most eighteen-year-olds, I put off doing anything about it. Aside from the usual childhood ailments and the time I shot myself in the collarbone, I'd always been as healthy as a colt in the Bluegrass.

But I hadn't been a Tiger rookie very long when my throat began to pain me like fury. Burly Germany Schaefer, the second baseman, watched me at the dinner table one night.

"Say, kid," he said curiously, "why do you grip the chair seat with both hands after swallowing your soup?"

"Because it hurts so much," I groaned.

I wanted to take my problem to Armour, but didn't dare. I had the well-founded fear that the small toehold I had on the position of right-fielder with the team would be stolen by another player if I reported sick. So I suffered and covered it up and suffered some more.

Ty Cobb joined the Detroit Tigers in 1905 as a fresh-faced eighteen-year-old out of Narrows, Georgia. Over the next twenty-four seasons, he would compile a career average of .367—the highest in history—while breaking the .400 mark in three different seasons. His 4,191 career hits stood as a record until Pete Rose broke it in 1985. (Some sources give Cobb's correct hit total as 4,189.)

Finally, when we made an exhibition game stop in Toledo, pausing at the Boodie House, I was running such a fever and in such agony that I hunted up the house doctor—who was neither a surgeon nor equipped for the treatment I needed. Germany came along to lend support.

"Tonsillitis, and an acute case," the doc diagnosed.

He sat me in a chair, tipped it back and went to work, without anesthetic. My tonsils were in such a condition that they had to be removed in sections. Each time a piece of them came out, blood surged into my mouth, choking me, and I had to demand a rest period. Putting a stranglehold on my neck, the doc would probe and cut for 10 or 15 minutes before letting me collapse on a sofa. Stretched out there, I'd wonder how I could ever take another round in that chair.

"Let's go, son," the M.D. would say cheerfully, brandishing his tonsil-chopper.

He cut me seven times before he was finished, after which I was so weak from pain, loss of blood, and shock that Germany had to half-carry me to bed. The Tigers had a game scheduled next day and you can bet I showed up for it—wobbly, but playing seven innings and making sure I was still around when the game was won. I don't remember getting any sympathy.

A few people remarked that the doc must have been crazy to extract the tonsils so informally. I wondered about that, and checked up on him the following season.

Sure enough, during the winter he had been committed to an asylum for the insane.

Let a modern-day player develop a bit of indigestion or a minor bone chip in his arm and he's clamped into a bed at Johns Hopkins, attended by world-noted specialists, fed by dieticians, and generally treated like a maharaja with the gout. His team pays all the bills. In my day, a sick ballplayer was just another liability—unless he got himself well in a hurry, and cheaply. As a new boy who didn't know how to protest, I even paid my own hospital tab on one occasion.

I'd been with the Tigers little more than a year when a "slider"—an abrasion caused by hitting the hard infield dirt too often in base-steals—became inflamed and filled with pus. Did Frank Navin, the Detroit president, offer me any assistance?

Cobb's aggressive play on the base paths helped him to accumulate record numbers of stolen bases and runs scored; he held the all-time mark in both categories until Lou Brock and Rickey Henderson came along decades later. His aggressiveness also led to conflict. His hard, spikes-out slide into Philadelphia third baseman Frank "Home Run" Baker caused much consternation among Athletics fans and players.

Not a nickel's worth. At a Fort Street hospital, the wound was lanced and drained and I paid for the privilege, at a time when I was earning $2400 a season. Navin visited me just once while I was invalided, and kept both hands in his pockets, clutching his bankroll, throughout.

Split a finger fifty years ago and you stuck it in the dirt and kept going. It gives me a wry laugh to hear players today complain about the conditions they labor under. They even find certain parks of the 1960s "tough to play in." In 1907, old Bennett Park in Detroit, as well as other arenas, sprouted grass which had been planted at the wrong time of year and was cow pasture rough and rutted with holes and soft spots. Where the infield grass met the skinned infield area, there were drop-offs that sent balls flying in all directions. Diamonds were given a quick once-over with a rake maybe once a week, where these days they are scientifically planted, cultivated, and manicured, and dragged smooth before, during, and after games. Drainage was crude and on wet days the outer pastures were marshy, if not worse. Danny McGann, who played for the old Baltimore Orioles, was galloping after a fly ball one day when he suddenly disappeared from sight. Then McGann's hand appeared above the turf, waving in distress. Dan had fallen into a long-abandoned sewer outlet over which a few thin boards, dirt, and grass had been placed.

In the old-time clubhouses, we had nothing. Whirlpool baths, electrotherapy, skilled trainers with all their healing apparatus and hot-water showers were luxuries the Wagners, Lajoies, Speakers, Mathewsons, McGinnitys, Radbourns, Planks, and Tinkers never experienced. We put on our uniforms in primitive quarters, waited in line for the single shower to be vacated and dressed next day in damp uniforms.

That's right—damp, if not wet. Uniforms were jammed into containers after a game in their natural sweat-soaked state and seldom saw a laundry. We wore them until they were a grimy disgrace.

Train travel was in non-air-conditioned chair cars and if you compare the jump of 16 to 18 hours from Boston to St. Louis with the modern magic carpet air trip, one wonders how it was that yesterday's baseball regularly produced dozens of hitters in the .350 to .400 class and pitchers who won 30 or more games per season as against today's sprinkling of .300 hitters and handful of 20-game winners. These days the player has everything in the way of comfort, consideration, and scientific assistance. We had no batting cages, motion pictures to record our form, pitching machines, coaching specialists, and multivitamin tablets. The pancake gloves we wore, the washboard fields we played on, the cramped upper berths we climbed into on endless rides over poor roadbeds, the need to wrestle with your own luggage, the four-men-to-one-bathtub system in hotels, and the crude equipment should have produced baseball which can't be compared to the modern brand. For instance, bases were left out there until they were spiked apart. They weren't anchored and strapped down firmly, giving you a solid cushion for sliding. Those sawdust bags would shift a foot or more when you tore into them. Pitchers dosed baseballs with licorice, talcum, slippery elm, and saliva flavored with tobacco until they came at the hitter so discolored that he could hardly pick them out of the shadows. If you tore a muscle or broke a bone, a long lay-off was out of the question—some eager rival would have your job in a minute. You played, whether you were lame, sick, or half-blind from pain. The first shin guards and sliding pads were coming into vogue when I was young, but we never heard of flip-down sunglasses, gloves with fantastic webbed extensions, outfield walls with cinder-track borders to save you from crashing the fence, finely clipped infield grass, and specially arranged backdrops to give the hitters a clear view of the ball.

Nevertheless, I'll take for my all-star line-up a group that includes George Sisler, Roger Bresnahan, Eddie Collins, Honus Wagner, Buck Weaver, Joe Jackson, Tris Speaker, Walter Johnson, Eddie Plank, Christy Mathewson, Grover Alexander, Ed Walsh, and Cy Young over any that can be named from a list of stars covering the past thirty years. Every index we have show their superiority over the fat-cat athletes of today. Why is this? I'll explain why it's true in another section of this book, but for now I'll put it in a few words: *The present-day boys lack the fighting dedication to the game that was entirely commonplace in my day.*

In short, we didn't have business agents out soliciting lecture dates, advertising testimonials, special bonuses, TV appearances, and autograph parties for us. We simply tried to hang onto our jobs by playing up to 100 per cent of our ability every inning, without distractions.

The men I jousted with in the early years were a strange breed that the United States of America never will see again—as long gone from the scene as the sodbuster, the hide-skinner, the riverboat gambler, and the map makers of the Old West. To them, baseball was a whole way of life, their reason for existence—not a means to another monetary end. They were poor boys from farms and villages, burning with ambition, who studied, practiced, threw themselves into games without thought of injury and who suffered rigors without complaint that would send a modern pro crying to the Players Association for relief.

If you had glanced down a hotel hallway fifty years ago, you'd have seen "ghosts" moving down those clammy corridors. These were ballplayers. They were wrapped in bedsheets, grimy and sore from the day's battle, and unable to find a bathtub anywhere. Sometimes we had to use public toilets in the second-rate hotels patronized by our nickel-squeezing owners. Detroit was a standout example. Bill Armour and Hughie Jennings, my first managers, rated a private tub in their room. We used to hang around their door in our sheets, hoping for a crack at just five minutes of soaking in hot water.

We dried out in our own sweat, put sticking plaster on open wounds and still managed to produce men like Kid Nichols of the Boston Nationals *who won 30 or*

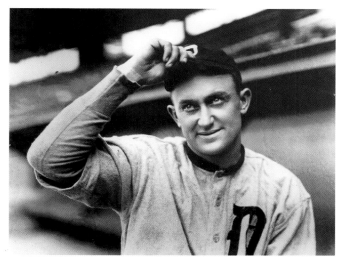

The "Georgia Peach" exhibits a rare, if partial, smile. Stating that "ferocious" was an adjective he would not quarrel with to describe himself, Cobb rarely backed down from a fight. In 1912, he climbed into the stands at New York's Hilltop Park and beat up a heckling fan; for this, he received an indefinite suspension from the league president. Cobb was ultimately reinstated, of course, but only after the entire Detroit Tiger team boycotted a game in protest.

more pitching decisions in seven seasons and 20 or more for ten years successively. How long since baseball has known a one-season 30-game winner? Not for a quarter-century, since Dizzy Dean.

Toughness. The old-timers had it in a measure the moderns don't even begin to understand. In having my tonsils jerked cold-turkey by a hotel M.D., I did nothing

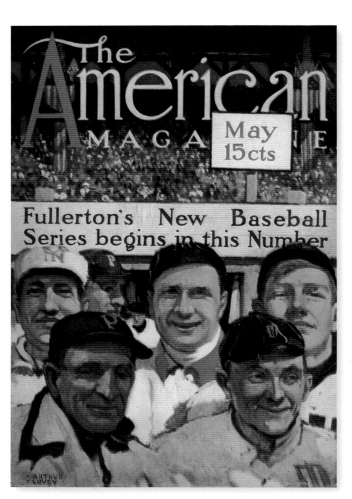

extraordinary. "Old Hoss" Radbourn once won 60 games in a season, pitching almost every day when his team ran shy of moundsmen—and did it with a sore arm. Hugh Duffy's leg was slashed open by spikes from ankle to knee, but he played out the season and compiled the highest batting average of all time: .438. So it went, back then.

In the beginning years, I didn't mind the hardships. Starting in 1907, a period of emergence began for me. That was my second full year with the Tigers and my third as a Major Leaguer, and it seemed to me that the concentrated, organized attempt of a certain clique of Detroit veterans to run me back to the minors was tapering off, if not ended. As I've already described, the clique had waged bitter war with me all through '06. I had been harassed to the point of hating to even show up at the park. Gradually, though, the antagonisms were fading . . . as a player I was progressing in skill . . . the formation of friendships with various Tigers was becoming a solid and warming thing.

But there remained Sam Crawford, our big outfielder-first baseman. Wahoo Sam, who'd trained to be a barber, chose to continue the feud. Sam had been the slugging star of the Tigers before my arrival, the fan's darling, after having earlier led the National League in homers while with Cincinnati. As 1907 rolled along, my bat average rose above .330. For the first time, Crawford was running second on his own club.

Just then some more of my bats turned up mysteriously broken. The vandalism infuriated me. It didn't take Sherlock Holmes to know that Sam was sicking the boys on me. He made no overt moves himself, preferring to agitate in the background.

At batting practice one day, I couldn't take another minute of it. I marched up to Crawford.

"You big —," I said. "You've been making trouble for me long enough. Now, put up your hands."

Crawford blinked and looked uncomfortable.

"Go ahead," I barked. "I'm calling you."

Sam muttered something about me having him all wrong, and edged away from there.

The one and only way I could see to settle the clique's hash was to outhustle and, if possible, outplay all members of the anti-Cobb faction, and this I bore down on with everything I had. By July, the Chicago White Sox had won 53 and lost 33 and led the American League over Detroit, with 49-33. In Boston, we knocked off the Red Sox in

Ty Cobb, Honus Wagner, and other early baseball stars grace the cover of *The American Magazine* from May 1911. The issue features an article by renowned sportswriter Hugh Fullerton called "Hitting the Dirt: The Science of Base Running and Stealing as Revealed by the Efforts of Ballplayers to Gain Ninety Feet of Ground." Cobb and Wagner both rank among the greatest base stealers of all time.

a nip-tuck game, aided by my eleventh-inning double off Charley Pruitt. Moving to New York, I was in right field when Frank LaPorte of the Highlanders sliced a drive that looked absolutely good for three bases. With two out, a pair of New Yorkers were on base and they went dashing for home. Tearing after the ball, I ran out of my shoes, but saw I wasn't going to make it, so I took off in a headlong dive and stabbed out barehandedly. Somehow the ball smacked my palm and stuck there long enough for me to clench it. Landing on my chest, I plowed up grass for half a dozen feet, somersaulted twice and held up the ball to the umpire.

It sounded like a gas bag had exploded. A vast *whoosh* of disappointment came from the crowd. Hughie Jennings, our new manager, did an Indian war dance on the sideline, uncorked his favorite yell of *"Eee-yah!"* and generally went crazy.

Two New York runs had crossed the plate while I was pursuing LaPorte's drive, but the catch ended the inning and the runs did not count. We went on to win a crucial game and move closer to the league lead.

About this time, I gashed my thumb and whenever I had to hit the dirt in a slide, the wound broke open and bled freely. It hurt, but I kept sliding. My bloody thumb became a sort of a symbol of the clawing, scrapping, determined Tigers and drew more newspaper space than my base hits. Charlie Schmidt, the 215-pound catcher who'd once broken my nose with a sneak punch, gave out an interview praising my "game" play. "Why," he told the newsboys, "Cobb loses a good pint of blood every time he slides!"

It was more like a thimbleful. But it helped break the ice with my teammates, and Schmidt, who'd been a tool of the clique that hated me, began to act like my press agent. He was even cheering for me to win the league batting championship. Hughie Jennings gave me *carte blanche* to run the bases as freely as I liked. Smiles replaced snarls, now that I was helping the Tigers toward that pennant money. In this happy atmosphere, I became a ballplayer.

Above: Honus "The Flying Dutchman" Wagner was the leading hitter in the National League while Cobb dominated the American League. Wagner topped the NL in batting eight times (a record he shares with Tony Gwynn); Cobb holds the AL record with eleven batting crowns. When Wagner and Cobb met head-to-head in the 1909 World Series, Wagner out-hit Cobb .333 to .231, and his Pittsburgh Pirates bested Cobb's Tigers in seven games.

Left: Napoleon Lajoie was another hitting rival of Cobb's in the early part of the twentieth century. In 1910, Lajoie seemingly nabbed the batting title from Cobb on the last day of the season, after the opposing St. Louis Browns' fielders left gaps for Lajoie to hit safely. An official recount gave Cobb the narrowest of margins—.3848 to .3841—but another tally years later noted that Cobb was credited with two extra hits, and Lajoie was the rightful winner. Both players were awarded a car by auto manufacturer Hugh Chalmers, who had promised the prize to the league's batting champ.

CHRISTY MATHEWSON, GENTLEMAN GIANT

from *The Celebrant* by Eric Rolfe Greenberg

CHRISTY MATHEWSON BELONGS on the short list of any ranking of all-time pitchers. His 373 career wins are third best in history, and his three shutout victories during the 1905 World Series remains one of the sport's most impressive pitching achievements. He was also an upstanding, well-educated man widely respected by his peers.

Eric Rolfe Greenberg's novel *The Celebrant* follows Mathewson's career through the eyes of jeweler and erstwhile amateur pitcher Jackie Kapp. During a business trip to St. Louis in the summer of 1901, Jackie and his brother Eli bring a group of clients to a game between the Browns and the Giants. The pitcher for New York is a young rookie named Mathewson.

Play had just begun when we arrived at League Park. We watched from the outfield as the Giants mounted an early attack. Sudhoff, the elfin St. Louis pitcher, began badly: a walk, a base hit, and then a drive that skipped under the rightfielder's glove and rolled to our feet. The tallest of our clients, a thin man with merry eyes, kicked the ball back toward the fielder. Far away, in the middle of the diamond, the umpire threw up his hands and shouted "Hold! Three bases!" Two Giants scored, and we moved with haste to the grandstand, a single-tiered wooden structure that rose along both foul lines. Having paid a quarter a head to enter the Park grounds, we were now charged as much again to gain the grandstand and needed fifty cents more for box seats beneath the low, shading roof. But an attendant at the box-seat turnstile swore there was no room for us in the shade, and when Eli protested he scolded us with Irish vigor: "You want to come out early these days, we're winning now, don't you know!" Finally we found room behind third base for three on one grandstand bench and for two more directly behind. The thin client and a bearded one flanked Eli while the stoutest squeezed in next to me. We doffed our jackets and loosened

Christy Mathewson was idolized by many New York baseball fans during his career. He won 20 games in his first full season in the majors, at the age of twenty, and went on to surpass that total in twelve consecutive seasons, including a career best of 37 wins in 1908. His screwball, or "fadeaway," pitch was legendary.

our collars. The Giants had scored no more, and the teams had changed sides. Little Jess Burkett stood in for St. Louis, hands high on the bat, feet spread wide. Behind him Patsy Donovan, who doubled as manager, picked at the tape around the handle of his bat. The sun burned down, the cries of the crowd floated in the humid air, and the umpire pointed a finger at the New York pitcher and bid him throw.

This pitcher was big—gigantic, compared to Wee Willie Sudhoff—yet his motion matched Sudhoff's for balance and ease until he pushed off the pitcher's slab with his right foot and drove at the plate with startling power. His follow-through ended in a light skip, and he finished on his toes, his feet well apart, his hands at the ready for a fielding play. I heard the umpire's call but didn't know if Burkett had swung and missed or taken the strike, for my eyes hadn't left the pitcher. He took the catcher's return throw and regained the hill in three strides. His broad shoulders and back tapered to a narrow waist; he wore his belt low on his hips, and his legs appeared taut and powerful beneath the billowing knickers of his uniform. A strong, muscular neck provided a solid trunk for a large head, and his cap was tipped rather far back on his forehead, revealing a handsome face and an edge of thick, light brown hair. He bent for his sign, rolled into his motion, and threw; this time I followed the ball and saw Burkett top it foul.

The fat man moved against me, reaching for his kerchief. "Who's your pitcher?" he asked.

"It's Mathewson," I said. "Christy Mathewson."

"That's Mathewson? Big kid!"

"He is that. He's bigger than [Amos] Rusie, that's for sure."

"Throws hard."

"Yes, he does."

"He's winning for you, isn't he?"

"Eleven games, best on the club."

"Not bad for new corn."

"Actually, he pitched a few last year," I said.

"Win any?"

"No. As a matter of fact he lost two in relief. Then he went back to school."

Another fastball: Burkett's swing was late, and the ball bounced to first base. Ganzel gloved it and tossed underhand to Mathewson, who caught it in full stride and kicked the base for an out.

"He got over there in a hurry, too," the fat man observed.

"Hey, sport, take this and bring back some wieners and beer for us all, won't you?" said Eli, pushing a silver dollar into my hand. He winked and clapped my arm. "Hurry back now, I'm going to need your advice."

I struggled to the aisle and headed along the walkway that divided the grandstand benches from the box seats. As I reached the ramp I paused to watch Donovan at bat. His red face was lined with a manager's web of worry. Patsy fought off the pitches with short, choppy swings, hitting several foul before earning a base on balls. Ganzel met him at first, and they exchanged a greeting. Ganzel was ancient, nearly forty, and Donovan beside him looked as old. I scanned the Giants in the field: Strang and Hickman, on either side of second base, were no striplings, and

Mathewson played for hard-nosed manager John McGraw from 1902 to 1916, during which time the Giants captured five National League pennants and one World Series title. In the Giants' championship season of 1905, Matty led the way with a 31-9 record. His 1.28 ERA was nothing short of dominant, and he threw the second no-hitter of his career against the Cubs in June of that year.

Davis, New York's playing manager at third, was older yet. They were all past thirty in the outfield. The catcher was Jack Warner, he of the awards dinner years before; already he was a veteran of years. Schriver, ready at the bat for St. Louis—enough to say that they called Schriver "Old Pop." At the center stood Mathewson, young as an April morning in that sweltering July, and I, small in the crowd at the top of the ramp, turned and walked down into the shadow beneath the grandstand.

The vendors at their sizzling grills cursed loudly as fat spattered on their aprons. All about, sports in checkered vests argued, passed money, and wrote betting slips. Every inning, sometimes every pitch, was worth a wager. With my dollar I bought five pigs-in-a-blanket and as many bottles of beer, and pocketed two bits in change. I worked my way back up the ramp with some difficulty. Near our seats the fans came to my rescue, passing the food hand over hand to Eli with the efficiency of a fire brigade. I couldn't resist an urge to toss the quarter to my brother, who snared it backhanded. The section resounded with cheers, and the ballplayers on the field turned at the commotion.

"Still two-nothing, sport. Donovan was caught trying to steal. Hey, here we go again!" Eli cried as a base hit began the Giant second. But their game was all sock-and-run; after Strang's single, Warner flied out.

"They don't believe in the bunt, do they?" said the fat man.

"They won't win 'til they learn how," said Eli. "You've got to be able to lay it down, right, sport?"

"Here's Mathewson," I said. "He'll be bunting."

Eli looked at me. "A dollar says he brings off the sacrifice. All around?"

The clients accepted the wager. Sudhoff pitched, and Mathewson pushed the ball onto the grass and ran to first with the spritely grace of a smaller man. He was narrowly out.

"He can bunt," the thin man conceded.

"Double or nothing that they score," said Eli.

Sudhoff walked a man, and the next nailed the first pitch on a low line over second base. Two Giants crossed home.

"Double or nothing they score again!" said Eli. I pushed my knee into his back, but he looked over his shoulder and winked. The three buyers took the bet and cheered when a fly ball ended the inning and wiped out their debts. Mathewson walked slowly to the pitcher's mound, dug at the slab with his toe, smoothed the dust, and worked into his warm-ups. Again his size and youth impressed. The bearded man beside Eli studied him.

"Mathewson, his name is?"

"College kid," said Eli. "Connie Mack signed him for Philly, but he jumped to New York."

"Where's he from?"

"Pennsylvania," said Eli, at the same time that I said, "Bucknell College."

"Imagine a college man playing ball for a living!"

I mentioned Lajoie and Plank, whom we'd seen in Philadelphia but the bearded man snorted that the new league would sign anyone, and while he knew Lajoie had played in a college uniform he doubted the boy had ever seen the inside of a classroom. Nor had Mathewson, he'd wager.

The fat man turned to me. "But you said he went back to school after last season!"

"Quit the team in September to do it," I said.

"You've seen him before?"

No, I explained; in recent seasons the more talented Brooklyn club had caught my fancy, and I hadn't been among the few at the Polo Grounds when the rookie threw his first big-league pitches that summer or won his first victories in the spring. What I knew of Mathewson came from notes in the newspapers: his age, a year greater than my own, and his home, the farming country of the Susquehanna Valley; his fame as a Bucknell footballer. I knew he'd pitched in professional leagues in New England and Virginia, and that while he'd put his name to a Major League contract with Connie Mack he'd never worn a Philadelphia uniform. Instead he'd come to New York, and now, in his first full year, he had a third of the club's victories. If his skills were the test he belonged in the National League, but like the bearded client I wondered why a true collegian would choose the life of a professional ballplayer.

The second inning ended quickly, and while Sudhoff hit his stride in the third Eli began to orchestrate wagers with every batter. If I thought the proposition doubtful

The film *Breaking into the Big Leagues* was a silent picture from 1913 featuring Mathewson and his manager John McGraw.

I'd signal by pressing my knee into his back, but he ignored my advice as often as he accepted it, and I came to understand that a deeper game was in progress. Eli was selling jewelry, and it wouldn't do to take too much of his clients' money. Each time he won he offered double or nothing on the next bet; at best he would finish little better than even, and at worst far worse. I engaged in chatter with the partisans around us when the Giants batted, or gazed over the midwestern crowd dotted with wide-brimmed western hats among the standard derbies and occasional boaters. Far down the right field line was the only uncrowded grandstand section; there the coloreds sat in overalls and yellow straw hats. When St. Louis batted I studied Mathewson. He could throw hard, and with excellent control, shading the edges of the strike zone, mixing his fastball with a curve that seemed somehow erratic. Sometimes it fell an astonishing measure, while other times—what did it do? Certainly it behaved differently from the drop, but from our location I couldn't track the pitch. When St. Louis came to bat in the fifth inning I excused myself and threaded my way to a spot close behind home plate. Now I could see the inner game, the fierce battle between pitcher and batter where power and control sought mastery over instinct and guess.

Polo Grounds, New York City, Home of the New York Giants.

Above: Located in the shadow of Coogan's Bluff in upper Manhattan, the Polo Grounds served as the Giants' home field from 1891 to 1957. The ballpark was rebuilt in 1911 after a fire destroyed the original wooden structure. The concrete-and-steel replacement featured decorative sculpting around the two-tiered grandstand.

Facing page, top: Over time, the Polo Grounds took on its distinctive horseshoe shape as seating was expanded around the entire field. The awkward setting of the ballpark within Coogan's Hollow created short distances down the foul lines (279 feet to left and 258 feet to right in its final configuration), while the center-field wall stood nearly 500 feet from home plate.

Mathewson began against Padden with a pitch that came in hard at belt level and dropped abruptly and dramatically, a superb overhand curve, and one which had wrenched my arm when I'd tried it. The second pitch was a fastball on the outside part of the plate, a second strike. Now another breaking ball, but so unlike the first, slower, and breaking in reverse, in the nature of a lefthander's curve; I'd never seen a righthander throw one. Nor had Padden, who swung late and was lucky to tip it foul. Padden stepped out of the box and shook his head like a man who'd just seen a rabbit leap out of his own hat. He took his stance a bit closer to the plate, leaning over to guard the outside corner. Then in an instant he was on his back in the dirt; comically, the bat landed on his head. Mathewson's fastball had reclaimed that disputed inside territory. Padden dusted off his knickers and took his stance farther off the plate. Mathewson stretched and threw another reverse curve, and Padden missed it badly. Strike three.

Mathewson worked through the St. Louis lineup just so. Always the first pitch was a strike, and usually the second; then a teasing pitch down low, or that strange fading curve thrown where no batter could hit it squarely, if at all. His rhythm and motion were balletic: a high kick, a swing of the hips, a stride forward, and finally the explosive release of the ball. There was intelligence as well as power behind the pitches: he had a four-run lead and found it to his purpose to walk Kruger with two out in the fifth and then retire the light-hitting Ryan, and to pass the dangerous Burkett in the sixth in favor of facing Donovan, who grounded out. When I rejoined Eli in the seventh inning Mathewson had allowed three baserunners, but no hits.

"Think they'll get to him, sport?"

I'd never witnessed a no-hit game. I'd come close to pitching one four years before, as close as the eighth inning, but a swinging bunt that squiggled up the first base line had foiled me, and in my disappointment I'd been racked for three runs. "He's doing pretty much what he wants," I said.

"A dollar says he gets by Schriver," Eli offered; the odds were heavily against a no-hitter, and betting with Mathewson seemed the safest way to protect the clients. Old Pop took a fastball for a strike, and the crowd booed. Its cries had taken on the anger of the heat and the temper of frustration. The fat man ground his cigar beneath his patent leather boot and muttered something about Schriver; the club missed its injured sluggers. Mathewson pitched, and Pop grounded weakly to Strang at second base. One out in the seventh.

"Double or nothing, all around?"

Now Padden again, and the first pitch a high strike, the second higher yet—but Padden had no wish to wait for another curve and swung, lifting a fly to center field where Van Haltren had hardly to move to glove it. Two outs now.

"Double or nothing?"

"It's a bet."

"What happens on a walk?" I asked.

"Do you think he'll pass him, sport?"

"He'll be careful with Wallace. It's his pattern."

Eli nodded. "I say he'll get him out. Double or nothing on an out." Mathewson's fastball flashed, and Wallace took it and jawed loudly at the umpire's strike call. Now that strange breaking pitch, and Wallace bounced it to third; he was out by two steps at first. The Giants came off the field as the crowd booed all the more, at Wallace, at the umpire, at the summer's merciless heat, at the cast of impending defeat.

The fat man tapped Eli on the shoulder. "It's four dollars now, right?"

"Two," said Eli.

"Four."

"No, the bet on Schriver brought us even."

"We were even before then. It's four."

Above: Walter Johnson joined Christy Mathewson as the first pitchers inducted into the National Baseball Hall of Fame in 1936. Johnson was a formidable American League hurler for two decades, winning 417 games— second only to Cy Young—while playing for the Washington Senators, a team that rarely finished above .500.

Walter "The Big Train" Johnson had one of the most overpowering fastballs ever thrown from a mound. He led the league in strikeouts a record twelve times, and his total of 3,508 stood as the all-time mark for more than five decades. Johnson didn't develop a curveball until late in his career; here he shows off his curveball form.

"Well, if you insist," said Eli, laughing.

The Giants went down swiftly in the eighth, but New York's efforts at bat hardly mattered now; we wanted Mathewson pitching. In the St. Louis half he began with a strikeout, and the buyer's debts to Eli doubled to eight dollars apiece. The total was nearly a month's salary to me. Next was Ryan, hardly a threat; after taking two strikes he chased a high fastball and lifted it to the centerfielder's range. Van Haltren loped easily across the grass and reached out to cradle it, but the web of his glove seemed to fail him, and the ball dropped at his feet.

Twenty thousand roared, but the fat man shook his head. "An error," he said.

"It's all the same," said Eli, attempting a mournful expression. "We're even."

"No, as far as I'm concerned, it's an out."

"The man's on second base," said Eli.

"But the bet is on a no-hit game, isn't it? The pitcher against the hitter. The man should have been retired. Now, double or nothing?"

It seemed it was a matter of integrity, for which the fat man had a reputation; when Eli made to forgive the debts of the men flanking him they proved no less upright than their colleague. They could play the inner game as well as my brother, for what might be lost in money was more than made in future favor. Word spread from the press benches that "error" was indeed the official call; the no-hitter was intact. Eli shifted ground: why not call the play "no bet?" The compromise was accepted, and the balance among the men reverted to eight dollars apiece.

While the party debated I studied Mathewson. He showed no annoyance in the wake of the misplay. His team still led by four runs, the inning was late, and the weak-hitting Nichols was at bat with pitcher Sudhoff to follow. Mathewson set, glanced at the baserunner, and threw. Nichols's bunt was a surprise; the score, the inning, the pitcher on deck all argued against it. Catcher Warner was slow to move after the ball, but Mathewson was upon it instantly, the ball in his glove, then in his hand, then at first base. Two outs, and sixteen dollars due to Eli from each of his clients.

"Double or nothing?"

Sudhoff, the little pitcher, hit the ball sharply, but Mathewson snatched it out of the air and the inning was over. At the Giant bench Mathewson greeted centerfielder Van Haltren with a forgiving slap on the rump. He was far more cheerful than Eli, a man due ninety-six dollars of easy money. When Mathewson batted in the Giant ninth he

was applauded by the home fans, and I cheered. Mathewson tugged at the bill of his cap in acknowledgment. "Imagine, a college kid!" said the bearded client. Most of the crowd had conceded the game, and many would prefer a defeat of special regard to a spoiling single in the home ninth. For myself, I wanted three clean outs and a glorious end; our clients' purses were of no matter.

"Double or nothing?"

Burkett led off. Mathewson started with a fastball; for the hundredth time he took Warner's return throw and climbed the mound. On the right knee of his knickers was a round smudge of red clay, the emblem of a hundred strides and a hundred pitches launched. He bent, stretched, and pitched again, a fastball in on Burkett's hands; it ticked the bat and sailed past Warner, who walked slowly in the heat to retrieve it.

"Oh, college boy! Oh, you college boy!"

Mathewson stood on the hill waiting for the catcher to return to position, his left leg slightly bent, his weight on the right. He gloved Warner's toss and bent for his sign, the ball resting in the pocket of his small brown glove. He seemed as fresh as when he

Honus Wagner remarked that, other than Mathewson, Grover Cleveland Alexander had the best control of any pitcher he ever faced. Throwing for the Phillies, Cubs, and Cardinals, Alexander matched Mathewson's career victory total of 373. Although he remained active into his forties—and twice defeated the Yankees of Ruth and Gehrig during the 1926 World Series at the age of thirty-nine—Alexander's later years were slowed by alcoholism and epilepsy.

had begun, and quite still: no heaving breath, no sleeve drawn across his face to clear the summer sweat. All question left me. This was Mathewson's place and moment; my whole being was with him. Burkett would not deny him, nor Donovan next, nor old Pop Schriver, that dark moving figure on the St. Louis bench.

"So young!" muttered the bearded man.

And I was old, I thought. I was older than Mathewson, older than Schriver, older than any of them in uniform. My youth had ended on a ragged lot by the Hudson when the curve ball had beaten my arm and my spirit—no, when I'd folded the contract into a drawer and reported for work at Uncle Sid's shop. I was on the road, yes, but as an old man, hawking samples in old men's hotels, learning how I might bet to keep old men happy. I watched Mathewson, and he became my youth; it was my fastball burning by Burkett, it was my curve that little Jess lifted to the outfield, and after the ball came back and around the infield I felt it was my glove closing around it, my arm that launched the fastball at Donovan's knees and the next that cut the black of the plate on the outside. My youth made him chase a breaking ball in the dirt, and there were two outs; here was Old Pop, and I had the game and the no-hitter in my hand.

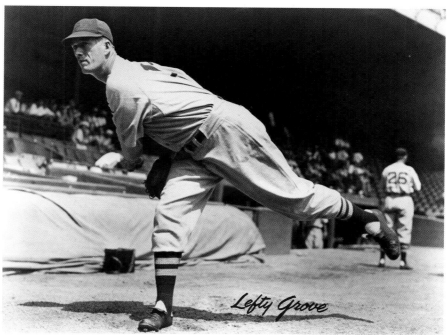

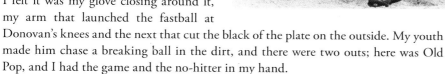

Curve ball: Schriver lets it pass for a strike.

The other, fading curve: Schriver, off balance, swings and ticks the ball foul. Ganzel picks it up barehanded and throws it to me. Schriver is nervous; I see his hands moving on the bat, his heel twisting in the dirt.

I waste a pitch high, ball one. I take Warner's toss, wrap the ball in my glove, jam the package under my arm, reach for the resin, dust my hand. There is a lone incomprehensible cry from the grandstand, then silence. I turn, I bend, I look for Warner's sign. I toe the slab. I stretch. I throw.

Ground ball.

I reach; it is past me—but Strang is there, he takes it on high bounce, he waits for Ganzel, old Ganzel, to set himself at first, he snaps a sidearm throw, and the ball disappears into Ganzel's mitt.

The crowd's hoarse voice rises in the heat, the Giant bench empties, the fielders race to the mound, and the team leaps to touch and embrace—

Mathewson.

Above: As the ace of Connie Mack's Philadelphia A's dynasty, as well as the Boston Red Sox, Robert "Lefty" Grove posted a career winning percentage of .680, highest among all pitchers in the 300-win club. Grove also led the league in earned run average a record nine times during an era when hitting dominated the game of baseball.

Facing page: Carl Hubbell is second to Mathewson in victories for the Giants franchise. The southpaw's notorious screwball pitch helped him to win 253 games in sixteen seasons. Hubbell's most notable achievement came in the 1934 All-Star Game, when he struck out, in succession, Hall of Famers Babe Ruth, Lou Gehrig, Jimmie Foxx, Al Simmons, and Joe Cronin.

REVOLUTION IN BASEBALL
RUTH REACHES NEW YORK
from *Babe: The Legend Comes to Life* by Robert W. Creamer

BABE RUTH NEEDS no introduction. Without question one of the greatest ever to play the game, he was also probably the most influential, forever changing the sport with his powerful swing and charismatic personality.

Author Robert W. Creamer, a senior editor at *Sports Illustrated* for thirty years, penned the definitive biography of this American icon. Among his many other books are *Baseball and Other Matters in 1941* and *Stengel: His Life and Times*, and he co-authored the memoirs of Mickey Mantle (*The Quality of Courage*) and broadcaster Red Barber (*Rhubarb in the Catbird Seat*).

America was in social revolution as the 1920s began—Prohibition went into effect on January 16, eleven days after the announcement of Ruth's sale to the Yankees—and baseball turned around as radically as the country did. The game changed more between 1917 and 1921 than it did in the next forty years. Despite the high-profile presence of such outstanding batters as Cobb, Wagner, Lajoie, Speaker, Jackson and a few others, during the first two decades of the century hitting was a lesser art in a game that honored pitching and low scores. The term "inside" baseball was almost sacred, and John McGraw was its high priest. It meant playing for a run, a single run. You bunted safely, stole second, went to third on a sacrifice and scored on a fly ball to win 1-0. An exaggeration, of course, but that was the ideal. Even after the cork-center ball was introduced in 1910, tight baseball continued to dominate.

All this changed after the war, after Ruth's breakthrough in 1919. It was not a gradual evolution but sudden and cataclysmic. Baseball statistics give dramatic evidence of this. For fifteen seasons before 1919, Major League batters as a group averaged around .250. By 1921 that figure had jumped above .285, and it remained steadily in the .280s throughout the 1920s. With this increase in hitting came an increase in scoring. Before 1920

The arrival of Babe Ruth in New York not only improved the fortunes of his Yankee team, it signaled a new era in baseball. The Bronx Bombers captured seven pennants and four world championships by the time Ruth left the team in 1934. Even as his career wound down, Ruth was a formidable presence in the dugout and at the plate.

it was a rare year when more than two or three men in both leagues batted in 100 runs; but in 1921 fifteen players did it, and the average for the 1920s was fourteen a year. Earned-run averages, the measure of a pitcher's run-suppressing ability, shot upward. Before 1919 the average annual ERA was about 2.85. In 1921 it was over 4.00, and it stayed in that generous neighborhood through the decade.

What caused the explosion? The end of the war, Ruth, money and the lively ball. Attendance in 1919 rose for every one of the sixteen Major League teams, in some instances doubling and even tripling. The release from war was largely responsible for the first burst of interest, and then Ruth's home run hitting came into focus. Babe was the most exciting aspect of the 1919 season, even more than the pennant races. New fans bubbling into the ballparks could not begin to appreciate the austere beauty of a well-pitched game, but they thrilled vicariously to the surging erectile power of the Ruthian home run. They wanted more. They wanted hits and they wanted runs, lots of hits and lots of runs. They wanted homers. The owners, delighted by the windfall at the ticket windows, were happy to give them what they wanted. They instituted legislation against the myriad trick pitches, like the spitball, that tended to befuddle batters, and they pepped up the ball. No hard irrefutable facts exist to verify this—indeed, a laboratory test in August 1920 "proved" the ball had not been changed—but the data cited in the preceding paragraph seem overwhelming circumstantial evidence.

Too, Ruth's full free swing was being copied more and more, and so was his type of bat, thinner in the handle and whippier, in principle something like a golf club. (Early in his career Ruth

This mighty swing produced 714 home runs and nearly 2,900 base hits during Ruth's career. In fifteen years in New York, Ruth was denied the league home run title only five times (never when he played in more than 140 games) and hit at least 34 homers every season in which he appeared in 100 or more games. His average also didn't dip below .300 in a full season until his final one in New York.

used a massive 52-ounce bat, but this slimmed down as Ruth himself ballooned.) Strategy and tactics changed. A strikeout heretofore had been something of a disgrace—reread "Casey at the Bat." A batter was supposed to protect the plate, get a piece of the ball, as in the cognate game of cricket. In Ruth's case, however, a strikeout was only a momentary, if melodramatic, setback. Protecting the plate declined in importance, along with the sacrifice and the steal (the number of stolen bases in 1921 was half the prewar average). The big hit, the big inning blossomed.

With them, so did attendance. It had been a good year in 1919, but 1920 was marvelous. Attendance went up again in every city in the majors except Detroit (the Tigers fell to seventh place that year) and Boston, where bitterness had replaced the Royal Rooters. Seven clubs established new all-time attendance highs in 1920, and the Yankees set a new Major League record. The old record was 910,000, by the 1908 New York Giants. No other club had ever drawn as high as 700,000, and for most of them yearly attendance was usually well under 500,000. In 1919 the Yankees had been like John the Baptist, preparing the way for the Lord. They were a powerful team, and their pre-Ruth batting order of Home Run Baker, Wally Pipp, Duffy Lewis, Ping Bodie, Roger Peckinpaugh, Del Pratt et al. was dubbed Murderers' Row by a newspaper cartoonist. The name seemed justified when the Yanks led the Major Leagues in home runs, with 45—only 16 more than Ruth hit by himself for Boston. They were in the race for the pennant a good part of the season, finished a respectable third and drew 619,000, more than 20 per cent above their previous high. But in 1920, with Ruth, they were in the pennant race all season long, finished a much closer third, hit 115 home runs (Babe had 54 of them) and drew phenomenally. The Polo Grounds had a seating capacity then of 38,000, and capacity was reached and surpassed time and again. The Yankees passed the Giants' old record in mid-summer, became the first Major League team ever to draw a million people, and ended the season with 1,289,422, almost 380,000 better than the previous high. The Giants drew well too, surpassing their 1908 mark themselves, and the two clubs together drew 2,219,031 to the Polo Grounds, almost a million more than ever before.

Ruth was made for New York. It has been said that where youth sees discovery, age sees coincidence, and perhaps the retrospect of years makes Ruth's arrival in Manhattan in 1920 seem only a fortuitous juxtaposition of man and place in time. Nonetheless, Ruth in that place at that time was discovery. And adventure. And excitement. And all the concomitant titillations. One of his famous nicknames, the Bambino, came about because New York's polyglot immigrants, and their children, found themselves strangely excited by Ruth and baseball. Many of those riding the subways and elevated trains and streetcars up to the thin northern neck of Manhattan where the Polo Grounds was, or who talked about Ruth on street corners and in the neighborhood stores, were Italian. The rhythm and alliteration and connotative impact of the Italian word for babe, *bambino*, made the nickname a natural. In time, headlines would say simply, "BAM HITS ONE."

Ruth did not come to New York as a Yankee until the day the club left for Jacksonville and spring training. He had dawdled in California, occasionally sounding off about getting more money from the deal, and sidestepped New York on the way back. In Boston he tried to wangle a percentage of the sale price from Frazee. He smoked cigars in a show window to promote the cigar factory, even smoking three cigars at the same time. He basked in the sad adulation of Red Sox fans at a testimonial dinner given in his honor at the Hotel Brunswick by the David J. Walsh Collegiate Club.

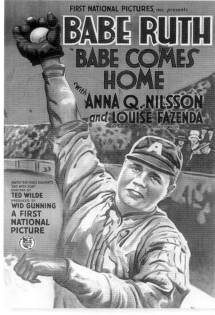

His "Ruthian" achievements on the field combined with his charismatic personality to make the Babe a star beyond the baseball diamond. He was the subject of songs, poems, and movies. He starred on the silver screen in the silent comedy *Babe Comes Home*—the only one of his ten film credits in which he didn't play the role of Babe Ruth. For this film, Ruth had to stretch his acting skills to play a baseball player named Babe Dugan.

Finally, on February 28, he took a train for New York to join the rest of the Yankee contingent at Pennsylvania Station, where the team was to catch the 6:20 sleeper to Florida. He did not appear in the station until ten past six, but when he did a mob of fans crowded around him trying to touch him or shake hands. Autograph hounds happily were still a rarity in those days. Ruth, hulking over the people around him, beamed, shook hands, exchanged greetings and obviously enjoyed the stir he was creating. He was wearing a heavy leather coat and was clinging to a new set of golf clubs he had bought in California.

The affable Ping Bodie took him around and made a great show of introducing him formally to each of the Yankee players, even though Babe knew most of them already. When a club official parceled out five dollars in expense money to each

Boasting a massive capacity of 58,000 seats, the "House that Ruth Built" brought in millions of fans in the 1920s. This game against the Philadelphia Athletics attracted a full house in 1928. Five years earlier, Ruth christened Yankee Stadium with a home run in the park's opening game in 1923.

player, Bodie said it would add up to just about enough for one fair-sized pot. Ruth grinned and said, "Let's get a game going." On the train he passed around Babe Ruth cigars and smoked some himself, as well as pulling at a handsome meerschaum pipe he said had cost him $12. He chewed gum incessantly ("He always had something in his mouth," Lee Allen wrote) and talked freely about his switch from the Red Sox to the Yankees. He cursed Frazee. When someone asked if he had managed to get part of the sale price from the Boston owner, he roared, "The son of a bitch wouldn't even see me."

In Jacksonville, whose chamber of commerce had advertised Ruth and the Yankees throughout Florida like a circus, he played golf with Bob Shawkey and Del Pratt and on one hole mis-hit the ball so badly he broke the head off his club. In early practice sessions at the ballpark he worked out at third base and surprised the other players with his left-handed agility. His winter of golf and baseball in California had left him in pretty good shape. His weight was just about 200. He quickly became an accepted member of the team and enjoyed himself hugely clowning about in practice. One day when the chunky five-foot, eight-inch, 195-pound Bodie cut in front of him to take a grounder away, Ruth yelled in mock anger, grabbed Bodie, turned him upside down, dropped him on the grass and sat on him. He and Bodie got along well. They were roommates and often ate together. Bodie had been considered the biggest eater on the club before Ruth came along, but now he admitted defeat. "Anybody who eats three pounds of steak and a bottle of chili sauce for a starter has got me," he said. Not everything was jovial. Ruth got fed up with the biting jibes of a spectator one afternoon and went into the stands after him. The man stood his ground and pulled a knife. Ernie Shore, then with the Yankees, pulled Ruth away, and the fan left quietly.

Off the field, except for an occasional round of golf with other players, Babe was gone most of the time. Lee Allen described Ruth years later as "a large man in a camel's hair coat and camel's hair cap, standing in front of a hotel, his broad nostrils sniffing at the promise of the night." The essence of that vivid picture suited him in spring training in 1920. There was an outsize complement of reporters from New York's dozen or more newspapers in camp, most of them there because of Ruth, and they had trouble catching up to him off the field.

He was never around. When the team would come into a town on its way north, the players' luggage would be delivered to the hotel and left in the lobby. Each player would pick up his own bag and take it to his room. But Ruth would go from the train directly into town, looking for a girl he knew, or knew of, or hoped to know. In the hotel the good-natured Bodie would pick up his bag and the Babe's and carry both up to their room. Ruth might look into the room for a change of clothing during his visit, but he was gone most of the time, and more often than not Bodie would dutifully bring Babe's luggage back downstairs when it was time to leave. An enterprising reporter, scraping around for some sort of new angle on the Babe, approached Bodie one day and asked him to talk about Ruth.

"I don't know anything about him," Bodie said.

"You room with him. What's he like when you're alone with him?"

"I don't room with him," Bodie said, in a remark that entered baseball legend. "I room with his suitcase."

One trip from Jacksonville down to Miami proved so riotous—Ruth, still hazy one morning, ran into a palm tree chasing a fly ball—that Ruppert never again let the Yankees play a spring-training game in that city. In any case, Ruth started slowly and did not hit his first home run until April 2. Happily, Ruppert was there and was delighted by the homer, which was especially Ruthian. The fence was 429 feet from the plate and ten feet high, and the ball cleared it by 50 feet. Ruth hit more homers and lifted his batting average above .300 before the season began, but even so it was not a particularly good spring for the Yankees. Bodie, beset by personal problems, jumped the club in March and did not return until the season was well under way. Another outfielder, the colorful Chick Fewster, was hit in the head by a pitched ball and was so badly hurt he was unable to speak for nearly a month. He was eventually sent north to Baltimore for surgery to remove a blood clot and was out almost all season. Before he was hurt, Fewster had inspired a choice bit of sports-page doggerel:

Said slim Chick Fewster to big Babe Ruth,
I haven't had a hit since Hector was a youth.
Said big Babe Ruth to slim Chick Fewster,
You don't hit the ball as hard as you uster.

With Bodie and Fewster gone, Ruth asked Huggins if he could play center field. He said he did not want to play left or right because he might run into the short

Wally Pipp, shown here sliding into third at Washington's Griffith Stadium in 1924, was the Yankees' starting first baseman for ten seasons, including Ruth's first five years with the team. Then, on June 2, 1925, he made the fateful mistake of asking manager Miller Huggins if he could sit out that game because he had a bad headache. He was replaced by twenty-two-year-old Lou Gehrig at first base, a position Gehrig would later give up—2,129 games later.

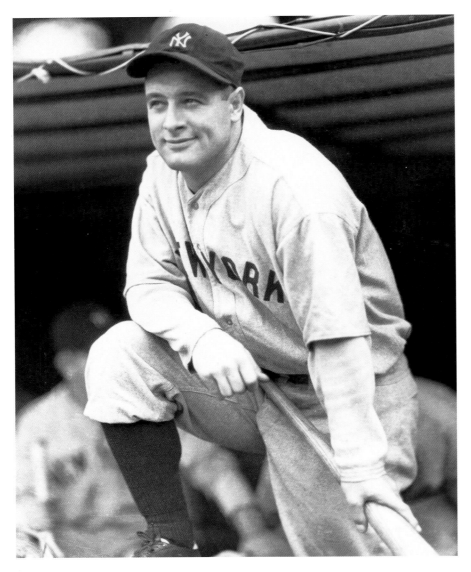

Though he spent much of his career in the shadow of his larger-than-life teammate, Lou Gehrig was one of the best the game has ever seen. Even after Ruth was out of the picture, Gehrig's Yankees won four straight titles from 1936 to 1939. A lifetime .340 hitter, Gehrig's 493 home runs ranked him second only to Ruth when he retired in 1939. (By 2004, Gehrig had slipped to twenty-first on the homer list.)

outfield walls in the Polo Grounds. "I'll get myself all smashed up going after a fly ball," he said. Huggins acceded to the request, and Ruth made his regular season debut with the Yankees as a centerfielder, although it was not an auspicious debut. The Yankees opened in Philadelphia against the Athletics, and Ruth gave the last-place A's the game-winning runs when he dropped a fly ball in the eighth inning with two men on base and two out. At bat all he could produce were two meek singles.

Joe Dugan, the Philadelphia third baseman (known as Jumping Joe for his practice of jumping the ball club at irregular intervals), hit the fly ball Ruth dropped, which pleased Dugan, who liked a laugh. He felt Ruth's muff could not be ignored. After the game he scraped around and found a brown derby, in those days a symbol of ineptitude (Al Smith had not yet made it nationally famous as a political trademark). He had it wrapped up and the next afternoon a messenger brought it onto the field when Ruth came to bat in the first inning. Such presentations were not uncommon, and the umpire dutifully called time. The other players gathered around and Ruth opened the package. When he lifted out the brown derby, the crowd and the players and even the umpires howled with laughter. Huggins tensed, waiting for Ruth's famous temper to explode. But after staring at the derby in stunned surprise for a moment, Ruth grinned, put it on and waved to the crowd.

His graceful acceptance of the joke did not help him at bat. He struck out three times and did not get a hit. The Yankees went on to Boston for three games before returning to New York for their home opener, and before his old fans Ruth's slump continued. And the Yankees lost three straight to the Red Sox.

When the club began its home season in New York a big crowd was on hand to see the hero's debut. Again there was disappointment. Ruth pulled a muscle in his rib cage in batting practice, hurt it again striking out in the first inning, and to the chagrin of the crowd left the game.

"How do you like that?" complained a fan. "I come all the way from Red Hook and they take him out five minutes after the game starts."

Babe was out for several days, disappointing big crowds on the first weekend of the season, and when he did get back he struck out twice in one game and made another error. Then the Red Sox came to town and in the opener of a five-game series beat the Yankees for the fourth straight time in the young season. New York was becoming uneasy. The Ruthless Red Sox, as they were being called, were leading the league with a 10-2 record, while the Yankees were in the second division. The Babe had not hit a single homer. Maybe Frazee was right. After all, Boston had finished sixth with Ruth the year before.

On Saturday, May 1, a skeptical crowd came to see the second game of the series with the Red Sox. And that was the day Babe started. With Huggins, coaching at third, shrilling, "Come on, big boy!" Ruth hit his first home run of the year, a truly amazing drive far over the Polo Grounds roof, even farther than the one he had hit there the September before for his record-breaking 28th home run. The Yankees shut out Boston, 6-0, won two of the remaining three games, and were on their way. The Red Sox balloon went pffft. Frazee's depleted team slipped and slipped and eventually finished fifth with a 72-81 record, while Ruth and the Yankees began their climb to glory.

Babe's home runs came with exciting regularity—he had 12 before the end of May, far more than anyone had ever hit in one month before—and the crowds followed. On Sunday, May 16, a record 38,600 jammed the Polo Grounds, and 15,000 others had to be herded away by police when the ticket windows were shut down well before game time. Ruth hit another dozen homers in June, and his batting average climbed as sensationally as his home run total. On June 20 it was .345; on June 28, .359; on July 1, .372. It was up to .385 by July 11—he hit safely in 26 straight games—and peaked at .391 on August 4. After that the fires banked somewhat, and he finished the season at .376, fourth in the league behind Sisler (.407), Speaker (.388) and Jackson (.382).

All around the league, fans jammed the ballparks to see him, and they booed their own pitchers whenever Ruth was given a base on balls, which happened often (he had 148 walks in the 142 games he played that season). Because he was walked so often, Huggins moved him up from fourth to third in the batting order and put Bob Meusel, a good cleanup hitter, in the fourth spot. Most of the bases on balls Ruth received were intentional, or all but intentional, and with good reason, for it seemed almost impossible to get him out. Typical was a game in June when the Yankees were losing, 5-3, to Boston in the eighth inning. The Yanks had men on first and third with one out, Ruth up. The Red Sox wanted to walk him, but a walk would fill the bases, put the winning run on first and move the tying runs to scoring position at second and third. So they pitched to him, and Ruth tripled against the exit gate in deep right center to drive in both runners. Meusel doubled Ruth home, Pratt singled Meusel home, and the Yankees won, 7-5.

As the season wore on, the bases on balls became more frequent. On July 11 Ruth went to bat four times against Howard Ehmke of Detroit and took his bat from his shoulder only twice. In the first inning, with men on second and third and no one out,

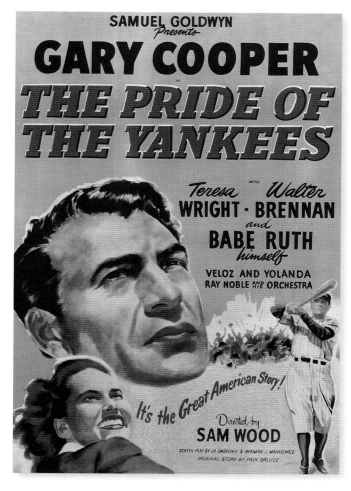

Gehrig's life story was brought to the big screen just one year after his tragic death from amyotrophic lateral sclerosis (ALS), the disease that now bears his name. With Gary Cooper playing the lead role, *The Pride of the Yankees* featured cameo appearances by former teammates of Gehrig's, including Bill Dickey, Mark Koenig, Bob Meusel, and Babe Ruth.

Jimmie "the Beast" Foxx was the only player to twice lead the American League in home runs during Ruth's tenure in the league, and he was the second player to join the 500-homer club. His 58 dingers in 1932 are as close as anybody came to Ruth's record of 60 until Roger Maris in 1961. (Hank Greenberg matched Foxx's 58 in 1938.) Foxx was also baseball's first three-time MVP, capturing the award in 1932, 1933, and 1938.

he walked on four straight pitches. In the third, with the bases empty, he swung and missed at the first pitch and hit a home run on the second. In the fifth and seventh innings, both times with the bases empty, he walked on four straight pitches. The crowd booed the walks.

He still had occasional bad days. He extended his hitting streak to 26 straight games in the first half of a doubleheader (before a capacity crowd on a Tuesday afternoon) but ended the streak when he walked twice and struck out twice in the second game. When he struck out on his last time at bat, which meant the streak was all over, he smashed his bat on the ground so hard that it broke. Such failures, which seemed rare, inspired one more bit of Ruthian verse:

There was a man in our town
Who was a baseball fan;
And who was always in his seat
Before the game began;
And every time the Yanks were here,
And Ruth came up to bat
And failed to bust the ball, he rose
And yelled and waved his hat.

He tied his own record of 29 homers on July 15. He hit his record-breaking 30th (the first time anyone ever hit that many in a season) on July 19 in the second game of a doubleheader, hit another in the same game and the next afternoon hit another. In those two games he made out only once; the rest of the time he either hit a home run or received a base on balls.

By the end of July he had 37. Maintaining that pace would have carried him past 60, but he slowed drastically and hit only seven during the next five weeks. In September he came alive again and hit 10 in his last 24 games to finish with 54. Second to him was Sisler, with 19. The National League champion had 15.

His performance in 1920 is a baseball landmark. He batted .376, hit 54 home runs, nine triples, 36 doubles, scored 158 runs, batted in 137, stole 14 bases. His slugging average was .847, [then] the Major League record. Sports researcher George Russell Weaver, quoted by David Willoughby in his book *The Super Athletes,* said it was the best single season any Major League hitter has ever had. Weaver based his opinion on a comparison of Ruth's home run performance with that of the league as a whole. As an example, Weaver noted that Bill Terry's oft-cited batting average of .401 in 1930 was achieved in a season when the league as a whole batted .303; Terry's performance was therefore nowhere near as impressive as Honus Wagner's .354 in 1908, when the league as a whole batted only .239. Only five men batted over .300 in 1908, whereas more than fifty batted over .300 in 1930. When Ruth hit his 54 home runs in 1920, Weaver noted, only one other *team* in the league hit more than 44.

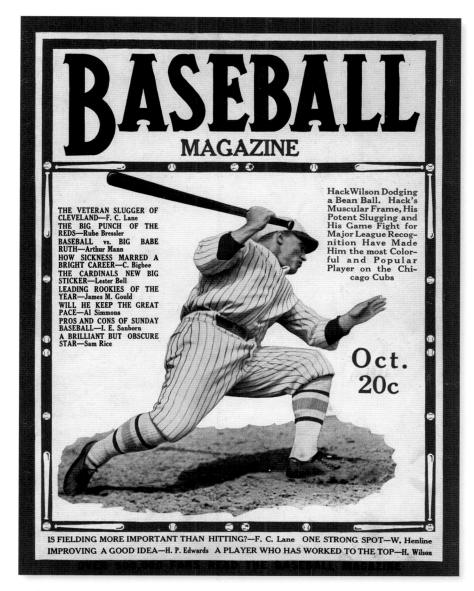

Above: The Hillerich & Bradsby Company, manufacturer of Louisville Slugger baseball bats, for years produced an annual booklet reviewing the baseball season. The 1933 edition of *Famous Sluggers* featured Jimmie Foxx and Chuck Klein. Both Philadelphia ball-players—Foxx with the Athletics and Klein with the Phillies—the two sluggers won the Triple Crown in their respective leagues in 1933.

Left: The powerful Hack Wilson was dodging bean balls even before he established himself as a premier hitter, as indicated by this *Baseball Magazine* cover from October 1926. Despite a relatively short career, Wilson was the longtime holder of two major offensive records. For nearly seven decades, no National Leaguer hit more home runs in a season than Wilson's 56 in 1930, and his 191 runs batted in that same year still stand as the Major League record.

WHAT MAKES A GREAT HITTER?

from *Ted Williams' Hit List* by Ted Williams with Jim Prime

TED WILLIAMS SAID he hoped his legacy would be that when he walked down the street, people would say, "There goes the greatest hitter that ever lived." True to that dream, many sportswriters, fans, and players alike praised "the Splendid Splinter" as such—and his career totals of 521 home runs, 1,839 runs batted in, and a .344 average are difficult to ignore.

But whom did Williams consider great? And what did he consider the qualities necessary for great hitting? In 1996, he laid out his own list of baseball's twenty-five all-time best hitters (himself excluded), with a summary of his criteria for hitting excellence.

I said it thirty years ago and I steadfastly believe it today. In fact I've said it so often it could probably serve as my epitaph: Hitting a baseball is the single most difficult thing to do in sport.

My golfing friend Sam Snead once tried to make a case for the unique skills needed to succeed in his genteel sport, but his challenge didn't really impress me. I pointed out that golfers are permitted to hit a stationary ball with a flat-surfaced club, while playing to galleries which remain silent during each swing and then applaud politely regardless of the result.

A hitter, on the other hand, is expected to hit a round ball with a round bat and adjust his swing in a split second to 100-mile-per-hour fastballs, backbreaking curveballs, and, occasionally, knuckleballs that mimic the flight patterns of nearsighted moths. All this, while 50,000 fans are questioning his ancestry and screaming for him to fail. Snead made a last brave attempt to defend the honor of his game—and don't get me wrong, golf is a great game—by suggesting that at least I never had to wade into the crowd to play my foul balls. Well, he wasn't going to convert me with that stuff. You'd have a better chance of convincing Norman Schwarzkopf that the Bolshoi Ballet is a tougher outfit than the U.S. Marines.

Ted Williams knew what it took to be a great hitter. He was an all-star every year except his rookie season of 1939—when he hit .327 with 31 homers and a league-best 145 RBIs. The two-time MVP could easily have been a five-time winner; amazingly, he was not granted the award in two Triple Crown seasons (1942 and 1947) nor in 1941, when he batted .406 but finished second to Joe DiMaggio in the voting.

I don't think you have to have been a Major League ballplayer to concede my point. Anyone who grew up facing the wild offerings of some rawboned hurler, whether it was in an uneven cow pasture in the Midwest or on a vacant lot in Brooklyn or San Diego, knows exactly what I'm talking about. And anyone who has been humiliated in the batting cage at the county fair, in front of his family or his girlfriend, knows the clear truth of my argument.

Even the vaunted Major Leaguer who hits at the magic .300 level—and as a result now earns a salary that resembles the gross national product of a small country—fails seven times in every ten at bats. That sort of production would not be tolerated in bowlers, quarterbacks, basketball players, or stockbrokers, and certainly not in golfers. But in baseball these athletes are dubbed superstars and their rookie baseball cards become investment-portfolio starter kits.

In hitting, a .700 futility percentage is a much coveted goal. That tells you something! The fans are willing to accept and appreciate such apparent mediocrity because they know the degree of difficulty involved in hitting a baseball. That's why they applaud such seemingly small mileposts. They know in their hearts that the difference between a .280 hitter and a .300 hitter is more than .020. It's the difference between Bucky Dent and Carl Yastrzemski. Hell, it's the difference between Dom and Joe DiMaggio.

It's obvious to me that those players who excel at such a demanding skill are deserving of special recognition, and that's what this book is all about. But first I'll tell you what this book is not. It is not a book which attempts to analyze the greatest all-around players of all time, although many of those included

The "Splendid Splinter" was such a formidable opponent at the plate that some teams employed the so-called Williams Shift against him. As demonstrated by the St. Louis Cardinals during the 1946 World Series, the shortstop would shift over so that three infielders stood between first and second base to close up any holes for the pull-hitting Williams. The strategy worked well in this series, as Williams managed only five hits in twenty-five times at bat.

certainly qualify on that count too. There are no "good field, no hit" shortstops or "defensive specialists" included here! Obviously there are no pitchers here either—with the spectacular exception of Babe Ruth, who probably could have made it to Cooperstown as a hurler or a hitter. Greats of the game such as Brooks Robinson, Joe Morgan, and Johnny Bench will not be found between these covers, despite their considerable hitting skills and Hall of Fame credentials in other phases of the game. It's not that those other facets of the game aren't important, but I was a hitter and that's what I know something about.

In fact a lot of truly fine hitters did not find their way onto my Hit List. Pete Rose is conspicuous by his absence. Roberto Clemente, a fine ballplayer and a finer human being, didn't make the cut. Neither did Ernie Banks, Al Kaline, Rod Carew, Hack Wilson, Paul Molitor, and a veritable galaxy of other bona fide hitting stars. I don't apologize for their absence. It's no oversight—and it's sure no disgrace. It only serves to underscore just how great my top 25 hitters really were.

This is a book about baseball's greatest hitters, a tribute from a fellow hitter to that special breed of athlete who has hit the ball harder, farther, and with greater frequency than anyone else in the history of the game. These are best of the best, the aristocracy of hitting.

Now what made them the best? Over the years much has been made of my three golden rules of hitting: 1) get a good ball to hit; 2) proper thinking at the plate; 3) be quick with the bat. To me those remain the real secrets of hitting. But they don't really tell you what personal characteristics are common to all superior hitters. In my experience all great hitters share certain strengths. I call them my five ingredients, and they practically define a great hitter.

THE FIVE INGREDIENTS

I've always had strong feelings about the attributes needed to become a great hitter. In 1950 *Time* magazine interviewed me for a cover story and asked me to divulge the "secrets of my success" at the plate. At that time I singled out four "ingredients" that I felt made me a successful hitter: courage, eyesight, power, and timing. Today I'd like to confirm those choices and add one more.

INTELLIGENCE

Those others are great ingredients, and they are all things that you have to have, but I was very young when I said all of that and there was one glaring omission in my analysis. Today I'd add one more very important component to the mix. The one ingredient that isn't there—the one that separates the really good from the great— is intelligence. And I'm not necessarily talking about rocket science here. I'm talking about baseballic intelligence.

The first four attributes certainly describe what you have to have, but they don't give you the whole meat. You can have those things in spades, but damn it, you've got to know what you're doing at the plate. You've got to be smart. Hitting is 50 percent from the neck up, and knowing what's going on is 50 percent of the battle.

It's a little game, knowing the pitchers, knowing their strengths and their weaknesses, studying their deliveries, and learning how you have to hit certain types of pitchers. Is there such a thing as a dumb good hitter? Well, I've seen guys who could swing the bat and were pretty good natural hitters, and you wonder why they're not even better, why they don't improve. Invariably it's because they're so damn dumb about what's going on. Before long the pitching fraternity catches on and it's all over. They start to go downhill instead of learning and improving. There are dozens of examples to draw from, guys like George Bell. He started out like gangbusters but didn't progress. After a while he just left me cold. I wouldn't have had him on my ballclub.

You see a lot of deficiencies in today's hitters. Some problems are just matters of style—or lack of style. In that regard the biggest fault is not getting their hips ahead

Williams had an often-rocky relationship with the public and the media, but he was truly worshipped by the Boston fans throughout his Hall of Fame career. On this particular day at Fenway Park in August 1958, Williams came through with a four-for-four day at the plate against the hated Yankees.

of their hands. It should be pretty basic, hips ahead of hands, but I don't always see quite the action there that I'd like. And the number of hitters swinging at too many bad balls has reached epidemic proportions. It makes me cringe to watch some of these guys. The thing is, those are things that can be corrected if you have a hitter who wants to learn and improve.

It's really a symptom of a much bigger malady. The fundamental problem is that hitters quite obviously don't know proper thinking at the plate. By that I mean, for instance, they get the count in their favor against a pitcher and still look like they've got two strikes on them. Hell, they may have a pitcher two and nothing and then let him off the hook by swinging at bad pitches. You know the script: Fooled on a pitch! Late on a fastball! Fooled on another pitch! Lunging at pitches that are outside and taking fastballs down the middle for strikes. For no reason. In most cases they didn't even know what the situation was, let alone what the pitcher might be throwing in that situation. This isn't some radical new idea. These are basic, elementary, 150-year-old rules we're talking about here.

So baseballic intelligence is a common thread that runs through all great hitters. For some it's almost instinctive, for others it comes about through hard work and a willingness to learn.

COURAGE

Courage you have to have, that little extra determination, especially when the going is tough and you don't see the pitcher quite as well as you should. Some pitchers have a tight-assed delivery and you don't follow those guys as well.

I was never really afraid at the plate. Good hitters can't afford to be. When you're young you have the really great reflexes and you're confident that you can get out of the road in time. Naturally if you faced a genuinely wild son of a gun, someone that you knew was wild, you might be a little more concerned.

1944 — Williams Wins His Wings

It's hard to imagine what Williams's career numbers might have been had he not lost four seasons in his prime to military service. He missed the entirety of 1943, 1944, and 1945 during World War II and most of 1952 and 1953 while flying for the U.S. Navy in Korea. Considering he hit 29 homers in his final season at the age of forty-one, it's reasonable to think he would have given Ruth's 714 a run for the money.

That's different from a good pitcher who just wants to brush you back and keep you honest. With those guys you might not worry too much; at least I know I wouldn't. But if a guy is just plain wild and you don't know where the hell he's going to throw it, you might be a little looser up there. Especially if he could really throw smoke.

I was beaned once, and all I kept thinking was, "This ain't gonna stop me! This ain't gonna stop me! This is not going to stop me!" I kept saying it and saying it. I wasn't going to let anything stop me from being the hitter I hoped to be. That's exactly the way I felt. In fact I remember right after the beaning incident in Milwaukee, we went directly to Kansas City and I played an afternoon game against a left-handed pitcher, and I hung right in there repeating that same phrase over and over: Nothing's going to stop me. And that's what happened. Nothing stopped me! Looking back forty years later, you have to say that it was a great attitude to have. I never really thought about it at that time, but it was pretty near storybook devotion to the goal I had set for myself. To become the best hitter I could be.

That kind of determination is common to all my top 25 hitters. Aaron had it. Gehrig sure as hell had it, and so did Robinson and the rest. They all overcame obstacles and persevered and eventually came out on top. All my great hitters have to have had courage.

EYESIGHT

Certainly good eyesight is necessary for a hitter. You need it in order to be able to pick up various pitches and see the spin on the ball. The writers were always quick to credit my eyesight for my hitting, and a lot of rubbish was written about just how good my eyes were. They made it sound as if I had Superman's vision. My eyesight was good, but not that good. I hurt my eye when I was a young kid, and there were plenty of times when I couldn't see well that day and still I'd get three hits. It takes a hell of a lot more than good eyesight to hit .400 in the Major Leagues. But it would be impossible to become a great hitter without it.

Hornsby had exceptional eyesight. So did Mel Ott. I bet if you could have tested the eyes of all of baseball's first-rate hitters, they would all show above-average eyesight.

POWER

In that same *Time* magazine story, I talk about power being in the "wrist and forearm." My power was actually generated from hip action. I'm not a muscular guy anyway, and neither was Hank Greenberg or some others on the list. The hips force you to go through the power zone with power. If you don't use your hips, you don't have that power. You just pull the bat through. I was certainly very aware of my strength, but more than anything else I wanted to be quick with the bat through the power zone.

The National Leaguers used to tell me what a great hitter Paul Waner was at 155 lbs soaking wet. Waner was a .340 hitter, and even though he didn't have that many home runs, he was so good that I'm not sure he doesn't deserve to be within a line drive of the top 25. For a couple of years he hit 15 or 18 home runs, and Dizzy Dean told me, "Without a doubt, Waner is the greatest hitter I ever pitched to." Now that's quite a statement coming from a Hall of Famer and one of the greatest National League pitchers who ever played. Dean could mow anybody down, but regardless of his lack of size, Waner wore him out with his quickness. So bat speed produces power, even in guys who aren't so muscular. You don't have to be built like Paul Bunyan—or even Jose Canseco—to hit home runs, and long ones too.

TIMING

As in many things in life, timing is everything for a hitter. Timing comes through practice, practice, practice, and through analyzing what you're doing. Hitting a baseball is difficult because there are so many variables involved, and that's why it requires so much practice in order to improve. As a youngster growing up in San Diego, I played every month and every day of the year. None of the hitters on my

Williams credits Mel Ott's eyesight and timing for his success at the plate. The lifelong New York Giant stood only five feet nine inches tall, but he was the first National Leaguer to hit 500 career home runs. He also was among his league's top ten home run hitters in eighteen different seasons. The only other players to finish in the top ten that many times? Hank Aaron and Babe Ruth.

list got there without hours and days and years of hard work. You need to take advantage of every opportunity to hone your hitting skills. You need to hit a lot of baseballs and have a lot of baseballs thrown to you. Eventually your sense of timing becomes sharp. It always amazes me—and this is as much a case for a hitter's intelligence as it is for timing—if you ask a lot of today's hitters, "When you hit the ball on the ground, are you generally late or early?" Well some of them are still trying to figure it out. There's no question about it: when you hit ground balls, you're much more apt than not to be early. Then you ask them, "When you hit the ball to the opposite field, do you tend to hit it in the air or on the ground?" Well, in the air of course! So if you're a little late on the swing, the tendency is to get it in the air; when you're a little early, the tendency is to hit it on the ground toward some Golden Glove infielder. Just knowing that basic fact puts you ahead of the game. Mel Ott, another little guy, hit over 500 home runs, and he gave most of the credit to timing.

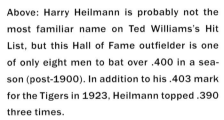

Above: Harry Heilmann is probably not the most familiar name on Ted Williams's Hit List, but this Hall of Fame outfielder is one of only eight men to bat over .400 in a season (post-1900). In addition to his .403 mark for the Tigers in 1923, Heilmann topped .390 three times.

Above, right: George Sisler—and his .340 lifetime average—is one who did not make Williams's list. Sisler twice hit over .400 for a season, and his mark of 257 base hits in 1920 stood as a record for 84 years, until broken by Ichiro Suzuki in 2004. He won the MVP in 1922 for his .420 average, 51 stolen bases, and 134 runs scored.

RESULTS ARE WHAT COUNT

If this were a recipe book, I guess you'd just mix those five ingredients together, put them in the oven at 350 degrees, and cook up a great hitter. Well obviously it doesn't work that way. While many players may possess some—or even all—of the qualities that I just identified, only a very select few make full use of them throughout their careers. A bad chef might have the best ingredients in the world, but the results can still prove disastrous.

After all, baseball is not a neat cause-and-effect kind of game. You can't apply a formula—great eyesight + great power + intelligence + courage + timing = a great hitter—to baseball. It's not an exact science. There are still things like heart and desire and dedication and hard work that enter into the equation too. Sometimes a player with only mediocre natural talent can outperform a guy with a ton of God-given ability. I've seen it many times.

That's why the proof of the hitter is in the numbers. Statistics and career records provide concrete, irrefutable evidence of those who were best able to take full advantage of their ability over the long haul. And while it's perfectly true that statistics don't tell the whole story and are incapable of measuring intangibles like heart and desire, they can provide you with a yardstick to compare the results of a hitter's skill and effort.

THE HIT LIST	
1	Babe Ruth
2	Lou Gehrig
3	Jimmie Foxx
4	Rogers Hornsby
5	Joe DiMaggio
6	Ty Cobb
7	Stan Musial
8	Joe Jackson
9	Hank Aaron
10	Willie Mays
11	Hank Greenberg
12	Mickey Mantle
13	Tris Speaker
14	Al Simmons
15	Johnny Mize
16	Mel Ott
17	Harry Heilmann
18	Frank Robinson
19	Mike Schmidt
20	Ralph Kiner
21	Duke Snider
22	Harmon Killebrew
23	Willie McCovey
24	Chuck Klein
25	Josh Gibson

Williams ranks Rogers Hornsby fourth on his Hit List, ahead of names like Cobb, Aaron, and Musial. Indeed, Hornsby's .358 career average is second only to Cobb's, and he holds the highest single-season mark (post-1900) with a .424 average in 1924. The second baseman also displayed some power, knocking 42 homers in 1922 and 39 in 1925, both seasons in which he won the NL Triple Crown.

THE LAST IMMORTALS
STAN MUSIAL AND BOB FELLER
by Marty Appel

IN THE EVER-PRESENT debate over baseball's best, the names Stan Musial and Bob Feller all too often slip down the list. Dominant figures during their careers, history has seen them placed in the shadows of names such as Williams, Aaron, Mays, and Bonds, Koufax, Gibson, Ryan, and Clemens in the popular consciousness. Indeed, neither Musial nor Feller cracked the top ten at their position in fan voting for Major League Baseball's All-Century Team in 1999.

Marty Appel, author and former public relations director for the New York Yankees, seeks to rekindle the legacy of these two Hall of Famers. Appel has written many books and articles on baseball, including his memoirs, *Now Pitching for the Yankees: Spinning the News for Mickey, Billy, and George.*

Baseball fans measure their own lives by the entrance and exit of players. There is the day the son of a Major Leaguer you saw play is suddenly in the big leagues. There is the day you realize that you knew every manager and coach when they were players. There is the day the last active player from your first year as a fan retires. And there are the days when your heroes turn sixty, then seventy, some eighty and more. And the days when the obituaries carry the names of players you could swear you just saw turn a double play last week. But, no, it was, in fact, a long time ago.

With the passing of Joe DiMaggio and Ted Williams as bookends around the turn of the millennium, in 1999 and 2002 respectively, there comes a renewed appreciation for the last survivors of a time when the game was played in flannel uniforms, mostly in daylight, always on grass, only on radio, and no farther west than St. Louis. They traveled by train, slept without air conditioning, experienced the Great Depression and World War II, worked second jobs in the winter, signed

autographs for free, and laid down a sacrifice bunt now and then. They considered doubleheaders routine, and they went from high school to the minors, where they might toil for six or eight seasons. It was also a time when the game was devoid of the gifts of players of color.

But they knew .300 was the demarcation line for a good season, knew 20 victories made you an ace, and tried like hell to beat the damn Yankees. Some things don't change.

And so it came to pass, as the Bible might say, that two superstars remained from that period of baseball history tucked between Babe Ruth and Jackie Robinson, and their names—nicknames included because we must—are Bob "Rapid Robert" Feller and Stan "the Man" Musial.

And with Joe and Ted having departed, it seems like a good time to turn our thoughts to Feller and Musial, who were so heralded in their time, but who, it seems, have not maintained their stature with the passing of the years.

Baseball does give one a sense of immortality, in that fans who love the game always carry memories. If you are "Squirrel" Reynolds who played shortstop for the 1945 White Sox, at least you are in *The Baseball Encyclopedia*. If the Squirrel had chosen to hang power lines across the nation, he would have found no such volume commemorating his hard work.

When friends can look at each other over a beer and say, "Remember Zeke Bella, and his '59 Topps baseball card," not only have these friends bonded, but Zeke Bella has achieved something approaching immortality. The best surgeon in Boston in the 1930s has no such fame.

This fresh-faced youngster out of Van Meter, Iowa, quickly grabbed the attention of the media when he struck out 15 batters in his first Major League start in 1936—at the age of seventeen. Bob Feller led the league in strikeouts at the ripe old age of nineteen and pitched his first no-hitter on the Opening Day of the 1940 season, the only no-hitter ever pitched on Opening Day. He went on to win the pitching Triple Crown in 1940, leading in wins, ERA, and strikeouts.

But fame, to some measure, can be fleeting. In 1950, *The Sporting News* polled sportswriters and sought the "all-time team" of the first half of the twentieth century. George Sisler was the first baseman. Rogers Hornsby was at second and Honus Wagner at short. Jimmy Collins was at third. Tris Speaker was in center, flanked by Babe Ruth and Ty Cobb in the outfield. Catcher Mickey Cochrane was behind the plate, and the pitchers were Christy Mathewson and Cy Young. John McGraw was the manager.

How did these guys hold up by the time the century came to a close? For Collins and Speaker, and perhaps Sisler, a lot of young fans might look quizzically at you. A poll taken today might not even place Speaker among the top twenty outfielders. Collins's reputation was long since buried by Pie Traynor, Brooks Robinson, and Mike Schmidt. And who among young fans today would even recall Traynor?

The point is Bob Feller and Stan Musial are two who let the train roar past them, but two who deserve to be revisited and appreciated anew for who they were. Feller, who lost three years to World War II service, was passed by many pitchers bound for 300 wins (he won 266), and by the strikeout aces of a later time who would pass 3,000 and even 4,000 strikeouts (he had 2,581, third behind Johnson and Young when he retired). Musial, who always had been spoken of in the same breath as his contemporary Williams, seemed dwarfed by the over-the-top personality of Teddy Ballgame as the years went on, so much so that Williams and DiMaggio became the subject of comparison, with Musial cast aside—despite seven batting titles and most of the National League records you could think of.

They deserve better. They are of "The Greatest Generation," as Tom Brokow wrote, and they played the game at a time when heroes were heroes.

The essence of Bob Feller was that he burst onto the public consciousness as an overnight sensation, hitting the big time before he had even graduated from high school. In his 1947 book *Baseball's Hall of Fame*, Ken Smith described baseball as "the greatest common denominator that the nation has ever known." That is probably not true any longer, but at that time, it was, and Feller became the talk of the land.

Every baseball fan knew the Bob Feller story. He was the American dream.

He came from the heartland of America in a time when much of the country was still rural, and long before the sophistication of scouting combines, the draft, baseball scholarships, *Baseball America* draft previews, and agents. Farm boys back then might throw the ball with blazing speed against the side of a barn and catch the eye of a traveling scout.

Tom Seaver once asked Feller how he threw his curve, and Feller said, "Well, just like you'd flick a buggy whip!" as though everyone would understand. It was a different era.

The story began in Van Meter, Iowa, population today under nine hundred, back then, about three hundred, located twenty miles west of Des Moines, on a 360-acre

When he retired, Stan Musial held National League records for career hits (3,630) and consecutive games played (895). He was the first three-time MVP in the NL, and nobody in that league had been an all-star as many times as Stan the Man (twenty). A .331 career hitter, Musial batted over .300 seventeen times. Sound like one of the greatest hitters ever to play the game?

farm owned by the Fellers. It doesn't get more heartland than this. Stick a pin dead center in a map of the continental United States, and you hit Feller's barn. (We speak figuratively; the geographic center is actually in Kansas.) Robert William Andrew Feller was born there on November 3, 1918.

When Feller was a teenage schoolboy in little Van Meter High (where he had sixteen classmates), it happened that he could throw the ball nearly 100 mph against the side of a barn, or if necessary, against opposing hitters from the area's other amateur teams, made up of much older players. A scout for the Cleveland Indians with the wonderful name of Cy "Slap" Slapnicka wandered upon the hard-throwing righthander and began to watch him dominate these amateur games. At the Iowa State Fair, Feller's team won the state tournament, and he fanned 18. Slap was onto something.

After Feller's junior year in high school, while his classmates were taking summer jobs as lifeguards or soda jerks, Feller was pitching for the Indians. It was 1936; he was seventeen. He was in the big leagues to pitch against Lou Gehrig, Jimmie Foxx, Al Simmons, Charlie Gehringer, and another rookie, Joe DiMaggio. Oh, did the nation love this story!

Feller made his debut on July 19, hurling one inning in relief at Griffith Stadium in Washington, D.C. In his first month, he made six relief appearances and gave up five runs in eight innings. On August 23, he made his first start, in front of a hometown crowd at League Park. He faced the St. Louis Browns—and struck out 15 of them for his first victory. Fifteen strikeouts! The record at the time was 17.

Feller ended his rookie season with a 5-3 record and 76 strikeouts in 62 innings. He went back to school, but left his senior year for spring training (accompanied by a tutor, so that he would graduate on time) and had a 9-7 season with 150 strikeouts in 148 innings. In April, he was on the cover of *Time* magazine. But there were critics, even for an eighteen-year-old wonder boy.

In 1938, now a poised veteran of nineteen, Feller struck out 240 batters, the first of seven strikeout titles he would capture. On October 2 of that year, in his final start of the season, Feller fanned 18 Tigers in a losing effort, breaking the Major League record for strikeouts in a game. He finished the season 17-11, giving him 31 victories as a teenager. A year later, he had his first 20-win campaign, going 24-9 with 246 strikeouts—a 51-20 record with 712 strikeouts before he was old enough to vote.

In Feller's first start after reaching the age of twenty-one, he pitched an Opening Day no-hitter, stopping the White Sox 1-0 in 47-degree weather at Comiskey Park. In that 1940 season, he won a career high of 27 games, but the Indians lost the pennant to Detroit by a single game.

That Opening Day gem would be the first of Feller's three career no-hitters, to accompany a dozen one-hitters. No one at that time could envision the coming of a Sandy Koufax (four no-hitters) or Nolan Ryan (seven!), and it was strongly believed that Feller's no-hit mark would stand forever.

In fact, the same was felt about his single-season strikeout mark of 348, set in 1946, another record that would live until Koufax snapped it. This was the magnitude of Rapid Robert—fans would anticipate no-hitters or dazzling strikeout performances with each outing. He was the circus coming to town: "Bob Feller, Cleveland Indians, here this weekend! Tickets now available!"

He was, unfortunately, saddled with control problems, and his walk totals were also enormous. In 1938, he walked 208. He lived in an era when pitch counts went

BOB FELLER

Above, top: This arm struck out more batters than any other in the majors for seven seasons—and it might have been more had Feller not missed four years in the middle of that stretch to fight for his country. In 1946, his first full season after the war, he struck out a career-best 348. Feller had a deadly curveball, which he demonstrates here, but his fastball was the stuff of legend.

Above, bottom: Bob Feller was honored as a "Baseball Great" for this series from Fleer Baseball Cards in 1960. The card cites Feller's many strikeout records, and although most of those records were eventually broken by the likes of Sandy Koufax, Nolan Ryan, and Roger Clemens, Feller still must be considered among the game's best.

As Bob Feller's Hall of Fame career was winding down, a new pitching phenom was emerging in a Cleveland Indians uniform. Lefty Herb Score had an immediate impact in 1955, striking out a league-best **245** batters and winning Rookie of the Year honors. He was even better in his second season, fanning **263** and winning 20 games. This promising career came to a sudden end, however, on May 7, 1957, when Score was hit in the head by a line drive and had to be carried off the field on a stretcher. He missed the remainder of the season and never regained his form, retiring for good in 1962 at the age of twenty-nine.

unrecorded, when starting pitchers just reared back and threw, the expectation being the complete game. There was never a "closer" associated with Feller, no "middle relievers" or "set-up men." He would hurl 279 complete games in 484 career starts, pitching as many as 371 innings in a single season. Pitch counts? He probably came close to two hundred in some games, then went back out there four days later and did it again.

Whatever overwhelming lifetime totals he might have recorded were thwarted when he went off to fight for his country in 1942 and essentially missed four seasons. Walter Johnson had the career strikeout mark for decades (3,509), and Feller ended up 928 short of that. He might well have hit that target had he pitched in those four years; he had averaged more than 250 strikeouts over the four seasons prior to the war. But, then again, how many pitchers got the head start that Bob did, striking out nearly five hundred batters while still a teen?

Feller never complained about missing those four seasons. A patriotic American, he did what most of those in his generation did: fight a popular war without asking questions. He never looked back, never had any regrets, never spoke of what might have been.

Bob entered the Navy in 1942, where he served as a gun-crew chief aboard the U.S.S. *Alabama*. Discharged in late 1945, he returned to start nine games as a prelude to the "second half" of his career.

He was now twenty-eight. Although still a young man, and not a college product, he had the maturity to become the first player to ever incorporate himself for tax purposes, to organize a winter tour against Negro League stars headed by Satchel Paige, and to involve himself in the early days of the fledgling Major League Baseball Players Association. His salary climbed to $80,000 a year.

In his first full season back, 1946, everyone was anxious to see whether the old Bob Feller would still be the one taking the mound every four days. What they got was perhaps a better pitcher, one who had added a slider to his repertoire.

Feller went 26-15 in that first full season home, when fans packed the ballparks in record numbers to see the old stars and return to normal routines.

In 1948, Feller pitched in his only World Series. In the opening game against the Boston Braves, he was locked in a scoreless pitching duel with Johnny Sain. In the eighth, Feller turned and fired to second to pick off Phil Masi. Masi was ruled safe, although newspaper photographs appearing that evening showed he was anything but. Tommy Holmes followed with a single for the game's only run, in what Feller would call his toughest loss. He also lost the fifth game. He did not appear in Cleveland's next trip to the Series, in 1954 against the Giants, and thus a World Series victory eluded him.

He pitched through the 1956 season, then embarked on a personal appearance career, which foresaw and set the stage for all the card shows and signings that players would do decades later. Piloting his own plane, Feller went from minor league town to minor league town, giving pitching exhibitions, signing autographs, speaking to the crowds. He was a one-man traveling enterprise. Even in his seventies, he was still pitching, by his count, eighty innings a year at Old Timers' Games and in personal appearances.

Outspoken in 1940 about Cleveland manager Oscar Vitt ("He makes us nervous"), he was just as outspoken in 2004 about sharing the Hall of Fame with Pete Rose ("Count me out").

Stan Musial, less outspoken to be sure, also started out as a pitcher. Born in the coal-mining town of Donora, Pennsylvania, on November 21, 1920, Stan excelled in baseball and basketball in high school. In those days, anyone gifted in both sports had no problem deciding which one to pursue. Musial signed in 1938 to pitch for Williamson in the Mountain State League as soon as he graduated.

In 1940, Stan came under the tutelage of Dickie Kerr, his manager at Daytona Beach. Kerr had an interesting pedigree in the game: he had been an "honest" pitcher on the 1919 Black Sox, winning twice in the World Series while his teammates were intentionally trying

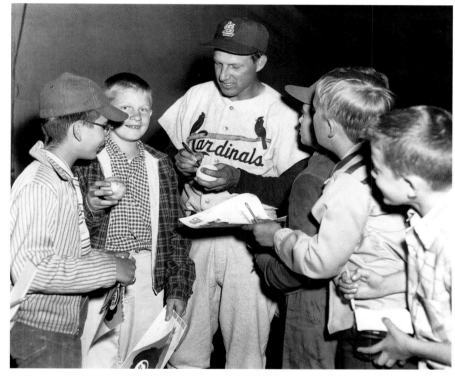

Revered by fans during his prime, Musial was known as a true gentleman. Even with his tremendous individual success and playing for three world championship teams in St. Louis, Musial never quite received the national attention of DiMaggio, Williams, and Mays playing on the East Coast.

to lose behind him. Talk about overcoming tough odds. It was Kerr who saw the hitting skills in young Musial, and who initiated his shift from the pitching mound to the outfield. Although posting a record of 18-5 as a pitcher that year, any hopes for reaching the big leagues as a hurler were dashed in '41, when he injured his throwing arm and lost whatever gifts were in there that might have kept him pitching. He became a full-time outfielder, and in 1941, playing 87 games, he batted .379 and hit a league-leading 26 homers. He was on his way.

He joined the St. Louis Cardinals as a regular in 1942 on a wartime team that was pennant-bound. He hit .315 that year, third best in the league, but didn't make the all-star team—a fact worth noting because for the rest of his career, another twenty seasons, he was selected annually. He was still an all-star in his forties, and at the 1962 midsummer classic, played in Washington, President John Kennedy said to him,

"They say I'm too young for my job, and you're too old. Maybe we'll both prove them wrong."

Stan's offensive numbers came to overwhelm observers. It was in Brooklyn's Ebbets Field, where he regularly killed the Dodgers, that he got the immortal nickname "Stan the Man."

STANLEY MUSIAL
Player of the Year
1946

FACTS, FIGURES AND OFFICIAL RULES

The Dell baseball handbook proclaimed Stan Musial player of the year for 1946. He won his second National League MVP by leading the league in batting, slugging, hits, runs, doubles, and triples, while finishing fifth in homers and third in runs batted in. Bob Feller—who set a new strikeout record that year, tied for the league lead in wins, and posted a 2.18 ERA—finished sixth in the AL's 1946 MVP race.

He won his first batting title in 1943, hitting .357, and went on to win six more. He led the league in hits six times, in runs scored five times, in doubles eight times, in triples five times, and in runs batted in twice. He led in on-base percentage six times and in slugging percentage six times. And although he would hit 475 home runs in career, sixth all-time at the time of his retirement, he never did manage a home run crown.

In 1948, Musial led the league in nearly everything but home runs: runs, hits, doubles, triples, RBIs, average, slugging, and on-base percentage. His 39 homers that year, a career best, were just one short of Johnny Mize and Ralph Kiner. With one more, he would have "run the table," so to speak. No one ever dominated a year offensively as did Stan in '48.

After three World Series appearances in his first three full seasons, Musial played in only one other, in 1946, and never appeared in a televised series. That, coupled with playing in the small market of St. Louis, suggests his national profile would be low. But Musial's abilities and cheery persona made him a perennial fan favorite, and the popularity of the Cardinals radio network throughout the Midwest brought him millions of admirers.

Musial didn't enter military service until 1945, playing service ball both at home and in the Pacific theater. In 1947, he was tempted to jump to the outlaw Mexican League when they threw a big contract at him, but he wisely decided to remain with the Cardinals and, as Feller with the Indians, never played for another team.

He won three MVP awards, and by the time his career came to a close, he had established a sizable number of National League career marks, virtually knocking Honus Wagner out of the record books. In 1958, he became only the eighth player to record 3,000 career hits, which was quite an accomplishment at the time. It had been sixteen years since the last man, Paul Waner, had accomplished the feat, and it wasn't nearly as frequently reached as it would come to be after Stan.

Between 1952 and 1957, Musial played in 895 consecutive games, a league record at the time.

In 1959, he fell below .300 for the first time in his career and, indeed, stayed there in 1960 and '61, as his career began to wind down. But in 1962, now a forty-one-year-old grandfather, Musial returned to hit .330, third in the league, assuring his fans that he would not retire on a long, steady decline. He hung up his spikes after the 1963 season, missing the Cardinal's next world title by one year, although he was a vice-president of the club during that championship run.

Throughout his career, it was Musial-Williams in the minds of fans. Stan and Ted, matching each other in statistical achievements, batting titles, MVPs, superlatives. But in retirement, Stan was just good ol' Stan, playing the harmonica at the Hall of Fame, puffing on a cigar, and glad-handing fans at his St. Louis restaurant. Williams thrust his larger-than-life personality out to the world and had people comparing him to DiMaggio, not Musial. Eventually, Stan became the forgotten superstar, the guy whose NL records fell to Willie Mays, then Hank Aaron, and then Pete Rose.

Feller and Musial. Magical names in their times, deserving of the immortality that baseball can bestow on its greatest stars. It was a joy to see them play, and it is a treat to still have them with us today.

Musial's Cardinals appeared in four World Series during the 1940s and won three of them. The 1946 classic against Ted Williams's Red Sox went in St. Louis's favor when outfielder Enos Slaughter motored all the way from first and slid home safely on Harry Walker's single in the final game. Slaughter's "Mad Dash," as it became known, broke a 3-3 tie in the eighth inning and helped clinch the title.

SATCHEL GETS HIS START

from *Maybe I'll Pitch Forever* by Leroy "Satchel" Paige as told to David Lipman

AS ORGANIZED BASEBALL pursued its unofficial policy of segregation through the first half of the twentieth century, many of the nation's best athletes and talents were excluded from the top ranks of the sport. While African-American players first organized their own leagues in the late 1800s, by the 1920s and '30s, the Negro National League and the Negro American League were the established showcase for the best black ballplayers.

Foremost among them was Leroy "Satchel" Paige, a lanky pitcher from Mobile, Alabama. In his autobiography, *Maybe I'll Pitch Forever*, Paige tells of the struggles and triumphs of his thirty years pitching in the Negro Leagues and, ultimately, the Major Leagues, beginning with his first tryout for a local team, just days after being released from reform school as an eighteen-year-old.

The next day I went looking for work, but those who knew where I'd been turned me down and those who didn't know didn't seem to have any steady work. Or maybe I wasn't really looking.

That afternoon I ended up over at Eureka Gardens, where the semi-pro Mobile Tigers still played, just like they did before I went up. My brother, Wilson, pitched and caught for them.

I sat down in the stands and leaned back to watch. The Tigers were getting ready for the regular 1924 season and were still trying out some guys for the club.

I looked all over but couldn't spot Wilson. He must not have come out that day.

The Tigers worked out about an hour and the longer I watched them the worse that itch to play got. Finally all the players except the catcher and the guy who'd been running the practice session left.

After the field was clear, a kid who'd been sitting down on the first row walked out on the field.

The kid went to the pitcher's mound and threw a few warmup pitches to the catcher. Then the Tigers' manager picked up a bat and stepped into the batting box. The kid started pitching again.

The Tigers' manager cracked those pitches all over the park.

He'd bat two thousand if he could come up against that kid every day, I thought.

One thing I was sure of was if that kid could try out for the Tigers, I sure could.

Then I got excited. Why not?

I looked close at that kid again.

I knew I could throw better than that shuffler.

Down I went, fast.

I waited at the side of the field until the kid walked off. I guess the manager had figured like me. That kid wouldn't cut it.

I walked up to the manager.

"You still looking for a pitcher?" I asked.

He just looked at me. "Go home, boy," he said. "I'm tired."

But when I told him I was Wilson's brother, he decided to let me pitch. He flipped a ball to me.

"Where've you been pitching?" he asked.

"Oh, around," I said.

He just nodded.

I felt good out on the mound. I whistled in a few of my fast ones, not bothering to wind up. They popped against the catcher's glove like they was firecrackers.

They never heard anything like that, I thought.

"I'm ready for you, mistah," I called to the manager.

He stepped into the box.

Leroy "Satchel" Paige played for at least a dozen different teams during his career in the Negro Leagues, often outshining his white counterparts in exhibitions and barnstorming games. He spent nine seasons with the Kansas City Monarchs, during which time they won five Negro American League pennants (1939–42 and 1946). Artist Lance Richbourg painted this watercolor portrait in 1986.

Above: Josh Gibson, the Negro Leagues' greatest hitter, crosses the plate after one of many home runs for the Homestead Grays. Gibson is believed to have accumulated more than 800 home runs in his career, including 84 in one season. His blasts were admired for their distance as much as for their frequency, regularly traveling more than five hundred feet. Gibson died at the age of thirty-five in 1947—less than four months before Jackie Robinson made his debut with the Brooklyn Dodgers.

Facing page: After starring in the Negro Leagues for a quarter century, Satchel Paige finally got his chance to pitch in the majors in 1948 at the age of forty-two, the oldest debut by a Major Leaguer. He spent two seasons with the Cleveland Indians and then signed with the St. Louis Browns for 1951–53. The durable Paige returned to pitch three shutout innings for the Kansas City A's in 1965—at the age of fifty-nine.

I threw. Ten times I threw. Ten times he swung. Ten times he missed.

I grinned. I stuck my foot up in his face and then tore the catcher's hand off with my blazer. He didn't have a chance against me.

The manager was grinning too.

"Do you throw that fast consistently?" he asked me.

"No, sir, I do it all the time."

That's the day I learned a new word.

• • •

The manager gave me a dollar and told me to come back with Wilson for the next game. I felt like that dollar was a thousand.

That was the point where I gave up kid's baseball—baseball just for fun—and started baseball as a career, started doing what I'd been thinking about doing off and on since my coach at the Mount'd told me about getting somewhere in the world if I concentrated on baseball.

And getting somewhere in the world is what I wanted most. Baseball had to be the way, too. I didn't know anything else.

• • •

Wilson, they called him Paddlefoot, and I were real tough for the Tigers. Actually, Wilson could throw about as hard as I could and we would have made one of the best two-man staffs you ever saw if he'd stuck with baseball, but he didn't.

First of all, he didn't want to leave Mobile then, and Wilson didn't love baseball like me. I'd do anything—practice for hours, watch and study for hours—just to get a little better.

While we were with the Tigers, though, we made a lot of people talk about us.

Wilson already was a big man around Eureka Gardens when I joined the team. It only took me a few games to become another hero. All the guys wanted to buy me drinks. All the gals just wanted to be around, squealing and hanging on my arms.

That's a mighty comforting feeling.

It's funny what a few no-hitters do for a body.

But those no-hitters don't make you rich. Not in semi-pro ball. I'd get about a buck a game when enough fans came out so we made some money after paying for expenses. When there wasn't enough money, they gave me a keg of lemonade.

I got to laugh at that now. Back in 1924, I'd get a keg of lemonade to pitch and just a few years later I was getting as much as $500 for pitching those same nine innings.

I won just about all the games I pitched for the Tigers. We had a pretty good club and one of our best players was my old buddy, Julius Andrews. He played first base.

Sometimes I pitched for other teams. I jumped whenever there was some green waved.

The Tigers didn't like it too much, but my pocketbook did.

And I don't like to be tied down. Never have. I like to fly free.

'Course playing for a semi-pro club ain't a job, so I had to get me some work too. I landed a job over at the Mobile Bears' stadium. That was the white team, a minor-league club. Pretty soon those guys over there started hearing about Ol' Satch.

They heard good.

But all of them weren't buying what they heard. One day about four of them came up to me and told me how they been told I was some pitcher.

"We made a bet you couldn't throw as good as all of them say," one of them told me.

He offered me a dollar to show them.

That's the easiest dollar I ever made.

We went down on the field and one of them grabbed a bat and another a glove to catch me. I threw four or five real easy like, just to warm up. Then the batter headed for the plate.

"No need for you to tote that wood up there," I yelled at him. "It's just weight. You ain't gonna need it 'cause I'm gonna throw you nothin' but my trouble ball."

I threw. Them little muscles all around me tingled. They knew what we were doing. The first guy up there swung and missed three fast ones.

Another tried it. He just caused a breeze.

"We sure could use you," one of them finally told me. "If you were only white..."

That was the first time I heard it.

Andrew "Rube" Foster was both a tremendous talent on the field and an early pioneer for the sport. He reportedly won 44 consecutive games as a pitcher in 1902, and he earned his nickname by defeating Hall of Famer Rube Waddell of the Philadelphia Athletics in an exhibition game that same year. Foster later formed the Chicago American Giants, acting as player-manager and winning multiple titles. In 1920 he founded the Negro National League, the first successful organized black baseball league.

SATCHEL PAIGE'S RULES FOR STAYING YOUNG

1. Avoid fried meats which angry up the blood.

2. If your stomach disputes you, lie down and pacify it with cool thoughts.

3. Keep the juices flowing by jangling around gently as you move.

4. Go very light on the vices, such as carrying on in society—the social ramble ain't restful.

5. Avoid running at all times.

6. And don't look back. Something might be gaining on you.

Before Satchel Paige arrived on the scene, the title of greatest black pitcher went to Smokey Joe Williams, who pitched from 1910 to 1932. He is credited with a 20-7 record against Major League competition, and Ty Cobb (no friend to African Americans) once said that Williams would have been a "sure 30-game winner" in the majors. While pitching for the Homestead Grays in 1930 at the age of forty-four, Smokey Joe struck out 27 and allowed only one hit in twelve innings against the Kansas City Monarchs.

A LONE NEGRO IN THE GAME

from *Baseball's Great Experiment: Jackie Robinson and His Legacy* by Jules Tygiel

It's DIFFICULT TO name an event that had a greater impact on the game of baseball than the signing of Jackie Robinson to a Major League contract. When Brooklyn general manager Branch Rickey made the bold move to break baseball's "color line," he chose a player who offered both the physical skills and the mental fortitude to handle the challenge. Robinson's influence on the field and off was immediate during his rookie season of 1947.

Jules Tygiel's acclaimed *Baseball's Great Experiment* explores Robinson's entrance into the league and the event's impact on baseball and on larger society. Tygiel, a professor of history at San Francisco State University, is an award-winning author of several books and articles, including *Past Time: Baseball and History*.

The evolution of Dodger attitudes toward Robinson reflected a process occurring throughout the nation. Robinson's aggressive play, his innate sense of dignity, and his outward composure under extreme duress captivated the American people. Only Joe Louis, among black celebrities, had aroused the public imagination as Robinson did in the summer of 1947. Robinson's charismatic personality inspired not merely sympathy and acceptance, but sincere adulation from both whites and blacks alike.

To black America, Jackie Robinson appeared as a savior, a Moses leading his people out of the wilderness. "When times got really hard, really tough, He always send you somebody," said Ernest J. Gaines's fictional heroine Miss Jane Pittman. "In the Depression it was tough on everybody, but twice as hard on the colored, and He sent us Joe [Louis] . . . after the war, He sent us Jackie."

Thousands of blacks thronged to the ballparks wherever he appeared. At games in the National League's southernmost cities blacks swelled attendance. Many traveled hundreds of miles to see their hero in action. The Philadelphia *Afro-American*

reported that orders by blacks for tickets for the first Dodger-Phillies series had "poured in" from Baltimore, Washington, and other cities along the eastern seaboard. For games in Cincinnati, a "Jackie Robinson special" train ran from Norfolk, Virginia, stopping en route to pick up black fans.

Throughout the season black newspapers continued to campaign for proper crowd behavior, and the deportment of the Afro-American spectators drew widespread praise. Blacks nonetheless found it difficult to restrain their enthusiasm. Robinson himself wrote that while the sight of so many blacks pleased him, their indiscriminate cheering sometimes proved embarrassing. "The colored fans applauded Jackie every time he wiggled his ears," complained one black sportswriter after a game in Cincinnati . . .

The scenes at the ballparks represented only the surface level of black adulation of Robinson. "No matter what the nature of the gathering, a horse race, a church meeting, a ball game," explained Sam Lacy, "the universal question is: 'How'd Jackie make out today?'" . . .

Robinson's popularity was not confined to blacks; white fans also stormed baseball arenas to view the new sensation. At the start of the season the St. Louis edition of the Pittsburgh *Courier* warned its readers that tickets for the Dodger games were "going like hot cakes and it isn't the Sepia fans that are buying the bulk of them." In Brooklyn, the fans rallied behind Robinson "350 percent," recalls Joe Bostic. "They were with him, not just Jackie, they were with the idea. He became a state of mind in a community that was already baseball-oriented." After the games at Ebbets Field, fans waited for more than an

As the first African American in the Major Leagues, Jackie Robinson was more than just a pioneer; he was a veritable superstar. He won the Rookie of the Year Award in his first season of 1947 and followed that with Most Valuable Player honors in 1949. He was a six-time all-star in a ten-year career. Who knows what his career might have been had he not been kept out of the majors until he was twenty-eight years old.

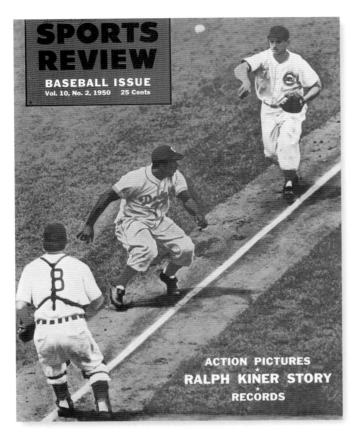

SPORTS REVIEW

BASEBALL ISSUE
Vol. 10, No. 2, 1950   25 Cents

ACTION PICTURES
★
RALPH KINER STORY
★
RECORDS

Robinson brought his own unique talents to the big leagues and introduced the kind of aggressive base-running that was common in the Negro Leagues. Disrupting the opposition on the base paths, he led the league in stolen bases twice and finished in the top ten in all but one season. Robinson also stole home 19 times in his career.

hour for Jackie to appear. "Many wanted autographs and others simply wanted to touch him," reported Sam Lacy. "It was just as though [he] had suddenly been transformed into some kind of matinee idol." . . .

The volume of letters that Robinson received also reflected his popularity. From the day of his promotion to the Dodgers through the end of the World Series, each day brought "piles of mail." The Dodgers hired a special secretary to handle his correspondence and Arthur Mann composed answers to all letters, both the inspirational and the insulting. Robinson reviewed, sometimes revised, and signed each response.

The Robinsons and the Dodgers disposed of most letters containing threats and insults, but a sample of the vitriolic language and personal attacks survive in letters to Branch Rickey. W. J. "Buck" Blankenship of Jackson, California, wrote criticizing the Durocher suspension, but added, "The blow that the commissioner dealt was not as severe as the one that the Brooklyn club handed itself when it signed Jackie Robinson." A Philadelphia writer told Rickey, "You should be ashamed of yourself . . . If you want to do something for the negro, why not give some educated negro *your* job," and added, "The next time you take a shower get a negro to take one with you or does that just apply to some other man's son?" After asking Rickey if he would want his children to marry a Negro, the disgruntled critic concluded, "Well Good-Nite Dictator and Happy Dreams." Drew Linard Smith, an attorney from New Orleans, voiced similar sentiments:

Your decision to break a big league tradition by playing a Negro on the Brooklyn team is indeed deplorable. In fact, it is inconceivable that any white man would force a Negro on other white men as you have done . . . I tell you Rickey anything the Negro touches he ruins and your club will be no exception . . . The first time Robinson steps out of line you will see what I mean. He will inevitably do this too because he will be egged on by a militant and aggressive Negro press forever propagandizing for the amalgamation of the races.

. . . The opprobrium heaped upon the central actors in the integration drama reflects the stereotypes and the deep-seated prejudice of the era. But the torrent of sympathy and acclaim which Robinson inspired drowned out these negative sentiments. The surviving sampling of letters to Robinson reveals the thoughts of people from all sections of the country and in many walks of life: a deputy sheriff from Detroit, a black teenager from Johnson City, Tennessee, an accountant from Ontario, Canada, and a dry cleaner from Bellevue, Ohio. Robinson heard from doctors, ministers, lawyers, and college professors; from black and white students at every educational level; from a magazine editor in Rockford, Illinois, and the president of a life insurance company in Durham, North Carolina. Twenty-four patients at the Oak Knoll Tuberculosis Sanitarium in Mackinaw, Illinois, wrote in support. Most letters, particularly after the early weeks of the season, contained words of advice and encouragement and reflected the impact of Robinson's ordeal upon the American public . . .

Robinson's correspondence reflected the changes in racial attitudes that he inspired. His dynamic presence instilled a sense of pride in black Americans and led many whites to reassess their own feelings. The affection for Robinson grew so widespread that at the year's end voters in an annual public opinion poll named him the second most popular man in America. Only Bing Crosby registered more votes.

• • •

On the field, meanwhile, Robinson had emerged as one of the crucial figures in the Dodger pennant drive. The Dodgers moved into first place in July, but in mid-August the Cardinals, recovered from their disastrous start, challenged for the league lead. The two clubs met at Ebbets Field on August 18 and Robinson again found himself surrounded by controversy. In the opening game of the series Cardinal outfielder Joe Medwick spiked Robinson on the left foot, leaving a bloody gash. Two days later Robinson barely removed his leg in time to avoid Enos Slaughter's spikes on one occasion, but on another, Slaughter slashed Robinson on the left leg, dropping the injured athlete to the ground.

Observers disagreed as to whether the spiking was deliberate. Bill Corum of the New York *Journal-American* called it "as normal a play as anybody, whose imagination wasn't working too fast, ever saw." Robert Burns, in the St. Louis *Gazette Democrat* argued, "If Slaughter had been trying to 'nail' Robinson, you can be sure Jackie wouldn't have been in condition to stay in the game." Slaughter, in a statement that must have surprised most National Leaguers, avowed, "I've never deliberately spiked anyone in my life. Anybody who does, don't belong in baseball." The incident, however, infuriated Robinson's teammates. Noting that the cut on his leg was located eight inches above the ankle on the outside of his leg, one player asserted, "How in the hell could Slaughter hit him way up on the side of the leg like that unless he meant to do it?" Several Dodger players threatened "dire consequences" if the Cardinals continued their attacks on Robinson.

Robinson started his Major League career at first base, because that's where the Dodgers had their biggest need. A year later, to make room for the up-and-coming Gil Hodges, Robinson moved to second base, where he formed a deadly double-play combination with shortstop Pee Wee Reese. After Junior Gilliam joined the team in 1953 and took over the pivot position, Robinson played primarily left field and third base in the last four years of his career. His versatility in the field was a tremendous asset.

. . . [T]he Dodgers continued to stave off the Cardinal pennant bid. When they arrived in St. Louis on September 11 for the final meetings between the two clubs, the Dodgers led the second-place Cardinals by four and a half games. The series marked the last opportunity for St. Louis to bring the Brooklyn club within striking distance.

As in the earlier series the first game was marred by a spiking incident. In the second inning Cardinal catcher Joe Garagiola caught Robinson on the heel. "I don't think Garagiola did it intentionally," Robinson said after the game, "but this makes three times in two games with the Cardinals that it's happened. He cut my shoe all to pieces." When Robinson came to the plate in the third inning he made a remark to Garagiola, who responded with a racial slur. For the first time during the long season, Robinson lost his temper. He and Garagiola "engaged in an angry teeth-to-teeth exchange" which brought coach Sukeforth out of the dugout to restrain Robinson, and required intervention by umpire Beans Reardon. *Time* magazine wrote of the episode, "That was the end of it; no fisticuffs on the field, no rioting in the stands. But it was a sign that Jackie had established himself as a big leaguer. He had earned what comes free to every other player; the right to squawk."

Time's celebration of Robinson's acceptance was premature. It would be another year before Robinson could freely retaliate against his tormentors. The outburst

against Garagiola merely underscores the pent-up anger and frustration that gathered within Robinson as he submerged his naturally combative instincts and channeled them into his performances. After the spiking Robinson powered a two-run home run to lead the Dodgers to a 4-3 victory. The following night Robinson had two hits and scored two runs in a losing cause and then stroked three hits in the series finale. "In the field," wrote Dan Daniel, "Robinson's tempo was a gradual crescendo which attained the truly spectacular in the eighth inning of the last game," when the rookie first baseman hurled himself into the Brooklyn dugout to make a "brilliant catch" of a foul pop-up. The Dodgers won, 8-7, virtually assuring themselves the pennant.

"This week as the Dodgers raced toward the finish, seven games ahead," attested *Time* magazine in its cover story on Robinson, "it was at least arguable that Robinson had furnished the margin of victory." Dixie Walker agreed. "No other ballplayer on this club, with the possible exception of [catcher] Bruce Edwards, has done more to put the Dodgers up in the race than Robinson has," claimed the once recalcitrant Walker who, despite his own personal ordeal, delivered another .300 plus campaign. Another skeptic also surrendered when Tom Spink and the *Sporting News* awarded Robinson the Rookie of the Year Award. The judges, wrote Spink, had "sifted only stark baseball values . . . The sociological experiment that Robinson represented, the trail blazing that he did, the barriers he broke down, did not enter into the decision." Spink personally flew to Brooklyn to present the award to Robinson at the pennant-clinching celebration at Borough Hall.

Three months after Jackie Robinson crossed baseball's color line, Larry Doby suited up for the Cleveland Indians as the first African American in the American League. Doby appeared in only 29 games his first year, but he hit his stride by 1951, knocking at least 20 homers in each of the next eight seasons. He collected 253 homers in his career and was a seven-time all-star.

Throughout most of the season Robinson maintained his batting average over .300, but a late season slump after the Dodgers had clinched the pennant dropped him to .297. He finished second in the league in runs scored and first in stolen bases. Robinson also led the Dodgers in home runs with 12. Despite his reputation for being injury prone, Robinson appeared in 151 of the 154 contests, more games than anyone else on the club.

Robinson's performance also benefited other National League teams. Throughout the season fans continued to watch him in record numbers. At Pittsburgh in late July spectators overflowed the stands and lined up along the outfield wall. The grounds crew posted ropes to establish the boundaries of the playing field. By the season's end Robinson had established new attendance marks in every city except Cincinnati. Thanks to Robinson, National League attendance in 1947 increased by more than three quarters of a million people above the all-time record set in 1946. Five teams set new season records, including the Dodgers, who attracted over 1.8 million fans for the first, and last, time in the club's Brooklyn history . . .

• • •

The saga of Robinson's first season has become a part of American mythology—sacrosanct in its memory, magnificent in its retelling. It remains a drama which thrills and fascinates, combining the central themes of the illusive Great American Novel: the undertones of Horatio Alger, the inter-racial comradery of nineteenth-century fiction, the sage advisor and his youthful apprentice, and the rugged and righteous individual confronting the angry mob. It is a tale of courage, heroics, and triumph. Epic in its proportions, the Robinson legend has persevered—and will continue to do so—because the myth, which rarely deviates from reality, fits our national perceptions of fair play and social progress. The emotional impact of Robinson's challenge requires no elaboration or enhancement. Few works of fiction could impart its power.

Above: One of the greats who came along too soon for the majors, James "Cool Papa" Bell was known for his incredible speed. Satchel Paige once said that Bell could turn out the lights and be in bed before it got dark. He also hit over .400 multiple times. He earned his nickname for keeping cool under pressure while getting his start as a pitcher with the St. Louis Stars in the 1920s.

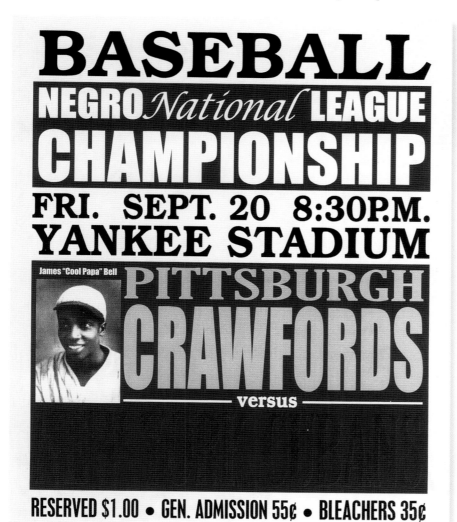

BASEBALL
NEGRO *National* LEAGUE
CHAMPIONSHIP
FRI. SEPT. 20 8:30P.M.
YANKEE STADIUM
James "Cool Papa" Bell
PITTSBURGH
CRAWFORDS
— versus —
RESERVED $1.00 • GEN. ADMISSION 55¢ • BLEACHERS 35¢

WHAT IS SO RARE AS A WILLIE MAYS?

by Tallulah Bankhead

THE CONCEPT OF the "five-tool player" is a popular measure of a ballplayer's all-around talent—the ability to hit for average, hit for power, field, throw, and run. Few players fit that label better than Willie Mays. A twelve-time Gold Glove winner, he is one of only two players to hit 500 homers, steal 300 bases, and bat over .300 for his career (the other is his godson, Barry Bonds).

Tallulah Bankhead, a star of the stage, screen, and radio, was also an avid baseball fan, who once said of her fellow Alabaman, "There have been only two geniuses in the world: Willie Mays and Willie Shakespeare." Bankhead's prediction in the pages of *Look* magazine in September 1954 proved accurate—not only did the Giants hold on to win the pennant that year, they also won the World Series.

Do you want to know why the Giants are going to win the pennant? Well, darlings, I can tell you in two words: Willie Mays.

Not since John McGraw snatched Frank Frisch off the Fordham University campus to play second base have the Giants boasted so dazzling a star, such box-office dynamite. I don't want to put the whammy on Willie, but it's my guess that before he shucks his Giant uniform in 1970 he'll be rated with Babe Ruth. But what am I talking about? Willie's right up there with the Babe now in my book. Let's not have any filibustering by Mickey Mantle and Duke Snider fans. They're both crack centerfielders and a credit to their parents. But they're not in Willie's class. When Willie's been around as long as those two laddybucks, he will have established a mass of new batting and fielding records—unless I miss my guess.

You think I'm getting too hysterical about Willie? Rubbish! We Giant fans haven't had a chance to gloat since Bobby Thomson sank the Dodgers with that home run in the play-off series in 1951. Last year, they straggled in a wretched fifth, 35 games behind the Dodgers. All season long, they wallowed around in second division with teams such as the Cubs, the Reds and the Pirates. If the guilt-by-association charge were generally accepted, they could have been jugged on suspicion.

The reason for their collapse? They lacked something. Out with it, woman, what did they lack? Again, I can tell you in two words: Willie Mays. Thirty-five games off the lead last October and out in front in '54. That gives you an idea of the difference. Willie hasn't done all this, but he certainly has helped. He has that priceless light touch and gay spirit that make people like to have him around. He makes them all feel good. He's done oodles for the team morale. True, John Antonelli has probably bagged ten or fifteen games we would have lost if he had stayed in Milwaukee.

I keep a radio going in my dressing room whenever possible so I can hear the Giant games. I have always been a rabid Giant fan. The name Giants is right for my team. Who could stand in awe of a team named the Cubs? Cubs are cute. Or the Dodgers? I never dodged anything in my life. Cincinnati? Too many Republicans. Pittsburgh always depresses me. They beat the Giants too often, and the elevators in the William Penn Hotel are too confusing for words. What I like best about St. Louis is the zoo. And the beer is fine in Milwaukee. But the Giants are a name to look up to. And I simply must know how they are doing every day. Last summer during the Giants' six straight over Brooklyn, I was on stage each day for most of the third act. So one of the cast wrote the inning score on a card and stuck it in his shirt where I could see it when he walked on stage.

"The Catch." Few plays are so readily known by such a simple label, but Willie Mays's running, over-the-shoulder grab of Vic Wertz's long drive in the opening game of the 1954 World Series was truly unforgettable. While Mays himself claimed that he made better catches in his career, this one—and the throw to the infield to keep the base-runners from advancing—turned the tide in the series and helped bring the Giants their first championship in more than two decades.

Above, top: Mays won only one batting title and four home run titles in his career, but his consistency over the years produced some impressive career stats. He topped 50 homers in a season twice and broke the 40 plateau four more times. He was also an immensely popular player and was selected to every all-star team from 1954 until he retired in 1973.

Above, bottom: Leo Durocher, the only man to skipper for both the Giants and the Dodgers, was at the helm for Mays's first four seasons in New York, leading the team to pennants in 1951 and '54. Durocher was known as a volatile, hot-tempered manager, but Mays always expressed respect and admiration for his first big-league manager and gave him credit for grooming him into the superstar he became.

Leo Durocher says Willie makes the pitching staff stronger because he can catch anything, if it stays in the air long enough. He can throw 'em out at home plate from deep center field, and he covers ground like a jack rabbit. When he has a good day, the Giants usually win.

Don't think Willie is just a long-ball hitter. He might well lead all National League outfielders in putouts this season. The right-center, center and left-center stands in the Polo Grounds are the most distant of any park in the league. Willie has a lot of territory to roam. It's 480 feet to the center-field bleachers. And Willie has taken long drives against the center-field fence. His belt-buckle catches are the talk of baseball. I guess he must play center field by ear!

Willie does everything with a flourish. He has the spectacular touch. Everything he does on a ball field has a theatrical quality. Even when he strikes out, he can put on a show. In the terms of my trade, Willie lifts the mortgage five minutes before the curtain falls. He rescues the heroine from the railroad tracks just as she's about to be sliced up by the midnight express. He routs the villain when all seems lost. Willie has that indefinable thing called color. Color blended with talent brings the highest prices in the amusement market. Those blessed with both have what it takes at the box office.

But I do have one qualm about Willie Mays. Can he stand the long and uproarious cheering without getting dizzy? The applause of thousands is pretty intoxicating stuff for a 23-year-old. But I think Willie can take it. I think he is the thoroughbred he looks. He will come through the wringer of publicity and acclaim unscathed. I'm convinced of this because I think he'd rather play ball than do anything else in the world. The joy and enthusiasm he puts into every play mark him as one dedicated. He goes all out on every swing of his bat, every racing catch. Not all players approach the game with such zest. A good many of them would rather be fishing or hunting. Ask any baseball manager. Willie is one of the fortunates of the world. He is paid for doing the thing he enjoys doing most. I wish I could say as much for Tallulah.

There's another reason I think Willie will become great without being spoiled. He has a tradition to live up to. It's the Alabama tradition. The Bankheads are long on Alabama tradition. I was brought up in Jasper, 30 miles from Birmingham. Willie was born in Fairfield, just a little south and west of Birmingham. Daddy's name was William Brockman Bankhead. But to family and friends (and voters, God bless them) he was Willie. My Grandmother Tallulah used to say when Daddy did something that pleased her, "Willie gets under my ribs." My Grandmother wouldn't have known a baseball from a beaten biscuit, but Willie Mays would have gotten under her ribs too.

The stars sort of fell on Alabama when it comes to Negro athletes. The great and ageless Satchel Paige was born in Mobile. Monte Irvin, Willie's roommate, is from Columbia. Joe Louis was from Lexington. And Jesse Owens, the great runner who upset Hitler so much in the 1936 Olympics, was from Danville . . .

When Jackie Robinson broke in with the Dodgers, he was the first player of his race ever to play in the big leagues. Jackie showed his appreciation and perhaps his sense of responsibility by belting a home run in the opening games at the Polo Grounds. I was among the thousands who rose to cheer him as he crossed the plate. Once Robinson hurdled the color taboo, democracy started to function in the Major Leagues. The Negro stars certainly have done something for baseball. There are Negroes on seven of the eight National League clubs. Not long ago, Brooklyn had five in the line-up in one day—five of the nine players on the field. The three top teams in the National League—Giants, Dodgers and Braves—have a total of thirteen, more in each case than any of the other clubs.

And baseball has done something for the Negroes too. If nothing else, it's unbigoted some bigots.

If the Giants win, it will of course be a team victory. They have good pitching, a good infield, good outfield and good hitting. It ought to be enough. But it takes more than just a platoon of players and Durocher to win a pennant. I believe Willie is the big difference. No one can improve on Willie's script, whether it's into the stands for a homer or three strikes and out. At least when it's the latter, you won't be seeing him do it with his bat on his shoulder.

There should be but one requisite for major-league ballplayers, just as there should be but one requisite for an actor or actress—quality of performance.

Quality is what Willie has in abundance.

Come on, you Giants. Come on, you Willie Mays!

In the 1951 World Series, the Giants made history by starting an all-black outfield of Monte Irvin, Willie Mays, and Hank Thompson. Thompson joined the St. Louis Browns in 1947 to become the third African-American player in the majors. Irvin had played with Mays on the Newark Eagles before the two were reunited in New York. Both Irvin and Thompson signed with the Giants in 1949.

PERFECTION: THE DOMINANCE OF SANDY KOUFAX

from *Sandy Koufax: A Lefty's Legacy* by Jane Leavy

EXCELLENCE IN SPORTS is often tied to longevity, the ability to succeed over time. For pitcher Sandy Koufax, his brilliance came from dominating so completely over a short period. Control problems made Koufax a late bloomer and devastating arthritis in his pitching elbow forced him into early retirement. But in between, Koufax strung together some of the most spectacular performances ever exhibited on the mound.

In *Sandy Koufax: A Lefty's Legacy*, journalist Jane Leavy explores Koufax's remarkable career by framing the story around an inning-by-inning account of his perfect game against the Chicago Cubs in 1965.

THE PREGAME SHOW

Sunset on September 9, 1965, was at 7:08 PM. The lights were on at Dodger Stadium, obliterating the last vestiges of smog and smoke lingering over Watts some ten miles away. It was that last moment before darkness compromises the light. But the absent sun still asserted its control over the ebbing day.

Sandy Koufax, the Dodgers' starting pitcher, knew he was in the gloaming of his baseball career. He had not won a game in three weeks. Not since black Los Angeles had exploded in rage. Not since he watched in horror as San Francisco Giants pitcher Juan Marichal bludgeoned John Roseboro with a baseball bat. Not since he had confided in his friend Phil Collier, the beat reporter for the *San Diego Union*, that the next season would be his last.

Traumatic arthritis in his left elbow required him to douse his body with Capsohn, a hot sauce derived from red hot chili peppers, before every game. Trainers used tongue depressors to apply it, smearing him with the stuff the way you'd spread mustard on a Dodger Dog. Bill Buhler, the head trainer, wore surgical gloves for this procedure; otherwise his wife wouldn't

Sandy Koufax's perfect game against the Cubs at Dodger Stadium in 1965 was his fourth no-hitter in four years. It was also one of eight shutouts for Koufax in a season in which he had a league-best 2.04 ERA (the worst ERA of his final four seasons, by the way). His 14 strikeouts, including the final six batters of the game, contributed to a record-setting 382 strikeouts for the season.

let him put his hands beneath the sheets when he got into bed.

All season, Koufax had been taking Butazolidine pills and cortisone shots. Empirin with codeine was a staple of his pregame diet. Afterward, he bathed his arm in a tub of ice water cold enough to chill three postgame beers left behind by the trainers. When the bottles were empty the treatment was done. But the inevitable erosion of time, bone, and cartilage had not yet compromised his ability. He could still throw the tantalizing curve that broke like a waterfall. And he could still blow.

There were times, many times, when he would come into the dugout before the game mindful of the Dodgers' paltry offense and tell his teammates: "Just get me one. All I need is one." No one thought he was bragging. Other times, he would emerge from the tunnel kvetching, "I can't get loose. I ain't got shit." They'd watch him dangle from the dugout roof trying to stretch, the only time he ever looked ungainly, and laugh: *"It's in the bag. Big Boy's got it tonight."*

This was not one of those times. It was just another Thursday night in September: an improbable confluence of lives, careers, dreams, and fates. There were no bullpen portents or predictions, only the usual great expectations. The Dodgers had lost their last two games to the hated, league-leading Giants to fall a half game behind in second place. A scheduling quirk had brought the dismal, last place Chicago Cubs to Los Angeles for a one-game visit. The U.S. Weather Bureau had predicted light to moderate smog and a game-time temperature in the seventies. The ball wouldn't carry; it never did at night. By the late innings, batting helmets and bullpen chairs would acquire a fine residue of condensation, as dampness settled into the

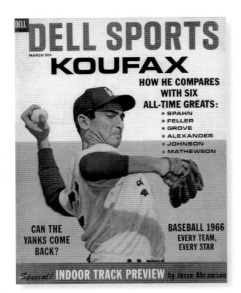

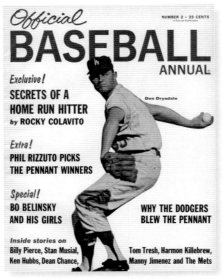

basin of Chavez Ravine. It was a forecast almost as providential as the scheduled pitching matchup: Koufax (21–7) vs. Hendley (2–2)

• • •

THE SIXTH INNING

Claude Osteen was lying in his shorts on a training table in the clubhouse listening to Jerry Doggett tout the virtues of Royal "76" Premium gasoline. It was getting late in the game and late in the season when arms tire and bodies need assuaging. Drysdale, who was scheduled to start against Houston the next evening, lay on the table beside him. It was Osteen's

Above, left: Few knew that 1966 would be Koufax's final season, but the experts were already comparing him to the all-time greats. In his final four seasons, he won 97 games against 27 losses. He led the NL in ERA all four years, with a combined 1.86 over that span. He struck out at least 300 batters in three of the four seasons and averaged 9.3 strikeouts per nine innings. He won the Cy Young Award in 1963, '65, and '66—all seasons in which his Dodgers won the pennant.

Above, right: The Cy Young Award winner for 1962, Don Drysdale formed with Koufax a fearsome righty-lefty duo for the 1960s Dodgers. Standing six feet six inches tall, the intimidating Drysdale wasn't afraid to pitch inside, and he finished among the top five pitchers in hit batters for twelve consecutive seasons. His 58⅔ consecutive shutout innings in 1968 was a record that stood for twenty years.

first year with the Dodgers, having escaped last place in the American League in an off-season trade with the ignominious Washington Senators. At twenty-six, Osteen was no rookie but he felt like one in Drysdale's presence. Everyone felt small in Drysdale's presence. He was the team enforcer; whether standing on the dugout steps, bat ominously in hand, the day-game sun glinting off his California-white teeth, or getting treatment in the training room. His entire being commanded authority. "Get up," Drysdale said suddenly. "Get your uniform on. You gotta watch this."

When Drysdale said "Get up," you got up—even if you were lying on the training table half naked and it was the sixth inning and a violation of baseball etiquette to do so. No one in the dugout or the press box could say how many times before Koufax had carried a no-hitter into the sixth inning. His teammates generally accepted the fact that he'd have one through four or five because it seemed like he always did. Later, they would count them up and be astonished all over again: nine times, not including the no-hitters, he had held the other team hitless through six innings.

The sixth inning of a no-hitter will either be remembered as the necessary pause before a classic denouement or it won't be remembered at all. The dramatic tension derives from not knowing which. The line between the mundane and the heroic is drawn with every pitch, every potential passed ball, every errant bounce. In this instance, the tension was compounded by the improbable symmetry of the line score. On the field, in the stands, on the respective benches there was a coming to consciousness of what lay ahead. Hendley was hanging on. Koufax was getting stronger. "You could smell that something big was about to happen," Osteen said.

It figures that Drysdale would smell it before anyone else. Their lives and fates were inextricably linked. After all, they virtually grew up together. They had been teammates for eleven years. The Dodgers were nothing without them. And without each other, neither would have been what each became. Righty, lefty, gentile, Jew. Everything about them was opposite except their purpose. Drysdale came sidearm; Koufax came over the top. Drysdale's ball beat you up, Koufax's rose to greet you. "Drysdale was like going to the dentist without Novocain," Joey A. liked to say. "Sandy had the Novocain." Facing him was painful only in retrospect.

If Koufax was a shooting star, Drysdale was a full moon. Both were essential but one was sublime. The closest Drysdale had ever come to throwing a no-hitter was a one-hitter against the Cardinals in May. A first-inning single removed all the anxiety from the effort. Big D knew better than anyone the infinitesimal difference between excellence and dominance; he inhabited that place. So there he was, all six feet six inches of him, climbing off the training table in his undershorts, going to his locker, and putting on the uniform, that big 53. That's what stunned Osteen most: "Drysdale's acceptance of what this guy could do that no one else, including himself, could do."

Drysdale's arrival in the dugout compounded the hush and the sense of occasion. Everyone knew what was going on. The Cubs were no longer just facing Koufax. They were facing an inchoate realization: *Uh-oh, he found it.* The curveball was breaking. The fastball was gathering force. "Each pitch," Osteen said, "harder than the last."

The Cubs were restive, jiggling with nervous energy, everyone desperate to change something, anything. For five innings, they had been telling themselves all the right things: We still got a chance. *We're only down one. One swing of the bat, you never know.* But due up in the sixth was the bottom of the order: Krug, Kessinger, and Hendley.

It would be human to weaken in the face of such tepid opposition. Koufax was unrelenting. "Two-hundred hitters hit two hundred for a reason," he liked to say. Drysdale knew if he got past the seventh, eighth, and ninth men in the batting order, the seventh, eighth, and ninth innings would be something to see.

The Dodger dugout exuded a studied nonchalance that soon gave way to superstition. The impulse was conservative. If you change nothing, then perhaps nothing will change. So you sit in the same seat, cross your legs the same way, tilt your cap in the same direction. If you're Maury Wills and you've been sitting beside Koufax on a stool in the runway between innings where you can have a smoke without being noticed, you make sure to sit there again. The one thing you don't do is mention the obvious.

We got a double no-hitter going here, Krug thought, swinging a bat in the on-deck circle. His errant throw was all that stood between what was and what could have been. It is baseball's way to juxtapose failure and redemption with comic regularity. Thus, Krug would remember this at-bat with uncommon specificity. How the pedestrian grounder he hit to short was gobbled up by Wills who threw it in the dirt to first baseman Wes Parker. And how Wills hollered thank you across the diamond after Parker dug it out. In truth, Parker had never been so scared in his life. God, he thought, I don't want to blow this guy's chance at immortality.

Kessinger, the shortstop, was next. After fouling back a fastball for strike one, Kessinger stepped out of the batter's box and exchanged a meaningful look with the home plate umpire. Vargo had seen that look before. Scully too: "Mitts are popping," he said. "The Cubs have a couple of fellas loosening up down there. But Hendley's out on deck."

As much as Koufax's career was short, Warren Spahn's was long and prosperous. In a career that spanned three decades, the Braves lefty won 20 or more games thirteen times, including a high of 23 wins at the age of forty-two. Spahn missed three full seasons to World War II, but he still won more games (363) than any lefthander in history.

Kessinger hit a hopeful dribbler down the third base line. It was a nothing ball—the kind on which so much can turn. Its weakness was its potential strength. In its timid trajectory Kessinger found cause for optimism. But Gilliam was playing in at third to guard against a bunt. "I thought I had a chance to beat it out," Kessinger said. "I got thrown out by half a step."

As he headed back to the bench, Kessinger couldn't help thinking about the Hollywood crowd: late to arrive, early to leave, slow to grasp what they were seeing. Arriving just as *we're* leaving, he thought, with a small smile.

The dugout lacked the usual baseball chatter, a form of surrender. Byron Browne kept waiting for someone to say something, break the spell: "This fool is trying to throw a no-hitter at us!" But he was a rookie. It wasn't his place.

With two down, Klein allowed Hendley to hit for himself. The man was still pitching a no-hitter. Besides, Klein was saving Amalfitano for later. As Hendley meekly and predictably struck out again, Richard Hume recorded the totals: no runs, no hits, no errors. Nothing had happened but everything had changed.

"In case you are speculating, down through the years, there's been one gem, one double no-hitter," Scully noted. "We'll tell you more about it if and when we get to

Left: Steve Carlton, a four-time Cy Young Award winner, battled Nolan Ryan head-to-head for the all-time strikeout record, and he grabbed the lead in 1983. Ryan took over the record a year later, though Carlton still ranks fourth on the list. Carlton's most remarkable season was 1972, when he finished 27-10 and won the pitching Triple Crown for a Phillies team that notched only 59 victories on the year.

Facing page, top: Nolan Ryan was the heir apparent to Sandy Koufax when he emerged in the late 1960s as a fire-baller with control problems. Ryan led the league in wild pitches a record six times, but he eventually mastered his delivery enough to break Koufax's single-season strikeout record, with 383 in 1973, and top 300 Ks in six different seasons. While pitching for Houston in 1981, Ryan passed Koufax with no-hitter number four; he would accomplish the feat a remarkable seven times in his career, including at the age of forty-four in 1991.

Facing page, bottom: On June 29, 2004, Randy Johnson became the fourth man in history to reach 4,000 career strikeouts. Six weeks earlier, the forty-year-old had become the oldest ever to pitch a perfect game. The six-foot-ten-inch-tall hurler known as "The Big Unit" holds many strikeout records for left-handed pitchers: most career strikeouts, most seasons striking out at least 200 batters and most striking out at least 300; and most strikeouts in a game. From 1999 to 2002, he struck out nearly five times as many as he walked, a better ratio than Koufax had during his prime years of 1963-66.

that stage. There's never been a perfect game on one side and a one-hitter on the other side . . . yet."

Musing aloud, Scully gave everyone within the sound of his voice permission to consider the possibilities. What had been murmured (or muttered) was now articulated. Adams, Davis, DeLury, Buhler, Hume, and God knows how many others were thinking the same thing. *I think he has a chance.* When Koufax returned to the dugout, Drysdale vacated the stool in the runway. In abdicating the seat, Drysdale was yielding not just to superstition but to reality.

In the Cubs dugout, Joey A. got up from his seat too and sought out Ron Santo: "Hey, Ronnie, somebody must have pissed him off." Santo nodded. Jogging back onto the field, he told Beckert, "Yeah, you're right. He doesn't have shit."

FINAL TWIST OF THE DRAMA
HANK AARON, HOME RUN KING
by George Plimpton

DONALD HONIG ONCE wrote that baseball's most celebrated record belongs to one of its least flamboyant stars. As sluggers came and went, decade after decade, in vain pursuit of Babe Ruth's mark of 714 career home runs, Henry "Hank" Aaron pounded away with quiet consistency to reach the Babe's doorstep in 1974.

Renowned author and journalist George Plimpton covered Aaron's historic home run number 715 for *Sports Illustrated*, providing a conclusion to what had been a tense and emotional journey for baseball's new home run king. Plimpton, longtime editor of the *Paris Review*, was the author of numerous articles and books, including *The Curious Case of Sidd Finch*, about a pitcher/Buddhist monk with a 168-mile-per-hour fastball.

It was a simple act by an unassuming man that touched an enormous circle of people, indeed an entire country. It provided an instant that people would remember for decades—exactly what they were doing at the time of the home run that beat Babe Ruth's great record, whether they were watching it on a television set, or heard it over the car radio while driving along the turnpike at night, or even whether a neighbor leaned over a fence and told them about it the next morning.

For those who sat in the stadium in Atlanta, their recollections would be more intimate—the sharp cork-popping sound of the bat hitting the ball, startlingly audible in the split second of suspense before the crowd began a roar that lasted for more than 10 minutes. Perhaps that is what they would remember—how people stood in front of their seats and sucked in air and bellowed it out in a sustained tribute that few athletes have ever received. Or perhaps they would remember their wonder at how easy and inevitable it seemed—that having opened the season in Cincinnati by hitting the tying home run, No. 714, with his first swing of the year, it was obviously appropriate that the man who has been called "Supe" (for

Superman) by his teammates was going to duplicate the feat in Atlanta with his first swing of that game. That was why 53,775 had come. Or perhaps they would remember the odd way the stadium emptied after the excitement of the fourth inning, as if the crowd felt that what it had seen would be diluted by sitting through any more baseball that night.

And then finally there were those few in the core of that immense circle—the participants themselves—who would be the ones most keenly touched: the pitcher, in this case a pleasant, gap-toothed veteran named Al Downing, who, of the more than one hundred National League pitchers, happened to be the one who threw a fastball at a certain moment that did not tail away properly; the hitter, Henry Aaron, for whom the event, despite his grace in dealing with it, had become so traumatic that he relished little in the instant except the relief that it was done; the Braves' announcer, Milo Hamilton, whose imagination for months had been working up words to describe the event to the outside world; and a young bullpen pitcher, Tom House, who would reach up in the air and establish contact with a ball whose monetary value as baseball's greatest talisman was pegged at $25,000 and whose sentimental value was incalculable . . .

THE PITCHER

The poor guy. All those years toiling on the mound, peering down the long alley toward the plate at those constant disturbers of his sense of well-being settling into their stances and flicking

---

Hank Aaron hit home run number 715 on April 8, 1974, at Atlanta's Fulton County Stadium in front of 53,775 fans. Though Aaron never hit 50 in a season and led the league only four times, his steady production over twenty-three Major League seasons took him to tremendous heights. Aaron hit at least 20 homers in twenty seasons and at least 30 fifteen times, both of which are records.

their bats—and then to look down one day and find Henry Aaron there, the large, peaceful, dark face with the big eyes and the high forehead, and to know that one mistake, one small lapse of concentration, would place the pitcher's name forever in the record books as having thrown the "immortal gopher."

Perhaps there are some pitchers around the league who would not mind being identified with Aaron's eclipsing of Ruth's record. Tracy Stallard, who was a young Boston Red Sox rookie when he gave up the home run to Roger Maris that broke Babe Ruth's record of 60 hit in a year, afterward rather enjoyed the back-of-the-hand notoriety that came with being a victim of Maris's clout, and he would announce, to the point of volunteering, that he was the pitcher responsible. Most pitchers, though, are sensitive enough about their craft to feel differently about such a role. Ray Sadecki once said of Stallard, "I don't want to be him. Everybody knows *who* he is. Nobody knows *where* he is."

Those scheduled in the rotation against the Atlanta Braves in the final weeks of last season and the opening days of the 1974 schedule were uncomfortably aware that they were involved in a sort of cosmic game of Russian roulette, it being inevitable that one of them was going to give up the 715th home run.

The pitcher opposing Aaron in Atlanta on the last day of the 1973 season was Houston Astro lefthander Dave Roberts. Before the game he sat in front of his locker looking crestfallen. "What I should be doing is concentrating on my 17th victory of the year," he said. "But I've been thinking about him. I thought about him all last night. He was just deposited there in my mind. What really got me was that I knew he wasn't thinking about me at all. I wished I'd known his home telephone number, so's I could have called him every 20 minutes—'How's it going, Hank?'—just to let him know I was around."

In that game Roberts survived three Aaron turns at bat by giving up three singles that raised the batter's average to .301. Then, perhaps with his nervous system betraying him, the pitcher pulled a muscle in his back in the middle of the seventh inning and was removed. In such a situation the relieving pitcher is allowed as much time as he wants to warm up. Don Wilson, Roberts's reliever, off whom Aaron had hit his 611th home run, said later that as he stood on the mound it crossed his mind just to keep on warming up indefinitely, shaking his head and saying, "No, not yet," to the umpire until the night fell and the moon came up, and perhaps at 10:30 the next morning some sort of statute of limitations would run out the season and he would be able to pack up and go home, sore-armed but assuaged.

The pitcher who through personal experience knows more about Aaron's specialty than anyone in baseball is the tall, sidearm, whip-motion Dodger righthander, Don Drysdale, now retired from active baseball and working as a broadcaster with the California Angels. Aaron hit the astonishing total of 17 home runs off him. Next down the line is Claude Osteen, who has been touched for 13, and when his rotation comes up against the Braves, Drysdale often calls him on the phone (the

The lead-up to home run number 715 was a period of considerable pressure for the unassuming Aaron. He received threatening letters, often with outwardly racist messages, during his chase of the beloved Ruth. When it was over, the sense of relief was evident on Aaron's face. The ball from the historic blast was delivered to the new home run king at home plate by Braves reliever Tom House, who caught the ball in the Atlanta bullpen.

two were Dodger teammates) to remind him that Drysdale would be delighted to be taken off the hook for being Aaron's special patsy. ("Now, Claude, don't let down. That record is within reach."

Drysdale has never felt it was possible to establish much of a "book" on how to pitch to Aaron. "Besides, there never is any set way to pitch to a great hitter," Drysdale says. "If there were, he'd be hitting .220. I always used to think that he had a lot of Stan Musial in his stance. From the pitcher's mound they both seem to coil at you. The only sensible thing—if you couldn't get the manager to let you skip a turn against him—was to mix the pitches and keep the ball low, and if you were pitching to spots, it was important to miss bad. If you missed good and the ball got in his power zone, sometimes you were glad it went out of the park and was not banged up the middle."

Drysdale remains in awe of the concussive nature of Aaron's power. He remembers a 250-foot home run Aaron duck-hooked over the short "Chinese Wall" screen in the Los Angeles Coliseum, hit so hard that Drysdale got a crick in his neck from turning abruptly to watch it go by. "It's bad enough to have him hit any home run off you—turning and looking and saying to yourself, 'My God, how far is *that* one going to go.' But with the Coliseum home run, I ended up not only in mental anguish but literally in physical pain."

At least Drysdale was not around to suffer the wrenching experience of facing Aaron at this stage in his career. As soon as Aaron was due at the plate, the crowd began to stir in anticipation. In the left-field seats a forest of raised fishnets and gloved hands rose and swayed in expectation. The pitcher was practically the only person in the park who did not want to see the home run hit. Even some of his own teammates would not have been displeased, though they might have been judicious enough to keep it to themselves. In the penultimate week of the 1973 season a scuffle almost broke out in the Los Angeles dugout when a couple of the younger Dodgers, casting aside their team affiliation, carried away in their hope to see a part of history, began urging a long Aaron drive out of the park—"Get on over; get out!" They got some hard stares and shoving from one or two of the more aggressively competitive among their elders, especially Andy Messersmith, who is not only a strong team man but a pitcher hardly agreeable to seeing one of his kind humbled.

The next presentiment that the pitcher had to deal with was the flurry of activity from the umpires as Aaron left the on-deck circle and approached the plate. Since home run No. 710, a ball boy had been rushing out to provide an umpire with a clutch of specially marked balls so that if the home run were hit, the ball could be positively identified to thwart a horde of people turning up for the $25,000 reward with fakes. Each ball was stamped, last year with an invisible diamond with a number within, this year with two sets of numbers, a marked pattern that lit up under a fluorescent lamp.

All of this could not do much to help the pitcher's confidence—the scurrying preparations of those attending to an execution. Last year Juan Marichal saw this activity, the plate umpire reaching in a special ball bag at his waist to introduce a

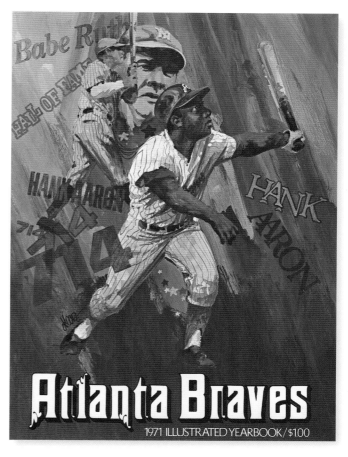

Atlanta Braves
1971 ILLUSTRATED YEARBOOK/$1.00

In the 1971 Braves yearbook, editor Lee Walburn wrote: "Once upon a time there were thought to be certain things that Man could not do without upsetting the divine order of the Universe. Like landing a man on the moon, or canceling the *Ed Sullivan Show*, or hitting 715 home runs. To hit 715 home runs would be to tear down baseball's most revered record. The Babe hit them and The Babe *was baseball*. There are those who still dislike Roger Maris because he dared to break Ruth's single season record of 60 homers. At least, they said, Babe Ruth still had his career record of 714 home runs, and that would never be challenged. Wrong again. Bad Henry is going after it." In 1971, thirty-seven-year-old "Bad Henry" was still 122 homers shy of the record.

special ball to the game, and not being aware of the procedure, Marichal felt that he was the victim of some odd plot, that perhaps the ball he would get from the umpire was going to pop in two and emit smoke as he gripped it for his screwball. This year it was decided that the base umpire closest to the Braves' dugout would handle the marked balls.

The ball Aaron hit in Cincinnati with his first swing of the season (into a deep enclosure between the outfield fence and the stands known as the pit) was marked with a pair of 14s and 1s. It was recovered there by a policeman named Clarence Williams, holed up in his canyon with just a piece of sky overhead so that he never saw the home run ball until it came over the fence and bounced at his feet, spattering his uniform

with mud. An attendant came rushing down the enclosure toward him, holding open a small paper bag and crying, "Drop it in here! Drop it in here!" And thus it was delivered to Aaron, the ball that tied Ruth's record, shielded as if contaminated from the view of the huge Opening Day crowd as the attendant, flanked by two guards, hurried in from center field.

Four days later in Atlanta, Al Downing handled two of the prepared balls. The first was marked with 12s and 1s, the 12 arbitrarily picked by Bill Acree, the Braves' equipment manager, and the 1 to show that it was the first of a series of 24 balls specially marked. Downing used it through the first inning, when he walked Aaron to massive hoots of derision. The same ball was tossed to him when Aaron came up again in the fourth. It was thrown out of the game after a pitch in the dirt. From the first base umpire, Frank Pulli, came a ball marked with a pair of 12s and two 2s.

Downing had realized in the middle of the previous week that he was to pitch the opener in Atlanta. It did not bother him much. Though he is not an overpowering pitcher, he has great

As soon as it became clear that Ruth's mark was within striking distance, the league began preparing for festivities to be held wherever the record-breaking homer might be hit. Aaron knocked the record-tying number 714 in Cincinnati on the opening day of 1974, in his very first at bat of the new season.

confidence. He relies on fine control and a good change of pace. His teammates call him Ace, an encomium for winning 20 games in 1971. He is also called Gentleman Al, for his bearing not only off the field but around the mound, where he behaves, according to Vin Scully, the Los Angeles broadcaster, "like a man wearing a bowler hat." Downing is very much his own boss. He shakes off his catcher's signs as many as 25 times a game, relying on his own concepts and on his sense that much of pitching is feel. ("If you don't feel you can throw a curve at a particular time," he says, "there's not much point in trying.") He is such a student of his craft that he has always made it a point to room with a hitter, rare in a society in which there is such a confrontation between the two specialists.

"It helps a pitcher to be exposed to the enemy camp," Downing says. "For years I roomed with Maury Wills, and it helped my pitching considerably just listening to him talk about hitting.

"Aaron? Well, I'm not sure that rooming with him for ten years would really help. You can have all the know-how, but if you make one small mistake, there's no one in the league who can take advantage of it like he does. He knows what I can throw. He hit two home runs off me last year. But I'm not going to change my pattern. I mustn't go against what I've been successful with . . . I shouldn't rearrange pitches that complement each other. If I throw 715, I'm not going to run and hide. There's no

Left: Hank Aaron, Willie Mays, and Roberto Clemente formed the National League's outfield for eleven of twelve all-star games from 1962 to 1972. Mays was pegged as the one most likely to break Ruth's home run record. Three years Aaron's senior, he had a 155-game head start on the Braves slugger and outpaced Aaron through 1970. At the start of the 1971 season, the forty-year-old Mays was sitting at 628.

disgrace in that. On the other hand, I'm not going to run to the plate to congratulate him. It's a big home run for him, for the game, for the country, but not for me!"

THE HITTER

On occasion, as Henry Aaron sits in the Braves' dugout, he takes off his baseball cap and holds it close against his face. He moves it around until he is able to peer through one of the vent holes in the crown of the cap at the opposing pitcher on the mound. The practice, like focusing through a telescope, serves to isolate the pitcher, setting him apart in a round frame so that Aaron can scrutinize him and decide how he will deal with him once he reaches the plate.

The thought process he goes through during this is deciding what sort of a pitch he will almost surely see, engraving the possibility in his mind's eye so that when the pitch comes he can truly rip at it. Home run hitters must invariably be guessers of some sort, since success at their craft depends on seeing a pitch come down that they expect, so they have time to generate a powerful swing. More than one pitcher has said that Aaron seems to hop on a pitch as if he had called for it. Ron Perranoski, the former Dodger relief pitcher (who in his first six seasons against Aaron held him to an .812 average, 13 for 16), once said, "He not only knows what the pitch will be, but where it will be."

Aaron describes his mental preparation as a process of elimination. "Suppose a pitcher has three good pitches: a fastball, a curve and a slider. What I do, after a lot of consideration and analyzing and studying, is to eliminate two of those pitches, since it's impossible against a good pitcher to keep all three possibilities on my mind at the plate. So in getting rid of two, for example, I convince myself that I'm going to get a fastball down low. When it comes, I'm ready. Now, I can have guessed wrong, and if

Above: Despite winning the home run crown only once, Frank Robinson is fifth on the all-time list. He slugged 38 in his first year in the bigs and surpassed the 20-homer plateau in each of his first twelve seasons. He also homered in his first game as player-manager for the Cleveland Indians in 1975, when he became the first African-American manager in Major League history.

Eddie Mathews was Aaron's teammate in Milwaukee and Atlanta for thirteen seasons, and from 1957 to 1961 they were the first teammates since Ruth and Gehrig to top 30 homers apiece for five consecutive seasons. The Braves claimed back-to-back pennants in 1957 and 1958 with this duo of sluggers.

I've set my mind for a fastball it's hard to do much with a curve short of nibbing it out over the infield. But the chances are that I'll eventually get what I'm looking for."

This procedure of "guessing" has many variants. Roger Maris, for example, always went up to the plate self-prepared to hit a fastball, feeling that he was quick enough to adjust to a different sort of pitch as it flew toward the plate. Most guess hitters play a cat-and-mouse game with the pitcher as the count progresses. What distinguishes Aaron's system is that once he makes up his mind what he will see during a time at bat, he never deviates. Aaron has disciplined himself to sit and wait for one sort of pitch, whatever the situation.

One might suppose that a pitcher with a large repertoire would trouble Aaron—and that indeed is the case. He shakes his head when he thinks of Marichal. "When he's at the prime of his game he throws a good fastball, a good screwball, a good changeup, a good slider, a good you-have-it . . . and obviously the elimination system can't work; you can't just throw out five or six different pitches in the hope of seeing the one you want; the odds of seeing it would be too much against the batter." What to do against a Marichal, then? "It's an extra challenge," Aaron says. "I've just got to tune up my bat a little higher. It's a question of confidence, knowing that the pitcher cannot get me out four times without me hitting the ball sharply somewhere."

It is this confrontation between pitcher and hitter that fascinates Aaron, and indeed it is what he likes best about baseball—what he calls "that damn good guessing game."

Obviously there have been the bad times. His manager in the mid-'50s, Fred Haney, was thinking of benching him against Drysdale, who was giving him fits in their early matchups. "I had a psychological block going there," Aaron says. "Drysdale was throwing from way out by third base with that sidearm motion of his, and he was mean, and it was hard to hang in there, knowing how mean he was. I had an awful lot of respect for him.

"So much of it has to do with concentration. On the day of a night game I begin concentrating at four in the afternoon. Just before I go to bat, from the on-deck circle, I can hear my little girl—she's 12 now—calling from the stands. 'Hey, Daddy! Hey, Daddy!' After the game she says to me, 'Hey, you never look around, Daddy, to wave.' Well, sometimes I look at her, I can't help it, but not too often. I'm looking at the pitcher. I'm thinking very hard about him. I started thinking about Al Downing of the Dodgers on the way home from Cincinnati. Basically, I knew what he would like me to hit—his fastball, which tails away and, if he's right, is his best pitch. I knew he didn't want to throw me curveballs, which from a lefthander would come inside, and which I could pull. So I set myself mentally for that one pitch I knew he'd rely on—his fastball. I can discipline myself to wait for that ball. I knew it would come sooner or later . . . "

There is nothing in Aaron's approach to the plate to suggest such an intensity of purpose. His stride is slow and lackadaisical. (He was called Snowshoes for a time by his teammates for the way he sort of pushes himself along.) He carries his batting helmet on his way to the plate, holding two bats in the other hand. He stares out at the pitcher. He drops the extra bat. Then, just out of the batting box, resting his bat on the ground with the handle end balanced against his thighs, he uses both hands to jostle the helmet correctly into position. He steps into the box. Even here there is no indication of the kinetic possibility, none of the ferocious tamping of his spikes to get a good toehold that one remembers of Willie Mays, say, or the quick switching of his bat back and forth as he waits. Aaron steps into the batting box as if he were going to sit down in it. Downing has said that looking at him during his delivery, he finds it hard to believe Aaron isn't going to take every pitch.

Downing's first pitch to him in the fourth inning was a ball, a changeup that puffed up the dirt in front of the plate. Umpire Dave Davidson turned the ball over, looking at it suspiciously, and tossed it out. He signaled to umpire Pulli at first base to throw in another of the prepared balls. Downing rubbed it up a bit, then turned and, as the clock on the scoreboard behind him showed 9:07, wheeled and delivered a fastball, aiming low and expecting it to fade away off the outside corner.

The ball rose off Aaron's bat in the normal trajectory of his long hits—the arc of a four-iron shot in golf—ripping out over the infield, the shortstop instinctively bending his knees as if he could leap for it, and it headed for deep left-center field . . .

Aaron never saw it clear the fence. Hard as it is to imagine, Aaron says he has never seen one of his home runs land. "That's not what I'm supposed to do," he says. "I've seen guys miss first base looking to see where the ball went. My job is to get down to first base and touch it. Looking at the ball going over the fence isn't going to help. I don't even look at the home runs hit in batting practice. No sense to break a good habit."

So, as he has done countless times, he looked toward first as he ran, dropping his bat neatly just off the base path, and when he saw the exultation of his first base coach, Jim Busby, he knew for sure that the long chase was over.

THE PITCHER

Al Downing did watch the ball go over the fence. He had seen the leftfielder and the centerfielder converge, and he was hoping the wind would hold the ball up. When the ceremonies began just off home plate, he went to sit in the Dodger dugout and looked on.

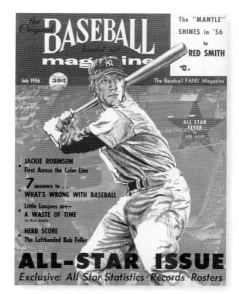

Had injuries not cut short several seasons in his prime, Mickey Mantle might have been the greatest challenger to the home run record. Instead, he retired in 1968 with 536 to his credit, the most by a switch-hitter. A three-time MVP, Mantle won a Triple Crown in 1956 at the age of twenty-four, with 52 homers, 130 RBIs, and a .353 batting average.

The delay was of no help to his control, and he was taken out that same inning. He went to the empty Dodger locker room and dressed. A taxi was ordered for him, and he stood in the stadium tunnel waiting for it. Downing has a very cheery voice that seems to belie the gravity of any situation one might connect him with. "Well, that's that," he said. "I didn't have the rhythm, and the fastball wasn't doing what it was supposed to, which is to drop slightly. I threw a changeup, low, and then I threw a fastball right down the middle. What did I think when he hit it? Damn, there goes our lead. So I went and sat in the dugout. Nobody said anything about the home run. Why should they? We're all grown men. We don't have to console each other. One or two people came by and said, 'We'll get the runs back for you.'"

A photographer appeared with a small souvenir placard handed out by the Braves, testifying that the bearer had been on hand to see the record home run hit. It had a picture of Aaron and the number 715. The photographer wanted Downing to pose with it, hold it up and smile. Downing shook his head quickly. "I don't think that would prove anything," he said. He looked up and down the tunnel for his taxi.

Above: Ralph Kiner played just ten seasons in the majors, but he made the most of them. Before hanging up the bat because of a bad back, he led the league in homers a record seven consecutive times, twice hitting more than 50. Kiner's home run ratio is the fifth highest in history, trailing such home run heroes as McGwire, Ruth, Bonds, and Sosa.

Right: All twenty members of the 500 home run club spent most of their careers playing the outfield or one of the corner infield positions. Although Ernie Banks played more games at first base (1,259) than any other position, nine of his nineteen seasons (1,125 games) were as a shortstop for the Chicago Cubs. All five of his 40-homer seasons came while playing short, spoiling the image of the all-field, no-hit position.

"I'm more concerned about my next start," he went on. "This thing is over. It's history. It won't bother me. There's only one home run hit off me that's ever stayed in my mind. That was a grand slam that Ken Boyer got in the sixth inning of the 1964 World Series—the one that beat the Yankees 4-3 and turned the whole Series around. I threw him a changeup, and there was a lot of second-guessing that I had thrown him the wrong pitch, that I should have challenged him. I thought about that for a long time. I was 23 at the time. It was a technical consideration. This one? It's more emotional. Well, pitchers don't ever like to give up home runs. But I'm not giving myself up to trauma. People will be calling to see if I've jumped out the window yet. I'm not going to wake up in the middle of the night and begin banging on the walls and looking over the sill down into the street. The next time I pitch against him I'll get him out."

A distant roar went up from the crowd. The Braves were having a good inning.

"Your team has made six errors," Downing was told.

"That so? They must be pressing," he said. "Everybody's edgy tonight." He craned his neck, looking for his taxi.

THE ANNOUNCER

At the sound of the ball hitting the bat, in the broadcast booth the chief voice of the Atlanta Braves rose against the tumult to describe the event over the air to his part of the outside world. The voice belonged to Atlanta's local broadcaster, Milo Hamilton, an announcer for the Cubs and the White Sox before coming to the

Braves. It was a tremendous moment for him. True, an NBC crew (Curt Gowdy, Tony Kubek and Joe Garagiola) was on hand and so was Vin Scully, the Dodger announcer for the past twenty-five years, sending the game back to Los Angeles. Through their combined broadcast outlets, many millions would be made aware of the instant, but none had a more personal involvement than Milo Hamilton. Being with the Braves, he was the only broadcaster in the country who had known for months that at some point he would be describing Aaron's historic home run. His situation was extraordinary. While he had to verbalize instantly into a microphone what he saw, in the case of Aaron's home run, because it was inevitable, Hamilton had an opportunity to prepare a sentence so perfect that if it worked, if enough people heard it and commented on it, it had an excellent chance to slip into *Bartlett's Familiar Quotations* alongside "One small step . . . "

It was a unique situation. Almost invariably, a momentous comment in sports reporting is made spontaneously, under pressure and against the crowd noise, so that a common characteristic is often that the key sentences are repeated. There was a flurry of repetitions when Russ Hodges, ordinarily a somewhat phlegmatic sportscaster, gave his on-the-spot report of Bobby Thomson's "miracle of Coogan's Bluff" home run in

Question: Who hit the most home runs during the 1960s? Not Hank Aaron. Nope, not Willie Mays, and not Frank Robinson either. It was Harmon Killebrew, who hit 393 of his 573 career dingers during the decade. Killebrew played in his first game for the Washington Senators as a seventeen-year-old, but his first full season came in 1959, when he was twenty-three. He hit a league-high 42 homers.

the Dodger-Giant playoff game in 1951: "The Giants win the pennant! The Giants win the pennant! The Giants win the pennant! The Giants win the pennant . . . I don't believe it! I don't believe it! I do not believe it!"

Describing the extraordinary home run of Ted Williams in his last at bat in the majors, Curt Gowdy had a brace of repeated sentences—"It's got a chance! It's got a chance! And it's gone!"—all said in a somewhat restrained fashion, since in an earlier inning Williams had hit a long fly ball that Gowdy had described as if it were going into the seats. He did not want to be fooled again.

Phil Rizzuto, the Yankee broadcaster, had a quasi-opportunity, much like Hamilton's, to prepare for Roger Maris's 61st home run, which was a strong possibility though hit on the last day of the 1961 season. Obviously, Rizzuto did not do so, since his radio commentary, utilizing his favorite epithet, was absolutely predictable. "Holy cow!" he cried. "That's gonna be it."

Sportscasters all take a dim view of preparing material in advance, feeling that spontaneity must be the key essential of their craft, the thing that so often produces the most noteworthy effect . . . "It's very much my cup of tea," Hamilton says. But on his speaking tours this past winter he realized that so much curiosity was being generated by what he was going to say at the climactic moment that he felt bound to work something up. In the evenings he would sit around and let his imagination take over: As he watched the Aaron home run arch into the seats his lips murmured; the sentences formed; the facts crowded his mind, especially the similarities between Aaron and Babe Ruth—that the two of them were born just a day apart in February, that both hit the 714th home run at the same age (40), both as members of the Braves' organization. Hamilton decided to announce much of this material as Aaron circled the bases after hitting 715, using each base as a marker along the way (" . . . he steps on second . . . and the Babe's great record, nearly two-score years old . . . and he steps on third . . . a great day for Aquarians! Both Henry and the Babe . . . ").

Many experts argue that Willie Mays would have had a better shot at Ruth's record had he not played in the pitcher-friendly Candlestick Park for much of his career. Willie McCovey, Mays's teammate from 1959 to 1972, managed to hit 521 while spending most of his days in San Francisco. The Giants are the franchise with the most members of the 500 club: Ott, Mays, McCovey, and Bonds.

As for the phrases at the moment of impact, Hamilton decided on "Henry has tied the Babe!" for home run 714, and for 715, the tiebreaker, he chose, after much thought, "Baseball has a new home run king! It's Henry Aaron!"—not earth-shaking (nor in the case of the latter especially grammatical), but functional. Hamilton realized that anything more ornate would sound hollow and forced.

When the great moment came, however, spontaneity took over despite Hamilton's best intentions. The planned sequence of comparing Ruth and Aaron was wiped out of mind because of the speed with which Aaron circled the bases (not being one to slow down and glory in the occasion), the tremendous crowd noise and a violent eruption of fireworks exploding above the center-field rim of the stadium. Even the word king, which Hamilton had intended to say, came out champion. "It's gone!" he cried. "It's 715! There's a new home run champion of all time! And it's Henry Aaron!" But mainly, Hamilton was startled during his commentary by something he had never seen before in his nine years of describing the Braves in action: As Aaron turned third base, his solemn face suddenly broke into a bright grin, as surprising to see, considering his usual mien, as if he had started doing an Irish jig coming down the base path toward the plate. Hamilton was struck by it, but he never had time to describe it to his audience; by the time he recovered, Aaron was running into the pack of players and dignitaries, with more streaming from both benches and the grandstand, and Hamilton had these things to describe to his listeners. But Aaron beaming was the one sight, he said later, that he would particularly remember of that day . . .

THE HITTER

Aaron himself does not remember smiling, or very much else about that run around the bases. The tension, the long haul, the discomfiture of the constant yammering, the hate mail—perhaps all of that was symbolized by 715, and to hit it produced a welcome mental block. Aaron has always said that the most important home run in his life was 109, an undistinguished number, but it was a home run hit in the eleventh inning of a 2-2 tie game that defeated the St. Louis Cardinals and gave the Braves the 1957 pennant. Aaron has a very clear memory of his reaction as he circled the base paths in that enormous tumult of rejoicing. He suddenly remembered Bobby Thomson's Miracle Home Run and how he had heard about it over somebody's radio as he was coming home from school in Mobile, Ala., and how he had begun running as if coming down from third toward his teammates waiting at an imaginary plate.

"That had always been my idea of the most important homer," Aaron said after hitting his pennant-winner. "Now I've got one for myself. For the first time in my life, I'm excited."

A home run of that sort, meaning one that produced a playoff or championship victory, is obviously Aaron's idea of an "important" home run. But about 715 he remembers only his relief that it was over with and a vague happiness; that his legs seemed rubbery as he took the tour of the bases, the Dodger second baseman and shortstop sticking out their hands to congratulate him. "I don't remember the noise," he said, trying to recall, "or the two kids that I'm told ran the bases with me. My teammates at home plate. I remember seeing them. I remember my mother out there, and she hugging me. That's what I'll remember more than anything about that home run when I think back on it. I don't know where she came from, but she was there . . . "

Above, top: Towering four-hundred-foot home runs get the crowds out of their seats and fill the highlight reels, but great fielding can be as important for winning ballgames. Brooks Robinson was the recipient of sixteen consecutive Gold Glove Awards while playing third base for the Baltimore Orioles, and the team won four pennants and two championships during his tenure. Robinson also clouted 268 homers in his career.

Above, bottom: At about the same time that Hank Aaron was closing in on the home run record, Lou Brock was chasing Ty Cobb's career stolen base mark. He passed Cobb in 1977, but he made headlines in 1974 by breaking the single-season record with 118 thefts. Here he slides in safely for number 105 on the season, putting him ahead of previous record-holder Maury Wills.

DISTANCE
THE ELUSIVE BOB GIBSON
from *Game Time* by Roger Angell

NO WORD WAS more often used to describe Bob Gibson's presence on the pitcher's mound than "intimidating." Staring down from his six-foot-one-inch frame, Gibson was a fierce competitor who instilled fear in opposing batters. His 1968 season is simply one of the best the game has ever seen.

Roger Angell, longtime fiction editor for the *New Yorker* magazine, is one of the pre-eminent baseball writers around. *Game Time* is a collection of many of his greatest writings from the last four decades. Previous collections of Angell's baseball essays include *The Summer Game*, *Five Seasons*, and *Late Innings*.

On the afternoon of October 2, 1968—a warm, sunshiny day in St. Louis—Mickey Stanley, the Detroit Tiger shortstop, singled to center field to lead off the top of the ninth inning of the opening game of the 1968 World Series. It was only the fifth hit of the game for the Tigers, who by this time were trailing the National League Champion St. Louis Cardinals by a score of 4-0, so there were only minimal sounds of anxiety among the 54,692 spectators—hometown rooters, for the most part—in the stands at Busch Stadium. The next batter, the dangerous Al Kaline, worked the count to two and two and then fanned, swinging away at a fastball, to an accompanying roar from the crowd. A moment later, there was a second enormous cheer, louder and more sustained than the first. The Cardinal catcher, Tim McCarver, who had straightened up to throw the ball back to his pitcher, now hesitated. The pitcher, Bob Gibson, a notoriously swift worker on the mound, motioned to his battery mate to return the ball. Instead, McCarver pointed with his gloved hand at something behind Gibson's head. Gibson, staring uncomprehendingly at his catcher, yelled, "Throw the goddam ball back, will you! C'mon, c'mon, let's go!" Still holding the ball, McCarver pointed again, and Gibson, turning around, read the illuminated message on the center-field scoreboard,

Bob Gibson was a force on the mound. His extraordinary 1968 season included 22 wins against 9 losses, 28 complete games, 13 shutouts, 268 strikeouts, and an ERA of 1.12—the best baseball had seen in more than half a century. Gibson was an all-around athlete, winning nine straight Gold Gloves from 1965 to 1973.

which perhaps only he in the ballpark had not seen until that moment: "Gibson's fifteenth strikeout in one game ties the all-time World Series record held by Sandy Koufax." Gibson, at the center of a great tureen of noise, dug at the dirt of the mound with his spikes and then uneasily doffed his cap. ("I *hate* that sort of thing," he said later.) With the ball retrieved at last, he went to work on the next Tiger, Norm Cash, a left-handed batter, who ran the count to two and two, fouled off several pitches, and then struck out, swinging at a slider. Gibson, a long-legged, powerfully built righthander, whose habitual aura of glowering intensity on the mound seemed to deepen toward rancor whenever his club was ahead in the late stages of a game, now swiftly attacked the next Detroit hitter, Willie Horton. Again the count went to two and two and stuck there while Horton fouled off two or three pitches. Gibson stretched and threw again, and Horton, a righty batter, flinched away from the pitch, which seemed headed for his rib cage, but the ball, another slider, broke abruptly away under his fists and caught the inside corner of the plate. Tom Gorman, the home-plate umpire, threw up his right hand, and the game was over. McCarver, talking about this moment not long ago (he is now a radio and television broadcaster with the Phillies), said, "I can still see that last pitch, and I'll bet Willie Horton thinks to this day that the ball hit him—that's how much it broke. Talk about a batter *shuddering!*"

Bob Gibson's one-game World Series record of seventeen strikeouts stands intact, and so do my memories of that famous afternoon. In recent weeks, I have firmed up my recollections by consulting the box score and the inning-by-inning

Right: In the opening game of the 1968 World Series, Gibson set a postseason record for strikeouts in a game, fanning eighteen Detroit Tigers. It was also Gibson's sixth consecutive series win going back to 1964 and his sixth consecutive complete game, records he would extend to seven in Game 4 of the '68 series. Gibson's 7-2 record with 92 strikeouts and a 1.89 ERA in four World Series place him among the best October mounds-men of all time.

Below: The powerful high-kick delivery of Juan Marichal caused many a batter to flinch as the ball came hurtling toward the plate. He never received the accolades bestowed upon contemporaries Gibson and Koufax—and is probably best remembered for hitting Johnny Roseboro in the head with a baseball bat—but Marichal was nearly as successful, topping 20 wins six times in a seven-year span.

recapitulations of the game, by watching filmed highlights of the play, and by talking to a number of participants, including Gibson himself. (He had had no idea, he told me, that he was close to a record that afternoon. "You're concentrating so hard out there that you don't think of those things," he said.) Gibson seemed to take absolute charge of that game in the second inning, when he struck out the side on eleven pitches. By the end of four innings, he had run off eight strikeouts. Not until I reexamined the box score, however, did I realize that there had been only two ground-ball outs by the Tigers in the course of nine innings. This, too, must be a record (baseball statistics, for once, don't tell us), but the phenomenally low figure, when taken along with the seventeen strikeouts, suggests what kind of pitching the Tiger batters were up against that afternoon. Most National League batters in the 1960s believed that Gibson's fastball compared only with the blazers thrown by the Dodgers' Sandy Koufax (who retired in 1966 with an arthritic elbow) and by the Reds' Jim Maloney. Gibson's pitch flashed through the strike zone with a unique, upward-moving, right-to-left sail that snatched it away from a right-handed batter or caused it to jump up and in at a left-handed swinger—a natural break of six to eight inches—and hitters who didn't miss the ball altogether usually fouled it off or nudged it harmlessly into the air. The pitch, which was delivered with a driving, downward flick of Gibson's long forefinger and middle finger (what pitchers call "cutting the ball"), very much resembled an inhumanly fast slider, and was often taken for such by batters who were unfamiliar with his stuff. Joe Pepitone, of the Yankees, concluded the All-Star Game of 1965 by fanning on three successive Gibson fastballs and then shook his head and called out to the pitcher, "Throw me that slider one more time!" Gibson, to be sure, did have a slider—a superior breaking pitch that arrived, disconcertingly, at about three-quarters of the speed of the fastball and, most of the time, with exquisite control. Tim McCarver, who caught Gibson longer than anyone else, says that Gibson became a great pitcher during the summer of 1966 (his sixth full season in the majors), when he achieved absolute mastery of the outside corner of the plate while pitching to right-handed batters and—it was the same pitch, of course—the inside corner to left-handed batters. He could hit this sliver of air with his fastball or his slider with equal consistency, and he worked the opposite edge of the plate as well. "He *lived* on the corners," McCarver said. A third Gibson delivery was a fastball that broke downward instead of up and away; for this pitch, he held the ball with his fingers parallel to the seams (instead of across the seams, as was the case with the sailer), and he twisted his wrist counterclockwise as he threw—"turning it over," in mound parlance. He also had a curveball, adequate but unextraordinary, that he threw mostly to lefthanders and mostly for balls, to set up an ensuing fastball. But it was the combination of the devastating slider and the famous fastball (plus some other, less tangible assets that we shall get to in time) that made Gibson almost untouchable at his best, just as Sandy Koufax's down-diving curveball worked in such terrible (to hitters) concert with his illustrious upriding fastball.

"Hitting is rhythm," McCarver said to me, "and if you allow major-league hitters to see only one pitch—to swing repeatedly through a certain area of the plate—eventually they'll get to you and begin to hit it, even if it's a great fastball. But anybody who can control and switch off between two first-class pitches will make the hitters start reaching, either in or out, and then the game belongs to the pitcher. Besides all that, Bob had such great stuff and was so intimidating out there that he'd make the batter open up his front shoulder just a fraction too fast, no matter what the count was. The other key to good hitting, of course, is keeping that shoulder—the left shoulder for a right-handed batter, I mean, and vice versa—in place, and the most common flaw is pulling it back. Gibson had guys pulling back that shoulder who normally wouldn't be caught dead doing it. Their ass was in the dugout, as we say."

Mike Shannon, who played third base behind Gibson in the 1968 Series opening game (he didn't handle the ball once), remembers feeling pity for the Detroit batters that afternoon. "Most of them had never seen Gibby before," he said, "and they had no *idea* what they were up against." Shannon, who is now a television game announcer with the Cards, told me that he encounters some of the 1968 Tigers from time to time in the course of his baseball travels, and that they almost compulsively want to talk about the game. "It's as if they can't believe it to this day," he said. "But neither can I. I've never seen major-league hitters overmatched that way. It was like watching a big-league pitcher against Little League batters. It was frightening."

Gibson, of course, was already a celebrated winning pitcher by 1968. Like many other fans, I had first become aware of his fastball and his unique pitching mannerisms and his burning intensity on the mound when he won two out of the three games he

Along with lefty Steve Carlton, New York's Tom Seaver succeeded Gibson, Koufax, and Marichal as the pitching superstars of the National League in the 1970s. After winning the Rookie of the Year Award in 1967, "Tom Terrific" went on to capture three Cy Young Awards, win over 300 games, and strike out more than 3,000 batters. He struck at least 200 batters in a record nine consecutive seasons (1968–76).

pitched against the Yankees in the 1964 World Series, including a tense, exhausting victory in the clinching seventh game. Then, in 1967, I had watched him capture three of the Cardinals' four October victories over the Red Sox, again including the seventh game—a feat that won him the Most Valuable Player award for that Series. I had also seen him work eight or ten regular-season games over the previous five years or more. Although he was of only moderate size for a pitcher—six feet one and about a hundred and eighty-five pounds—Gibson always appeared to take up a lot of space on the mound, and the sense of intimidation that McCarver mentioned had something to do with his sombre, almost funereal demeanor as he stared in at his catcher, with his cap pulled low over his black face and strong jaw, and with the ball held behind his right hip (he always wore a sweatshirt under his uniform, with the long, Cardinals-red sleeves extending all the way down to his wrists), and with his glove cocked on his left hip, parallel to the ground. Everything about him looked mean and loose—arms, elbows, shoulders, even his legs—as, with a quick little shrug, he launched into his delivery. When there was no one on base, he had an old-fashioned full crank-up, with the right foot turning in midmotion to slip into its slot in front of the mound and his long arms coming together over his head before his backward lean, which was deep enough to require him to peer over his left shoulder at his catcher while his upraised left leg crooked and kicked. The ensuing sustained forward drive was made up of a medium-sized stride of that leg and a blurrily fast, slinglike motion of the right arm, which came over at about three-quarters height and then snapped down and (with the fastball and the slider) across his left knee. It was not a long dropdown delivery like Tom Seaver's (for contrast), or a tight, brisk, body-opening motion like Whitey Ford's.

The pitch, as I have said, shot across the plate with a notable amount of right-to-left (from Gibson's vantage point) action, and his catchers sometimes gave the curious impression that they were cutting off a ball that was headed on a much

Bottom, left: Perhaps the man that most closely resembles Bob Gibson's aggressive style and belief that home plate belongs to the pitcher, Pedro Martinez never shies away from throwing high and tight. As a result, he has the highest winning percentage among active pitchers and the lowest career earned run average of any starting pitcher since World War II. Five times he has led the league in both fewest walks per nine innings and most strikeouts per nine innings.

Bottom, right: Roger Clemens won his first three Cy Young Awards pitching in Boston for the Red Sox. He won his sixth award while donning the uniform of the arch-rival Yankees. In between he picked up two with the Blue Jays. Aside from being the only man to win seven Cy Youngs—across three decades, no less—Clemens is also just one of three men to strike out 4,000 batters and win 300 games. (Carlton and Ryan are the others.) Clemens's competitive fire allowed him to remain dominant into his forties.

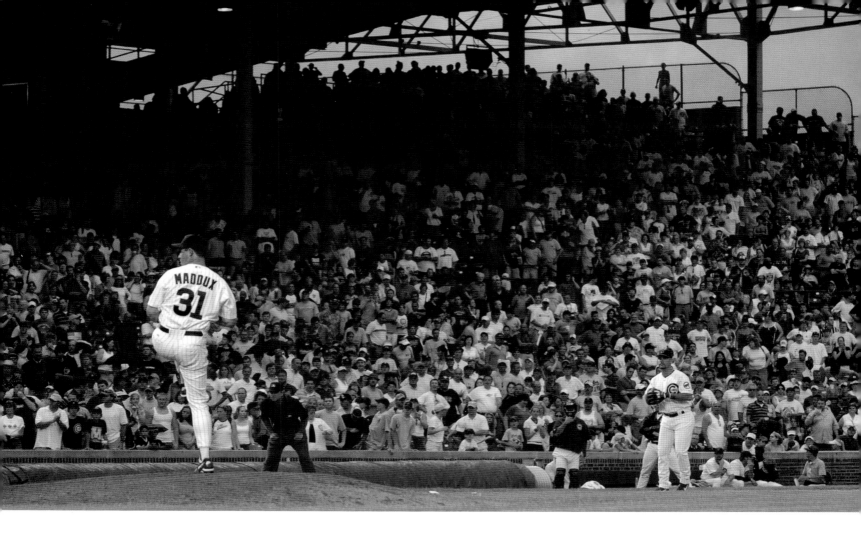

longer journey—a one-hundred-foot fastball. But with Gibson pitching you were always a little distracted from the plate and the batter, because his delivery continued so extravagantly after the ball was released that you almost felt that the pitch was incidental to the whole affair. The follow-through sometimes suggested a far-out basketball move—a fast downcourt feint. His right leg, which was up and twisted to the right in the air as the ball was let go (all normal enough for a right-handed pitcher), now continued forward in a sudden sidewise rush, crossing his planted left leg, actually stepping over it, and he finished with a full running step toward the right-field foul line, which wrenched his body in the same direction, so that he now had to follow the flight of the ball by peering over his right shoulder. Both his arms whirled in the air to help him keep his balance during this acrobatic maneuver, but the key to his overpowering speed and stuff was not the strength of his pitching arm—it was the powerful, driving thrust of his legs, culminating in that final extra step, which brought his right foot clomping down on the sloping left-hand side of the mound, with the full weight of his body slamming and twisting behind it. (Gibson's arm never gave him undue trouble, but he had serious difficulties with his knees in the latter stages of his career, and eventually had to have a torn cartilage removed from the right knee, which had pushed off to start all the tens of thousands of his pitches over the years and had then had to withstand the punishing force of the last stage of his unique delivery.) All in all, the pitch and its extended amplifications made it look as if Gibson were leaping at the batter, with hostile intent. He always looked much closer to the plate at the end than any other pitcher; he made pitching seem unfair.

Greg Maddux has used a combination of pitches and precision placement to leave hitters helpless at the plate for nearly two decades. He won at least 15 games in every season from 1988 through 2004—a record seventeen in a row. His ERA was a full run under the league average in ten of eleven seasons, and in 1994 and 1995, his sub-2.00 ERAs were more than two runs below the league average. He was the first pitcher ever to win four consecutive Cy Young Awards.

THE EDUCATION OF SAMMY SOSA

by Tom Verducci

AT THE HALFWAY **point of the 1998 baseball season,** *Sports Illustrated*'s Tom Verducci wrote that Sammy Sosa was having a "highly impressive" year to that point. Of course, that was only the beginning. Sosa finished the season with 66 home runs (second to Mark McGwire's 70), a league-high 158 RBI, and a .308 average in his MVP campaign. A year later he joined McGwire as the only players to twice hit more than 60 homers; in 2001 Sammy Sosa created a category all to himself by posting a third season with 60-plus homers.

Tom Verducci is a senior writer for *Sports Illustrated* and co-author of Joe Torre's autobiography, *Chasing the Dream*.

Sammy Sosa, who [in 1993] became the first Chicago Cub to steal 30 bases in a season while hitting 30 home runs, has recorded a highly impressive first half of the 1998 season. Sosa has hit for a .339 average, and in a one-month stretch hit 21 home runs.

Having learned that his personal goals and those of the team can be reached with a single stroke, the Cubs slugger produced the greatest home run streak the game has ever seen.

Sammy Sosa used to wear a millstone around his neck. It was a gold pendant approximately the size of a manhole cover, hung from a chain that seemed fashioned from a suspension-bridge cable. The bauble was inscribed with a drawing of two crossed bats and bore the numbers 30-30, inlaid with diamonds. The Chicago Cubs outfielder wore it when he drove to Wrigley Field in his sports car, the one with the SS 30-30 license plates. Then he would place the pendant in a safe before games. "Did he play with it on?," says Chicago first baseman Mark Grace, shaking his head. "No way you could run with that on."

Sosa had commissioned the Liberace-style accessory in 1993, after he became the first Cub to hit 30 home runs and steal 30 bases in a season, a milestone he reached thanks to 26 frantic stolen base attempts (20 of them successful) in the last two months. Never before, it seemed, had anyone been so ecstatic about finishing in fourth place.

Sammy Sosa has replaced Ernie Banks as "Mr. Cub" in the eyes of many Chicago fans. He led the team in homers and runs batted in every year from 1994 to 2003, and he passed Banks for the franchise record in career home runs in 2004.

What a piece of work! And the pendant, too—unintentional symbol of a vacuous career—was something to behold. Numbers? Sure, Sosa had them. So did World B. Free, Eric Dickerson and Imelda Marcos. Partly a creation of Wrigley Field's cozy dimensions, the notoriously undisciplined Sosa through his first nine seasons racked up nearly as many strikeouts as hits and approached his defensive responsibilities as if he thought "cutoff man" was a John Bobbitt reference. At week's end he had played 1,159 games without getting to the postseason—more than any active player except the Devil Rays' Dave Martinez (1,502) and the Indians' Travis Fryman (1,166).

Last season was vintage Sosa, beginning in spring training, when in response to a question about the possibility of his hitting 50 home runs, Sosa replied, "Why not 60?" His was most probably the worst year ever by anyone with 36 dingers and 119 RBIs. Behind that impressive-looking facade, Sosa hit poorly with runners in scoring position (.246), was virtually an automatic out on any two-strike count (.159), whiffed more times than anyone else in the National League (174), had a worse on-base percentage than Atlanta Braves pitcher Tom Glavine (.300 to .310), and again ran with such recklessness trying for 30-30 (he didn't get there, finishing with 22 steals in 34 attempts) that manager Jim Riggleman was once forced to scold him in the dugout in full view of the television cameras. Oh, yes—and the Cubs finished 68-94.

"I think there comes a time in every player's career when he plays for the team and doesn't worry anymore about getting established or putting up numbers," says Chicago shortstop Jeff Blauser. Sosa's time is now. Buoyed by the best lineup that's ever surrounded him on the Cubs, Sosa has put together a monster first half as rich in substance as it is in style. At 29 and in his 10th big league season, Sosa has at last begun to take more pitches, hit the ball to the opposite field and realize that the only piece of jewelry that really matters is a championship ring. Only his numbers are gaudy now.

At week's end he was hitting .339—82 points better than his career average—and had cut down on his strikeouts, increased his walks and launched one of the most outrageous power streaks the game has known. From May 25 through June 21, Sosa slammed 21 home runs in 22 games. In four weeks he exceeded the career seasonal highs of every one of his teammates except leftfielder Henry Rodriguez.

What's more, in June's first 21 days Sosa hit more home runs (17) than any man ever hit in the entire month, blasting Babe Ruth (1930), Bob Johnson (1934), Roger Maris (1961) and Pedro Guerrero (1985) from the record book while closing in on the record of 18 for any month, held by the Detroit Tigers' Rudy York (August 1937).

He popped home runs like vitamins last week: three on Monday, one on Wednesday, two on Friday and two on Saturday. Of course, he hit all of them at Wrigley, where in the last three years he has hit twice as many as he has on the road (71 to 35). So hot was Sosa that Grace jumped on his lap in the clubhouse last Thursday, rubbed against him and yelled, "Gimme some of that!" And that was before Sosa hit a 375-foot missile on Friday with a splintered bat and a 461-foot lunar probe Saturday—the June record-breaker—that crashed a viewing party atop an apartment building on Waveland Avenue. Just call him Babe Roof. "I think he ruined the barbecued chicken," Blauser says.

Says Grace of Sosa's June explosion, "I've seen a lot of things in this game, but I've never seen anything like this. The game of baseball has never seen anything like it. I really don't have words for it."

While Sosa wore out pitchers and thesauruses alike, the big payoff was that the Cubs were still hanging within four games of the first-place Houston Astros in the National League Central at week's

Sosa's trademark "home run hop" has been seen countless times by the Wrigley Field faithful. Although he has led the league just twice, Sosa is one of only two players in history to top 35 homers in nine consecutive seasons, accomplished from 1995 to 2003; the other is Jimmie Foxx. Sosa and McGwire are the only sluggers to hit 50-plus in four straight years.

end. For the first time in his life Sosa was hearing his faithful flock of right-field fans chanting, "M-V-P! M-V-P!" More telling, when reporters asked him about possibly outgunning Ruth and Maris over the full season, Sosa rolled his eyes in embarrassment and said quietly, "Oh, God. I'll just let you people take care of that. I don't want you to put me in that kind of company."

Why not 60? This time Sosa said, "I'll let you know after the year is over."

Grace says, "He's done 30-30, been player of the week, player of the month, an all-star, but now I think he knows there's nothing like having a good season and winning."

Sosa has reached a comfort zone. That it took so long in coming should not be such a surprise. Not when you consider that he didn't play organized ball until he was 14. Not when you take into account that he grew up selling oranges for 10 cents and shining shoes for 25 cents on Dominican street corners to help his widowed mother make ends meet. Not when you learn that home for him, his mother, four brothers and two sisters was a two-room unit in what once served as a public hospital. Each night when he put his head down on that wafer of a mattress on the floor, he didn't dream of playing baseball in a tailored uniform on manicured fields. He dreamed of his next meal.

The scout invited two kids to a field in San Pedro de Macoris for a tryout in 1985. Sosa was the one in the borrowed uniform and the spikes with the hole in them. He was sixteen years old and carried only 150 pounds on his 5'-10" frame. The scout made a mental note that the boy looked malnourished.

The scout timed him at 7.5 seconds for 60 yards. Not great. The kid's swing was, by his own admission now, "crazy"—all long and loopy. But the scout liked the way the ball jumped off his bat, and he liked the way the kid did everything on the field aggressively. So the scout, Omar Minaya of the Texas Rangers, eventually made his way to the Sosa home ("No bigger than the average one-bedroom apartment or large studio," Minaya recalls) and came up with an offer of $3,500. Sosa took it. He gave almost all of it to his mother, Lucrecia, allowing himself one modest extravagance: He bought himself his first bicycle.

Sosa's lighthearted, easy-going attitude toward baseball and life has made him popular with fans around the league and around the world, particularly in his home country of the Dominican Republic. Here he signs autographs for kids and adults at Busch Stadium, home of the longtime Cubs rivals, the St. Louis Cardinals.

The following year he was at the airport leaving for some place called Port Charlotte, Fla., without knowing a bit of English. As he looked over his shoulder, the last thing he saw was Lucrecia crying.

Only three years after that—only five years after he took his older brother Luis's advice to play baseball—he was in the big leagues. By the time he was 23, Sosa was playing for his third team, the Cubs. The Rangers and the Chicago White Sox each chose not to wait to see if he would acquire polish, trading him for veterans.

"When he first got here [in 1992], you could see he had great physical skills, but he was so raw," Grace says. "He didn't know how to play the game. He didn't understand the concept of hitting behind runners. He didn't understand the concept of hitting the cutoff man to keep a double play in order. So many little things he just didn't know."

This much he did know: If he was going to support his mother and family, it wasn't going to happen with the bat on his shoulder. "It's not easy for a Latin player to take 100 walks," Sosa says. "If I knew the stuff I know now seven years ago—taking pitches, being more relaxed—I would have put up even better numbers. But people have to understand where you're coming from.

"When I was with the White Sox, Ozzie Guillen said to me, 'Why do you think about money so much?' I said, 'I've got to take care of my family.' And he told me, 'Don't think about money. Just go out and play, and the money will be there.' It takes a while."

Sammy Sosa and eight fellow Dominicans from the Cubs and Cardinals line up with Hall of Fame pitcher Juan Marichal and President Leonel Fernandez of the Dominican Republic at Busch Stadium in 1999. More than 350 Dominican-born players have reached the Major Leagues since the 1950s, including more than 60 from Sosa's hometown of San Pedro de Macoris.

Says Minaya, "You've got to understand something about Latin players when they're young—or really any players from low economic backgrounds. They know the only way to make money is by putting up offensive numbers. Only now is Sammy at a mature stage. Only now is he becoming the player he always could have been."

Midway through last season the Cubs provided Sosa, already a millionaire, with $42.5 million of added security by way of a four-year extension, a contract that astonished many observers. Sosa had never scored 100 runs, had never had 175 hits and had made fewer all-star teams in the '90s (one) than Scott Cooper. Atlanta Braves manager Bobby Cox refused to add him to the all-star team in 1996 even though Sosa was leading the league in home runs at the break. Equally unimpressed fans had never voted him higher than ninth in the balloting. Even this year he is running only sixth among National League outfielders.

"We saw a five-tool player who was coming into what are the prime years for most guys, and who probably couldn't find the trainer's room because he's never [hurt]," says Chicago general manager Ed Lynch, explaining the thinking behind the extension. "The one important variable was Sammy's maturity as a player. We were banking that he would continue to improve."

Upon signing his new deal, Sosa did not buy a bicycle. He bought a 60-foot yacht that he christened *Sammy Jr.* By then he also owned, he says, "eight or 10 cars"—he can't remember exactly, though he is sure he has a Rolls-Royce, a Ferrari, a Viper, two Mercedes, a Hummer, a Navigator and an Expedition. Lucrecia is now living in the third house her son has bought for her, each one bigger than the last.

Cubs hitting coach Jeff Pentland gave Sosa a video to take home after last season, though he did so without great expectations. "I don't think he knew I existed last year," Pentland says.

The video included batting clips of three players: the Braves' Chipper Jones, Grace and Sosa. The tape showed that all three tapped their front foot on the ground as a trigger mechanism for their swing. But while Jones and Grace tapped their foot as the ball was halfway to the plate, Sosa would tap his when the ball was nearly on top of him, resulting in a wildly hurried swing. "We needed to come up with some way for him to read and recognize pitches sooner," Pentland says, "and that way we'd be able to slow him down."

A few weeks later Pentland called Sosa in the Dominican Republic. "All I care about are two stats: 100 walks and 100 runs scored," Pentland told him.

"And one more," Sosa said. "I want to hit .300."

Sosa spent much of the winter working on hitting the ball to right field. Meanwhile, the Cubs traded for or signed veterans Blauser, Mickey Morandini and Rodriguez, their first bona fide left-handed power threat since Rick Monday a quarter of a century ago. Since the season began, centerfielder Brant Brown and utilityman Jose Hernandez (22 home runs combined) have emerged from

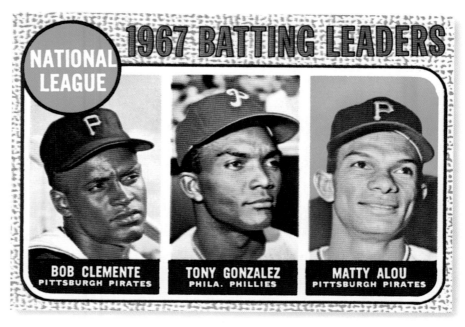

1967 BATTING LEADERS

NATIONAL LEAGUE

BOB CLEMENTE
PITTSBURGH PIRATES

TONY GONZALEZ
PHILA. PHILLIES

MATTY ALOU
PITTSBURGH PIRATES

Left: Roberto Clemente was one of the first true superstars from Latin America. Born in Puerto Rico, he debuted with the Pirates in 1955 and went on to collect 3,000 career hits and four batting crowns before he died tragically in an airplane crash delivering relief supplies to earthquake victims in Nicaragua in 1972. The spectacular-fielding Clemente won twelve consecutive Gold Glove Awards.

Above: The changing demographics of Major League baseball was evident by the late 1960s. In 1967, the top hitters in the National League were Puerto Rican–born Clemente, Cuban-born Tony Gonzalez, and Dominican-born Matty Alou. The previous year saw three players from the Dominican Republic top the NL batting list: Matty Alou, his brother Felipe, and Rico Carty.

Above: The Cleveland Indians were one of the first teams to fully make use of the talents of Latino ballplayers. In 1951, the roster featured (left to right) Orestes "Minnie" Minoso, Mike Garcia, Bobby Avila, Jesse Flores, and manager Al Lopez. (The Spanish-speaking Garcia and Lopez were both born in the United States.)

Facing page: Ichiro Suzuki, one of more than a dozen Japanese-born Major Leaguers in 2004, represents baseball's growing international flavor. Known simply as Ichiro, he burst onto the scene in 2001 as the first Japanese position player in the majors, capturing Rookie of the Year *and* Most Valuable Player awards. This multi-tool talent led the league in steals his rookie year and has won a Gold Glove in each of his first four seasons. In 2004, he set a new single-season hits record, with 262, breaking George Sisler's eighty-four-year-old mark of 257.

part-time roles as full-time surprises, and Grace, who bats behind Sosa against righthanders, was third in the league in hitting at week's end.

"There was too much pressure last year," Sosa says. "Pressure from the contract, pressure to do it all. I felt if I didn't hit a home run, we wouldn't win. I was trying to hit two home runs in one at bat. Now I don't feel that anymore."

Said Philadelphia Phillies manager Terry Francona last Friday after a 9-8 win over the Cubs, "Sosa's scary, especially when he puts the ball in the air in [Wrigley]. He doesn't chase pitches the way he used to. And the guy behind him scares me, too. I went out to talk to my pitcher, and the guy on deck [Grace] was smiling at me. He was dying to get up there. He was basically telling me, Go ahead and walk him. I'll drive him in. It's pick your poison."

Not once in 16 straight plate appearances against Philadelphia last weekend did Sosa swing at the first pitch. (Last year he had 84 one-pitch at bats; almost halfway through this season he has 16.) Two strikes aren't deadly for him anymore, either. In those counts, through Sunday, he had improved to .232 with 13 home runs, four more than he hit in such situations all of last year. The tried-and-true strategy for retiring Sosa—getting ahead on the count and making him chase pitches farther and farther off the plate—no longer applies.

"And he's not missing mistakes," says Phillies catcher Mark Parent, a former teammate of Sosa's. "That's the big thing for all good hitters—McGwire, Griffey and those guys. They don't swing at bad balls, and they hammer mistakes. They make you pay for every mistake. That's what Sammy's doing.

"The other day, [Mark] Portugal tried to sneak a fastball by him on the outside, and boom—home run, right field. You didn't have to worry about those homers to right in the past, because he pulled off those balls. But he ain't pulling off now."

Every day before batting practice Sosa and Pentland meet in the batting tunnel under the right-field bleachers at Wrigley. Pentland flips him baseballs to hit. He tosses them not on a line, as normally occurs with this drill, but in a high, slow arc. That way Sosa must wait, with his hands back, before finally unleashing his swing and belting the ball into a net where the right side of the field would be. The drill teaches patience. Sosa at last understands. The 30-30 pendant is a relic now, no longer found around his neck but in a display case at his home in the Dominican, like some artifact from another era.

BARRY BONDS
IS HE THE GREATEST EVER?

by John Thorn

TY COBB, BABE Ruth, Ted Williams, Willie Mays, Hank Aaron. It's difficult to deny that Barry Bonds belongs right up there with those legendary names in the pantheon of all-time greats. But where, exactly, he ranks is *the* question among baseball experts in the twenty-first century.

John Thorn has written, edited, and contributed to countless baseball works over the last three decades, including *The Hidden Game of Baseball* and *The Complete Armchair Book of Baseball*. In the seventh edition of *Total Baseball*, he explores Bonds's place in the lexicon of baseball immortals. (And keep in mind, this was written *before* Bonds captured MVP trophy number seven in another remarkable season in 2004.)

Barry Bonds has surpassed long-held records, changed the way his opponents play the game, and distanced himself from the performance level of his peers to a degree not thought possible, let alone made real, since the days of Babe Ruth. Over the course of half a century of paying serious attention to baseball, I have never seen anyone like him.

Through 2003, the man won six MVPs. He holds the single-season record in batting's most significant categories: home runs, slugging percentage, on-base average, and on-base plus slugging (OPS), that now ubiquitous measure of total batting excellence. He might have topped other important columns too, if he didn't also hold the record for bases on balls in a season (198). And while the all-time home-run record may prove to be his monument, the intentional base on balls is his enduring tribute.

Convinced that Bonds is the greatest? I didn't think so.

In fact, it is only once we put forward a reasonable answer that the question posed by the title begins to reverberate down the canyons of baseball history. Other gods of the past, not only Ruth but also Honus Wagner and Ty Cobb, rise up in protest. King Kelly and Buck Ewing wonder how they could have been forgotten when once they had been immortals. Until the day before yesterday, it seems, there was general agreement that in the "modern era"—the years after baseball integration—Ted Williams was the best pure hitter and Willie Mays the most complete player, while Hank Aaron was left to puzzle what he had to do to get a nod. Today's fans may support Alex Rodriguez as the greatest player in the game and perhaps one day the greatest ever, as Bonds will have turned forty before A-Rod hits thirty. And then there is Albert Pujols, who has accomplished so much in so short a time . . .

If one required proof that fame is fleeting and fortune fickle, consider that only three years ago this essay might have been titled, "Ken Griffey: The Greatest Ever?" At the All-Star Game in 1999, when Major League Baseball announced the fan balloting for the twenty-five spots on its All-Century Team, Griffey was the only active position player elected, with 645,389 votes; Bonds, who did not make the cut despite three MVPs in the decade, had 173,279.

In baseball the question "Who is the greatest ever?" is answered by a hero with a hundred faces, depending upon: (a) what we are measuring, (b) how we are measuring it, (c) when the measurement is made, (d) whom the plausible contenders may be, and (e) what recent development occasions the exercise.

The one knock against Barry Bonds early in his career was his failure in the postseason. Indeed, in three Championship Series with the Pittsburgh Pirates from 1990 to 1992, Bonds batted .191 with just one home run in 20 games. He redeemed himself in 2002, however, scorching Anaheim with four homers and a .471 average in the World Series. He took Jarrod Washburn deep in his first World Series at bat in Game 1.

DEFINING GREATNESS

There's no getting around it. We are going to have to agree what we mean when we talk about greatness. Are we naming the greatest hitter, pitcher, fielder, or all-around player? What factors constitute greatness—Branch Rickey's "five tools" (run, throw, catch, hit, and hit with power), or should we throw in some additional points for timely performance, especially in the World Series? Do we consider a man's present value only, or do we extrapolate his future proficiency as well as longevity? Do we care about what previous generations thought and why they thought it? Does character count? Are statistics the true-north guide to greatness?

When we say "great," do we really mean to say "best"? This is not merely a semantic quibble but the yawning gap between celebrity and skill. Achilles will always be a greater warrior than Patton, in no small measure because he had Homer as his advance man.

To assess skill it is invaluable to possess a sophisticated understanding of statistics, including the use of adjustments for era and home ballpark; we may look at the player panels in *Total Baseball* and count up the "black ink" entries that indicate league leadership in a category; we may tote up World Series and All-Star Game appearances; or we may look for a hidden code in arcane sabermetric figures as a key to greatness certain. To assess celebrity, on the other hand, it is necessary to learn how a player was viewed in his day, not

Bonds continues to rack up new honors and accomplishments as he approaches forty years of age. In 2004, the thirty-eight-year-old Bonds won his second batting title; he posted his record thirteenth consecutive season of 30-plus homers; he accumulated more than 200 free passes to shatter the record for walks in a season, while also striking out fewer than 40 times; and he became the first player ever to compile an on-base percentage above .600.

merely how he may be regarded at present. Yet to identify fame—an enduring place in the game's lore that is informed by the facts but stands outside and above them, like legend and myth—no metric is sufficient and no explanation fully satisfies.

Over the past two decades baseball sophisticates have derided the voting patterns and special selections of the Baseball Hall of Fame as a measure of nothing except sentimentality, foolishness, and cronyism. How did Rabbit Maranville get a plaque? Or Joe Tinker? Or Roger Bresnahan? Yet the Hall's purpose in honoring worthies of a bygone age, no longer famous but once so, has been to secure for them a sure pedestal in the pantheon, beyond challenge from future savants or the mere forgetfulness of a later generation. Examining the concept of a baseball pantheon, where renown may endure beyond records, provides a valuable context for understanding just where Barry Bonds fits in the grand scheme of things.

A BRIEF HISTORY OF FAME

The phrase "Baseball Hall of Fame" made its first appearance in the December 15, 1907, *Washington Post,* in a story about the top managers of the day, "the greatest galaxy of baseball brains." Barely three years later, *Baseball Magazine* announced its intention to form (in print, anyway) "The Hall of Fame for the Immortals of Baseball; Comprising the Greatest Players in the History of the Game." Inspiring the magazine's editors, no doubt, was the Hall of Fame for Great Americans, founded in New York City in 1900 (many mistakenly think that the Baseball Hall of Fame in Cooperstown was the nation's first such institution).

In the previous century Henry Chadwick had often rambled about the best players he had seen in his long exposure to the game, and he had done much to espouse statistics as the superior way to judge a player: "Many a dashing general player, who carries off a great deal of éclat in prominent matches, has all 'the gilt taken off the gingerbread,' as the saying is, by these matter-of-fact figures," he wrote in 1864. "And we are frequently surprised to find that the modest but efficient worker, who has played earnestly and steadily through the season, apparently unnoticed, has come in, at the close of the race, the real victor."

Chadwick's statistics, rudimentary as they were, were a necessary corrective to the flowery praise that came to so many early players for their pluck, their headiness, their dash and daring. As the number of statistics exploded in the 1870s, it became increasingly difficult to credit such intangibles; who was the greatest player of the age might still be left to those of a poetic bent, but identifying the best batter or fielder at a position was now a matter of record, in the *New York Clipper* and elsewhere. Not until the 1890s did newspapers begin to conduct surveys among veteran players as to who had been the top player of all, and the answers were most often Kelly, Ewing, and Cap Anson. The *Reach Guide* of 1894 featured a section entitled "Who Is the King Player?" that contained the opinions of such stalwarts as George Wright, Al Spalding, Fred Pfeffer, and Frank Selee, supporting the claims on fame of, respectively: Cal McVey; Wright and Ross Barnes; Kelly; and Ewing and Kelly.

Baseball Magazine's editors, notably Jacob C. Morse, took a new tack by moving beyond naming all-star teams of the season just past or soliciting old-timers to wrap

Although he has never led the league in stolen bases and, remarkably, only twice in home runs, Bonds is the only person in history with 500 career homers and 500 career stolen bases. The seven-time MVP has had five seasons with 30 thefts and 30 dingers, including the first-ever 40-40 season in 1996. Rounding out his otherworldly talents, Bonds collected eight Gold Gloves from 1990 to 1998.

themselves in nostalgic reverie. They sought to create a pantheon of heroes that would make Olympians of the best exponents of the national pastime, securing their places for all time, and they would take suggestions from their readers rather than

Even as a relatively scrawny youngster, Bonds was a premier player from the start. His first two MVP trophies came in a Pirates uniform in 1990 and 1992. (He finished second in 1991.) His lowest home run total was during his rookie year, when he hit 16 in 113 games, but he averaged 27 over his first six full seasons in Pittsburgh.

flog statistics or the opinions of one-time teammates. "It is a universal trait of humanity," they wrote in the January 1911 issue, "to wish to know who are the leaders, the tiptop men, in all kinds of human activity. We have ourselves felt a keen interest in selecting the All-America nine for the past season; and we know by the large degree of enthusiasm displayed in the public press, as well as in our own correspondence, that the general public was interested too.

"But the problem of selecting an All-America nine is a slight one compared with the task of picking out the greatest players in history. Here it would seem that the most ardent fan has the haziest kind of a notion, and the conflict among such opinions as are expressed, is very great.

"The older generation of fans is pretty much of the opinion that the old-time ball players were in a class by themselves, while the younger generation can see nothing but the brilliant feats of some of our present-day stars. The real unprejudiced truth, we imagine, lies somewhere between these two extremes . . .

"We can think of nothing more interesting in all baseball than a discussion of the greatest players which the game ever knew."

Over the next six months, *Baseball Magazine* named eighteen men to its Hall of Fame, beginning with "three names of famous ball players who, we feel sure, would be entitled to almost universal consent, to a place in our list." These three were Cap Anson, Ed Delahanty, and King Kelly. The last three named were the first whose careers were principally if not entirely in the new century: Nap Lajoie, Honus Wagner, and Ty Cobb. Of the twelve in between, six may come as a surprise to modern fans: pitcher Charlie Ferguson and outstanding fielders Ed Williamson, Charlie Bennett, Fred Pfeffer, Jerry Denny, and James Fogarty. Although these six were all well known to fans of 1911, only twenty-five years later, when Cooperstown began its election process, they were consigned to the dustbin of history, their reputations never to revive (as those of, for example, Roger Connor, Mickey Welch, and Sam Thompson would in the 1970s, thanks to *The Baseball Encyclopedia*'s unearthing of their statistical records).

As *Baseball Magazine* froze its Hall of Fame at eighteen immortals with the July issue, sportswriters for the daily newspapers began series on the greatest players. Most notable of these was former player Sam Crane's "Fifty Greatest Ball Players in History," for the *New York Evening Journal*, commencing in November 1911. Crane stopped the series at thirty, and included a few choices that may have stumped even his contemporaries (Archie Bush, Dupee Shaw) but by and large his subjects may have had more lasting influence with the public than the *Baseball Magazine* picks, as evidenced by their eventual elevation to Cooperstown: Harry Wright, Jim O'Rourke, Dickey Pearce, Candy Cummings, Hughie Jennings, Cy Young, John McGraw, and

Left: With his all-around talent, Ken Griffey Jr. was viewed as the successor to Aaron, Mays, and the rest when he joined the Mariners as a nineteen-year-old in 1989. He hit over 40 homers in every season from 1993 to 2000 (except the injury-shortened 1995) and had 400 for his career by the time he was thirty. Junior's aggressive play in the field brought him ten Gold Glove Awards, as well as many injuries. This leaping catch at the wall ended in a broken wrist that sidelined him for much of 1995.

Left: Vying with Bonds for the label of baseball's best player in the twenty-first century is Alex Rodriguez. While exhibiting grace and mastery with the glove, the six-foot-three-inch A-Rod brought power to a position traditionally known for defense—forgoing the Ozzie Smith mold of great shortstops for the Ernie Banks/Cal Ripken Jr. model. Along with Derek Jeter and Nomar Garciaparra, the American League of the late 1990s boasted as good a group of shortstops as the game has ever seen.

After coming to New York in 2004, Rodriguez shifted to third base while former rival Derek Jeter held the shortstop spot. Despite the change, A-Rod has maintained his superstar play. Considering that he has not even reached thirty years of age and is just shy of 400 career home runs, you can be certain that many records will fall by the wayside at the hands of Alex Rodriguez.

Roger Connor. Crane also named his twenty best of all time, including some players who weren't among the first thirty stories (such as Bill Lange and Willie Keeler) perhaps because he had arranged his fifty chronologically and had stopped at thirty.

In 1936 the Baseball Hall of Fame conducted its first elections, one polling 226 members of the Baseball Writers Association, the other an old-timers' committee of 78. The writers elected the "founding five" of Ruth, Wagner, Cobb, Christy Mathewson, and Walter Johnson; failing to get the required 170 votes were Lajoie, Tris Speaker, and Cy Young, all of whom were elected the following year. Grover Cleveland Alexander made the cut in 1938, and George Sisler, Eddie Collins, Willie Keeler, and Lou Gehrig entered in 1939. (Keeler thus became the only nineteenth-century player to be elected to the Hall; all the others were selected by committee.) In the veterans' election of 1936, no one garnered the necessary seventy-five percent. The two top vote-getters (tied at forty) were Anson and Ewing. By the time the Hall opened its doors on June 12, 1939, they were joined by old-timers Morgan Bulkeley, George Wright, Connie Mack, John McGraw, Henry Chadwick, Charles Comiskey, Candy Cummings, Al Spalding, Ban Johnson, and Alexander Cartwright.

Where *Baseball Magazine* had tabbed eighteen men in 1911, Cooperstown welcomed twenty-five—but only eight were honored in common. The early candidates for baseball's greatest player appeared to have been placed on not marble pedestals but greased poles.

When the Associated Press conducted a poll in 1950 to select the "Ten Most Outstanding in Sports," four were baseball players, if you count Jim Thorpe, the leading vote-getter; the three fulltime players were Ruth (second), Cobb (fourth), and Gehrig (ninth). When the AP conducted its Athlete of the Century poll in 1999, Ruth stood atop the heap, with Thorpe dropping to third. No other baseball player made it into the top ten. Of the one hundred athletes named, the only baseball players who commenced their careers after 1965 were Cal Ripken (82) and Mark McGwire (84). The message was clear: baseball is your father's game.

ESPN's Sports Century poll of that same year seconded the sentiment. Of the top one hundred athletes, twenty were selected for their baseball accomplishments alone, while three were multi-sport stars whose baseball exploits would not have been enough to place them on the list. Although twenty is a very respectable number, more than that for any other sport, this was a list topped by Michael Jordan and including many athletes only recently retired; ESPN's baseball players *all* had commenced their careers before 1965.

But 1999 also produced another poll, one unconcerned with other sports and designed to display the diamond of the present amid the glories of the past: Major League Baseball's All-Century Team. In a dry run in 1969, the centennial of professional baseball, the Baseball Writers Association had named Ruth the game's all-time outstanding player, outdistancing Cobb, Wagner, and DiMaggio, who was named the greatest living player. Thirty years later Joe was gone from the scene and, at a memorable All-Star Game at Boston's Fenway Park, an ailing Ted Williams, surrounded by the giants of the game, was its heartwarming embodiment of greatness.

A "blue-ribbon panel" (of which I was one) had selected the one hundred all-time greats from whom the fans, in a nationwide poll, would choose twenty-five. Then, because the popular vote had predictably given short shrift to some indisputable luminaries, the panel added five more (Warren Spahn, Lefty Grove, Stan Musial, Mathewson, and Wagner), plus four stars to honor the Negro Leagues (Oscar Charleston, Cool Papa Bell, Josh Gibson, and Buck Leonard; the absence of Satchel Paige was impossible to explain, unless he somehow integrated himself into oblivion by pitching in the "big leagues" after the age of forty-two).

The outcome was fascinating, as much for who was out as who was in, and for the disparities in vote totals among players who were statistically quite comparable. Ruth pulled in the most votes, with 1,158,044, but Aaron trailed him by less than 1,300. Williams, Mays, DiMaggio, Mantle, Cobb, Griffey, and Rose rounded out the outfield allotment. Where was Barry Bonds? Nowhere—eighteenth place in the vote totals, behind the no-less-snubbed Rickey Henderson.

During the 1980s, Andre Dawson displayed the power-speed combination that only a rare few have offered. One of four players in the exclusive 300-300 club (career home runs and stolen bases), Dawson also garnered eight Gold Gloves from 1980 to 1988. In his first season with the Chicago Cubs in 1987, Dawson won the league MVP with 49 round-trippers and 137 runs batted in, both league highs—and the Cubs still finished in last place.

The Evolution of Fame: The "Greatest" Through the Decades

1850s	Joe Leggett	Charles DeBost	Pete O'Brien	Louis Wadsworth	Frank Pidgeon
1860s	Charley Smith	Joe Start	**George Wright**	Dickey Pearce	**Jim Creighton**
1870s	Ross Barnes	Deacon White	**George Wright**	**Cap Anson**	Al Spalding
1880s	**King Kelly**	**Buck Ewing**	Ed Williamson	**Cap Anson**	John Clarkson
1890s	Ed Delahanty	Hugh Duffy	Willie Keeler	Bill Lange	Amos Rusie
1900s	Nap Lajoie	**Honus Wagner**	**Ty Cobb**	Rube Waddell	**Christy Mathewson**
1910s	Eddie Collins	Tris Speaker	**Ty Cobb**	Grover Alexander	**Walter Johnson**
1920s	**Babe Ruth**	Tris Speaker	Rogers Hornsby	George Sisler	Frankie Frisch
1930s	Jimmie Foxx	**Joe DiMaggio**	Lou Gehrig	Carl Hubbell	Lefty Grove
1940s	**Ted Williams**	**Joe DiMaggio**	Stan Musial	Ralph Kiner	**Bob Feller**
1950s	**Ted Williams**	Mickey Mantle	**Willie Mays**	Ernie Banks	Eddie Mathews
1960s	Frank Robinson	**Hank Aaron**	**Willie Mays**	Roberto Clemente	**Sandy Koufax**
1970s	Pete Rose	Joe Morgan	Johnny Bench	Reggie Jackson	Tom Seaver
1980s	Mike Schmidt	George Brett	Cal Ripken	Rickey Henderson	Nolan Ryan
1990s	Frank Thomas	Tony Gwynn	**Barry Bonds**	**Ken Griffey, Jr.**	Greg Maddux
2000s	Sammy Sosa	**Alex Rodriguez**	**Barry Bonds**	Albert Pujols	Vladimir Guerrero

At first base Lou Gehrig more than doubled Mark McGwire's vote but both made the team. George Sisler and Bill Terry brought up the rear with puny totals. Going around the horn, Jackie Robinson and Rogers Hornsby filled out second base, leaving no room for Collins or Lajoie. Shortstop went to Cal Ripken and, in an upset, Ernie Banks over not only Wagner but also Ozzie Smith. Third base went to Mike Schmidt and Brooks Robinson, far outdistancing Eddie Mathews.

As to the battery, catcher went to Johnny Bench and Yogi Berra by wide margins, with Gabby Hartnett, a sabermetric star, registering on only 24,196 ballots. Nolan Ryan topped all pitchers with 992,040 votes, with Sandy Koufax coming in second. Cy Young polled a very healthy 867,523 to come in third, proving that it is good have an award named after you.

The Hall of Fame's founding five all made the team (though Wagner and Mathewson required a boost from the panel). One active player made it (Griffey) and six others who had commenced their careers after 1965. Of the original pool of one hundred players, six were active and eighteen others had commenced their careers after 1965. The undertow of baseball's past was strong but the modern generation held its own.

Think of the All-Century One Hundred this way: if the Baseball Hall of Fame had not started up when it did, but instead at the end of the twentieth century, these are the men whose plaques would be on the wall. Sure, we would name some token representatives of the nineteenth century—maybe Anson, Ewing, Kelly, and Cartwright—and we could name Mack and McGraw as managers and maybe Ban Johnson and Bill Klem, and then look to the future for fresh nominees. But something irreplaceable would be lost. With mammoth statistical compendia available to us, we may be better equipped than our forefathers to assess achievement, but in perception of greatness they may have had an edge on us, because theirs was a more romantic age and they loved stories more than stats.

Is Bonds the greatest ever? Let's look at those who were once honored, as part of such a question. Every one of the men in the chart on the facing page, was once hailed as the greatest in his decade. Some, highlighted in **bold**, were called the greatest ever, regardless of position or era, and were still held high long after their playing days ended. Remember, this chart portrays not necessarily the men who were *the best,* as might be indicated by their statistics, but who won acclaim as *great* players—men of character, vigor, magnetism.

Studying what people believe to be true is often far more interesting than ascertaining what may actually be true, for even generally accepted falsehoods (the Abner Doubleday concoction, for example) reveal much about the hopes of an age. Legends are not mere falsehoods, however, but the end product of a process that begins in fact, extends to story, ascends to history, and ultimately transcends all of these to approach the realm of myth. From those heights, legend binds and nourishes a culture worn down and bored by humdrum fact . . . and thus becomes socially useful, as history used to be, and as embellished story captivated our forebears around the campfire. Barry Bonds may retain hold of his records for generations, but will

Above: Known for his ego almost as much as his baseball talents, Rickey Henderson played Major League baseball for twenty-five seasons, long enough to establish career records for stolen bases and runs scored. His steal of second base on April 28, 1991, brought him even with Lou Brock at 938; he passed Brock four days later. By the time he played his final season, at the age of forty-four, Henderson had nearly 500 more thefts than Brock.

Facing page: Similar to Barry Bonds, Eddie Murray came across as distant and aloof, particularly with the media. Consistent production on the field, however, put the switch-hitting Murray in rare company, with Aaron and Mays, for 500 homers and 3,000 hits. In his twenty full seasons, Murray had fewer than 20 homers only four times (never fewer than 15) and never fewer than 75 RBIs. He is the all-time RBI leader among switch-hitters.

Vladimir Guerrero has been a force at the plate since entering the league. In his first seven full Major League seasons, he drove in *and* scored at least 100 runs six times, hit more than 30 homers six times, hit over .300 seven times, stole more than 35 bases twice, and three times collected 200-plus hits. In the field, his powerful arm has been compared to that of legendary rightfielder Roberto Clemente.

stories attach to him the way they do to Kelly, Ruth, Cobb, Williams, and Mays? Or will his statistics have to speak for him, as they do for Rogers Hornsby or Jeff Bagwell?

EVALUATING THE CONTENDERS

Looking to the chart above, we may narrow the field. Kelly, Ewing, and Anson were the greats of their century. Creighton and Wright were the game's first heroes, and Creighton's role rapidly transformed to legend because he died in his prime; however, neither man was selected to the *Baseball Magazine* pantheon in 1911, so we may reasonably remove them from consideration now. Anson and Ewing made their mark in a game with very different rules, including in Anson's case a pitching distance that increased twice over the course of his career. For me, Kelly is the greatest player of the century: his on-field heroics were burnished by a folkloric combination of jester, knave, and fool, capped by a picturesque if premature demise (falling off a stretcher as he was taken to hospital with a fatal case of pneumonia, he is said to have remarked, "Boys, I've made me last slide"). Like Yogi, not half the things he said or did were so, but it doesn't matter.

When the game's rules stabilized in the first decade of the new century, two stars emerged who must still be considered today when we assess the greatest player ever: Wagner and Cobb. John McGraw, who had seen all the stars including Ruth, went to his grave in 1934 still favoring Wagner, in large part because he was not only a great hitter and baserunner but also splendid at the most difficult position in the field, excluding catcher. (That view—a good-hitting shortstop must be more valuable than a good-hitting outfielder or first baseman—has come around again, in support of Alex Rodriguez's candidacy.) All the same, in the Hall of Fame writers' ballot of 1936, Cobb's vote total was higher than that of either Wagner or Ruth, and it's impossible to ignore his all-time-high batting average and twelve batting titles in thirteen years. The greatest pitcher of the years before World War II was surely Walter Johnson, but he and his most excellent kin (Grove, Feller, Mathewson, Koufax) are excluded from consideration because their contribution to team success isn't as great as that of the top position players.

This brings us to Ruth, DiMaggio, and Williams as all-time greats who began or, in Ruth's case, completed their careers before racial integration, night ball, air travel, relief pitchers, or the proliferation of the slider. DiMaggio was esteemed for his style, his grace, his pinstripes, his World Series rings, his singular batting streak, and his silence, which was taken for grandeur. But he's not the batting equal of Williams, who maintained excellence over a much longer career, and the New York media that celebrated his ethereal charm is long gone. While DiMaggio's reputation dwindled over the last twenty years, that of Williams soared: statisticians were awed by his on-base average and younger fans embraced him as The Last American Hero; the gruff style that had irked the knights of the keyboard, as Ted derisively labeled them, was now colorfully authentic. The fans had changed, but in truth so had Ted; mellowing with each passing year, he was becoming beloved, like the Babe.

What's left to say about Ruth? He revolutionized the game, making even Cobb's lofty batting averages seem a wasted effort, and he was voted the top American athlete in 1999 and the top player of all time in that year's All-Century Team election. He no longer has his home-run records, nor his formerly unassailable slugging percentage marks of 1920 and 1921 (.847 and .846), nor his walks record of 1923 (170). But he retains this unique trump card: before he became the game's greatest slugger he was the American League's best left-handed pitcher, winning 94 games and twice—1916 and 1917—throwing over 300 innings while winning 23 and 24 games, respectively. And until Bonds no one dominated the game the way Ruth did: he hit 60 homers in 1927 when no other team in the American League hit that many; he led the league in slugging percentage thirteen years out of fourteen; and more.

Yet I maintain that Williams is the superior hitter, Aaron the better home-run slugger, and Mays the best all-around player. Reflect that Ruth faced pitchers who threw complete games about half the time (today it is about five percent), and thus faced the same delivery through four to six plate appearances (not to mention that he faced no relievers as we understand them today). Reflect that Ruth never had to hit at night. Reflect that African Americans never graced the same field as Ruth; had they done so, many white players would have lost their positions and the overall level of competition would have risen. One could add that Ruth never faced a slider or a split-fingered fastball; rarely faced a pitcher who would throw a breaking ball when behind in the count, and on. Ruth may have been better than any baseball player ever was or will be; however, it defies reason to claim that Ruth's opposition was likewise better.

Ruth's dominance was not only the measure of Ruth; *it was also the measure of the competition he faced.* To the extent that the league performs at an average level that from a later perspective seems easily attained, a colossus may so far outdistance his peers as to create records that are unapproachable for all time. When Williams retired, it was beyond imagining that we could reasonably compare batters of one era against batters of another simply by measuring the extent to which they surpassed the league average; now it is commonplace. But the large question that remains unanswered, and is perhaps not perfectly answerable, is: how to compare one era's average level of play to that of another. In swimming, track, basketball, football, hockey, golf—any sport you can name—the presumption is that today's athletes are bigger, stronger, better trained, and, on average, more proficient. World athletic records—in such competitions as the 100-meter dash, the 1500-meter run, the shot put, discus, javelin, high jump, 100-meter freestyle in swimming—have all been bettered by at least fifteen percent and in some events far, far more.

Only baseball, with its Punch and Judy battle between pitcher and batter to entertain the public while rules makers and ballpark architects invisibly pull strings from above, labors to maintain the illusion that nothing changes in the grand old game. A dollar in 1905 may not bear much resemblance to a dollar in 2005, but a .300 batting average remains the mark of a good hitter. Only in baseball do fans bemoan expansion, deride talent dilution and deteriorating fundamentals, and imagine that a 1927 team such as the New York Yankees would defeat all comers if they could be teleported to the American League East. (Strangely, no one thinks that about the 1906 Chicago Cubs.)

BARRY BONDS: BEST OR GREATEST?

Baseball was better in Williams's day than it was in Ruth's; it is better yet today. If you could transport Cobb, Wagner, Ruth, or Williams to the twenty-first century, they would benefit from improved training and nutrition, and because they would be smart enough to adjust to present conditions, they would be stars. But they wouldn't perform the way they did in their own day, and thus they would no longer be the Cobb, Wagner, Ruth, and Williams of the record books. Maybe they would be as good as Hank Aaron and Willie Mays; my guess is they would not.

Bonds, especially in 2001 through 2003, has exceeded the average batting performance in the National League to an extent greater than Ruth managed in his best years . . . while playing in a pitchers' park where home runs other than his are scarce. This is an astounding accomplishment, for with the average skill level increasing, it is mathematically ever more difficult to exceed it by a large margin. As Stephen Jay Gould memorably demonstrated, it is harder to post high rates of success in an era with a high level of average performance. Once .400 hitters were plentiful because it was relatively common to exceed the norm by forty percent or more when many less-skilled players competed with a few exceptional ones. In baseball's pre-WWII period, when the league batting average was .260, there was a slim chance that someone would hit .400; as the league average ascended to .280 or .300, someone could reasonably be expected to surpass that by forty percent. When Ruth slugged .847 in 1920, the American League slugged .388. When Bonds slugged .863 in 2001, the National League slugged .425, a comparable level of dominance, but in an era marked by greater average proficiency.

Yet for a number of reasons—aloof personality, whispered steroid use, no World Series ring, age-reduced effectiveness in the field, an armored right elbow that permits him to peer over the plate with little fear of harm—neither media nor fans seem willing to call Barry Bonds the greatest player ever, only "one of the greats." The steroid issue swirling around Bonds, in particular, has risen to a higher volume with less substance than Mark McGwire's use of the legal strength supplement androstenedione or such wink-nudge cheating as Gaylord Perry's spitball or Whitey Ford's scuffball, which carried them to the Hall of Fame; or the near-universal use of greenies (amphetamines) in the clubhouses of the 1970s.

That title of "Game's Greatest Player" seemed easier to affix to Alex Rodriguez, the shortstop who signed the biggest contract in history, $252 million over ten years, and then proceeded to live up to it, hitting 52, 57, and 47 home runs in his three years with the Texas Rangers. But when Rodriguez joined the New York Yankees for the 2004 season, he prepared to shift to third base, where power bats have been more common over the past half-century than at shortstop. He will be great at any position he elects to play, but the shift to third makes his historical competitors Mike Schmidt and Eddie Mathews, not Honus Wagner and Cal Ripken, and his batting record does not yet compare to that of Bonds.

Albert Pujols is a dark-horse candidate, only because of his youth, to become the greatest player ever. Certainly no one has ever done what he has in his first three years. But for now the proper comparisons for Pujols are to Hal Trosky and Cesar Cedeno, not Ruth, Williams, Aaron, and Mays.

No, the competition for Bonds is not from his contemporaries. It's the fat guy, the one who changed the way batters approach their task and thus changed the whole game of baseball. Bonds has not yet done that, but he may. In 2001 his batting stroke was so grooved that he hit 73 home runs against only 49 singles. In 2002, at the age of thirty-eight, he batted .370 to win his first batting crown and walked a record 198 times. In 2003 he took 65.9 percent of the pitches thrown to him yet still managed to hit 45 homers in only 390 at-bats. He has learned plate discipline, as Ted Williams did, and he cannot be induced to widen his strike

zone. When Bonds gets a pitch to hit, he does . . . and, choking up for greater bat control, he not only has a compact swing but also, with his maple mace, a larger sweet spot. Also like Williams, he is a consummate guess hitter, smacking home runs off pitches so high and so tight that they could not have been hit into fair territory unless he had begun to turn his hips and hands in advance. Truly, Bonds is not a slugger with a big swing like Ruth or Mantle or Jackson, but a technician like Williams, with the fastest swing and most powerful torque ever seen in the game. He is the perfect hero for a cold analytical age that prizes excellence over legend.

In previous times, people liked their heroes to be larger than life, to surround their prodigious feats with story; the feats were never enough. Folks preferred Ruth to Gehrig, Cobb to Heilmann, Kelly to Ewing, Waddell to Mathewson, even Doubleday to Cartwright. Bonds's accomplishments outstrip everyone's, including Ruth's, but the Babe lives in memory and we will tell his stories, or our ancestors' stories about him, as if they were our own.

Nobody has ever jumped out of the gate as strongly as St. Louis's Albert Pujols. He is the only player in baseball history to bat over .300, knock 30 home runs, score 100 runs, and collect 100 RBIs in each of his first four seasons. He set a rookie record with 137 RBIs in 2001, and he won his first batting title in 2003. A perennial Triple Crown threat, Pujols is sure to win multiple MVP awards—once Barry Bonds is out of the way . . .

TEXT CREDITS

ILLUSTRATION CREDITS

We wish to acknowledge the following for providing the illustrations included in the book. Every effort has been made to locate the copyright holders for materials used, and we apologize for any oversights. Unless otherwise noted, all other illustrations are from the author's collection.

AP/Wide World Photos: page 2, photo by Amy Sancetta; page 23, photo by James Finley; page 24, photo by Lynne Sladky; page 32, photo by Harry Harris; page 36; page 37; page 44; page 46; page 50, photo by Mark Lennihan; page 65 top, photo by Anthony Camerano; page 65 bottom; page 71; page 72; page 75; page 76; page 78; page 79; page 81 bottom, photo by Mark Duncan; page 82, photo by Rusty Kennedy; page 83; page 94, photo by John Gaps III; page 97, photo by Denis Paquin; page 101; page 104, photo by Rusty Kennedy; page 107 bottom, photo by Winslow Townson; page 112, photo by Amy Sancetta; page 114, photo by Ben Margot; page 144; page 145; page 150; page 157; page 161, photo by Matty Zimmerman; page 167; page 169; page 173; page 174; page 178 top, photo by EFK; page 178 bottom, photo by Matt York; page 182; page 184; page 194 top; page 196, photos by Jim Rogash; page 197, photo by Jeff Roberson; page 198, photo by David J. Phillips; page 200, photo by Paul Sancya; page 201, photo by James A. Finley; page 202, photo by Bill Boyce; page 203 bottom; page 205, photo by Ted S. Warren; page 206, photo by Mark J. Terrill; page 208, photo by Marcio Jose Sanchez; page 209, photo by Julie Jacobson; page 210, photo by Craig Fuji; page 211 top, photo by Gary Stewart; page 211 bottom, photo by Kevin Frayer; page 212, photo by Aaron Harris; page 213, photo by John Swart; page 214, photo by Nick Wass; page 215, photo by John Mabanglo; page 216, photo by Matt York; page 219, photo by David J. Phillips.

Berkshire Athenaeum, Pittsfield, Massachusetts: page 16

Bettmann/CORBIS: page 84; page 103

Carlisle DeWitt: page 34, page 45 left, page 56, page 64, page 70, page 86, page 87, page 88, page 89 top, pages 90–93, page 98

Chris Faytok/Star-Ledger/CORBIS: page 106 top

Library of Congress, General Collections: page 12

Library of Congress, Prints and Photographs Division, George Grantham Bain Collection: page 40; page 60; page 100; page 121 top; page 122; page 129

Library of Congress, Prints and Photographs Division, Benjamin K. Edwards Collection: page 26, pages 28–31, page 39

Library of Congress, Prints and Photographs Division: page 38, E. T. Johnson & Co; page 41; page 52, lithograph by Tuchfarber, Walkley & Moellmann, Cincinnati; page 54 top, photo by Charles H. Williamson; page 58 right; page 61; page 89 bottom; page 127 bottom; page 137.

National Baseball Hall of Fame and Library, Cooperstown, N.Y.: page 19 top, page 58 left, page 66, page 102, page 118, page 124, page 136, page 140, pages 147–149, page 160, page 162, page 163, page 164, page 172 top, page 180, page 185, pages 188–191, page 192, page 194 bottom

O.K. Harris Works of Art, New York: page 158, *Satchel Paige* by Lance Richbourg. 1986. Watercolor on paper, 65 x 51 inches.

INDEX

Hall of Fame catcher Mickey Cochrane.